To Sol & Herm,
Who are striving at
all times to understand
and clarify "the Jewish Paradox"

Love
7/16 F3

Rabbi

The Jewish Paradox

NAHUM GOLDMANN

The Jewish Paradox

TRANSLATED BY
STEVE COX

FRED JORDAN BOOKS/GROSSET & DUNLAP
NEW YORK

To My Wife Alice

Translation copyright © 1978 by Weidenfeld & Nicolson
Originally published in France under the title
LE PARADOXE JUIF, copyright © 1976 Editions Stock

Library of Congress Catalog Card Number: 78-58073
ISBN: 0 448 15166 9

Fred Jordan Books/Grosset & Dunlap

Grosset & Dunlap, Inc.
51 Madison Avenue, New York, N.Y. 10010

First Printing 1978

Printed in U.S.A.

Contents

Introduction

How DO YOU set about describing a man like Nahum Goldmann?

One of the best definitions of his line of action is to be found in his own comparison between the politician and the statesman. The politician, he says, cares only about satisfying his supporters or electors; the statesman's first consideration is for the aspirations of his opponents, so as to find an acceptable compromise with them.

That concept of the statesman is the fruit of copious experience, because for three-quarters of his life Nahum Goldmann has fulfilled the arduous mission of being the representative of a people whose very existence as a people was denied, and of being accepted as the ambassador of a country that remained to be created.

Nahum Goldmann delivered his first speech in public at the age of thirteen, and at once became active in the German Jewish community. While still a pupil at a very progressive Frankfurt school he was a propagandist for Zionism and made speeches in all kinds of settings—to the point of nearly failing his school certificate by turning up late after one of his speeches.

From then on, he was at the heart of all the major activities undertaken by the Jews on an international level: in the League of Nations from 1933 to 1939, and later on in the United Nations.

In 1934, with Stephen Wise, he laid the foundations of the World Jewish Congress, which he subsequently chaired. By creating the WJC in 1936, Nahum Goldmann endorsed the idea of the existence of a single Jewish people, an idea which had been abandoned by Jews and non-Jews alike. In that way he forced the big Jewish organizations and their leaders to integrate into a single structure at a level above the power struggles of the various factions.

During the last world war Nahum Goldmann emerged as one of the leading figures in the turbulent Jewish community of the

United States. He brought together the Zionists and those who wanted to keep their distance from the Jewish national movement.

Between 1956 and 1968 he combined the presidency of the World Jewish Congress with that of the World Zionist Organization.

A contemporary of Ben Gurion, Weizmann and Sharett, with them he was an architect of the creation of Israel, although he never involved himself in the quarrels of the Zionist parties. In order to preserve his own freedom of action and keep apart from partisan attitudes, he chose to refuse the high-level ministerial or diplomatic posts which were offered to him.

As a representative of the whole Jewish people, Nahum Goldmann was sometimes referred to as *Resh Galuta*, 'Leader in exile' (translated by the Greek word 'exarch'). This was the name given to those leaders of the Jewish community who, in the days of their people's exile in Babylon, in the sixth century BC, laid the foundations which enabled the Jewish people to survive its more than two thousand years of dispersion.

Nahum Goldmann is the image of the cosmopolitan Jew in the best sense of the word, an exotic and attractive blend of great cultures. At an early age he seems to have acquired a vision reaching so far beyond the horizons of his fellows that it is hard to say whether it reaches a planetary or a prophetic level.

Circumstances (I would say vocation) have impelled Nahum Goldmann to work on behalf of a single people, when his intellect would otherwise have made him an innovator in the field of the law of nations, as he showed when he became the driving force of the League of Nations' Minority Rights Committee.

As philosopher and historian, Nahum Goldmann can call upon encyclopaedic knowledge backed by an infallible memory. This tireless fighter for the Jewish cause has exerted the power of his lively mind, his charm and humour over the world's greatest statesmen. From Roosevelt to Adenauer, Mussolini to Litvinov, Ben Gurion to Kissinger, he has been in touch with and more than once influenced dozens of those leaders who have modified the history of our times.

Yet, for the interviewer, the single most striking element in the personality of Nahum Goldmann is his extraordinary gift as a raconteur, his appetite for anecdotes and lavish use of them throughout his life.

He is an art lover and collector, with a keen sensibility for music, poetry, literature and the theatre, a man who can appreciate a good text or an apt interpretation.

But there is too an ever-present irony towards himself, an awareness of his own limitations, a candour and zest which often make him say what he detests even before saying what he loves. Yet he is conscious of having no absolute truth in his possession, and displays real interest and a respectful tolerance towards other men and other ideas. If theological questions do arise for him, he knows that the search for the absolute is one which no human being can possibly conclude.

The Nahum Goldmann who charms his interlocutors also has the great defects of those gifted with the power to charm—which is to say egocentricity, a tendency to authoritarianism, and impatience. His gifts as a statesman and a stubborn negotiator do not free him from contradictions, procrastination and harsh criticism.

Nahum Goldmann practises a pragmatism occasionally taken to the very limit; this calls for prudence, dissimulation and astuteness. The statesman has been known to fall victim to the temptation to wheel and deal at a congress, ousting a centre-left president by means of a right-wing vote, only to get himself elected later, against the right, by the vote of the left.

His thinking is at once synthetic and analytic, and is based upon an associative, digressive mind.

Combining as he does the tradition of several thousand years and a compelling belief in progress, of all statesmen it is Nahum Goldmann who seems most genuine in his insistence on the need for change. Moulded by the great dramas in contemporary history and by the tragedy of the Jews of his generation, Nahum Goldmann is nevertheless a resolutely forward-looking man.

But this does not mean that he saddles himself with intellectual fashions, and he does not hesitate to stand up now and then against prevailing notions. He rapidly grasps the problems involved in any situation, and for that reason is an exceptional debater.

Nahum Goldmann seems to illustrate the Hasidic tale: 'A famous Master used to spend days and nights in study, and slept only two or three hours a night. When a disciple expressed surprise that he could make do with so little sleep, the Master replied: "When we are studying together I often read faster than you and find the meaning of the text before you. It's the same with sleep: I also sleep faster than other people." '

Beneath a calm exterior Nahum Goldmann conceals real scepticism towards himself and towards people and events. This sceptical spirit gives rise to moderation; that is why he holds that all objectives must be pursued without excessive bias. In a very lucid self-analysis he says: 'A goal to be reached is like a woman: if you want it, don't chase it too hard.' This way of thinking keeps him clear of any dogmatism.

In his effort to adapt Jewry to the transformations of the world, which affect Jewish communities in all countries, he prefers to cling to reason rather than to be right at any price.

He realized very early that assimilation was a real threat to the survival of Judaism. Even in 1936, in the midst of the struggle against Nazi discrimination, he was appealing to the Jews to take steps not to be melted into a liberal world in which there would be no more barriers between Jews and non-Jews.

In addition to his political achievements, Nahum Goldmann's contribution to the survival of Judaism has been felt mainly in the sphere of Jewish culture and learning. In 1928 he began preparations to publish the ambitious *Encyclopaedia Judaica*, of which ten volumes were to appear before Hitler's accession to power in 1933.

After resolving to create a Jewish state at the age of sixteen, Nahum Goldmann did not rest until that goal had been achieved. But his own conception of the Jewish state has often been at odds with the reality. By giving priority to the spiritual development which alone, in his view, is capable of assuring the continuity of Judaism and a special place among the nations for a Jewish state, he is in opposition to the rulers of Israel who, preoccupied by the state of war, have exaggerated the importance of military power.

At the same time, by advocating neutrality for Israel he opens the door to greater understanding between the Jewish state and countries that resent their dependence on the 'superpowers'.

Nahum Goldmann believes that in the Arab–Israeli conflict, as in any conflict between 'normal' human beings or peoples (which excludes Nazism), none of the antagonists is entirely right or entirely wrong. Taking account of the adversary's views seems to him to be the key to any negotiation.

He feels it as a major frustration of his life that he was not able to carry through a peace negotiation with the Arabs, so that contacts with Tito, Nehru and Hassan II, and the unachieved meeting with Nasser, constitute so many frustrating and inconclusive steps in his life.

Nahum Goldmann, who has chosen as his motto the Delphic inscription 'Nothing too much', seems to have picked his way as if by magic through the excesses of the history he has lived out, and which he has contributed to creating.

There is a constant discrepancy between his real power and the results he has achieved—he has no united people, no state, government or armed force behind him. His very fragility seems to serve him as a shield.

In spite of everything, optimism overcomes realism, eliciting once again the traditional Jewish belief that 'the Strength of Israel will not lie'. So it is not surprising that Nahum Goldmann should accord a forward place in the march of history to the irrational.

An enemy of demagogy (he finds committee meetings tedious), he dislikes the crowd—contact with it is painful to him. An intellectual, he detests those mass meetings where people express themselves through slogans rather than through any argued appeal to reason. His lack of respect for the masses is also prompted by their changeable character.

A statesman, he detests the idea of the sovereign state: he hopes for its decline, and longs for its progressive disappearance. This man, whose motto is also 'Serenity through action', nevertheless spent thirty years in an ideological battle against Ben Gurion.

A man with eight passports, and a loyal citizen of his successive countries, Nahum Goldmann lives in conformity with the concept of Talmudic Jewry which holds that: 'The law of the state (where you live) is the law.'

A character brimming with humour, and amazingly youthful both in mind and body, Nahum Goldmann's features sometimes assume the look of the impish little boy he used to be so long ago. And sometimes, in order to illustrate an idea, he will sing an old Jewish air.

Will Nahum Goldmann have a successor in the new situation in which the interests of world Jewry and of the State of Israel are quite distinct and require separate representation?

To know the answer it is first necessary to undertake a re-definition of the role of the World Jewish Congress in the system of international relationships, in world politics, and in the new condition of the Jews in the world.

On the other hand, now that the affairs of the Jewish state have been taken in hand by a new generation of native-born leaders and diplomats, is there any room still left for action by exceptional men whose personal relations may sometimes replace and surpass the influence of a state and a government?

Whatever the answer to that question may be, the ideas of Nahum Goldmann, all of them oriented towards the future of the human race and the Jewish people, will long continue to serve as a model for those who are called to shape the future.

In this book we have chosen to adopt a non-chronological order and to situate the events in each of the main categories of Nahum Goldmann's activities.

Some facts are already recorded in Nahum Goldmann's auto-biography, *Memories* (which first appeared in German under the title of 'Statesman Without A State'), others appear for the first time, either because they post-date the book, or because the time is now more ripe to reveal them. Nahum Goldmann's views on Jewry and its future prospects, on Zionism and the State of Israel, and on the great ideological and political debates that divide humanity, are representative of an independent, inventive, non-conformist mind. They look forward to a world in which the development of the Jews and of mankind intermingle for the greatest benefit of all.

Leon Abramowicz

Preface

My friend the late Prime Minister of Israel, Levi Eshkol, who had a great sense of humour, had a habit, when he was busy, of asking visitors to start at the end. 'If we have time,' he would say, 'we'll come back to the beginning.'

This seems to me an excellent method either for a speech or a book, because it means that the listener or reader knows what he is going to get, right from the start. My title, *The Jewish Paradox*, refers both collectively to the Jewish people to which I have devoted so much of my lifetime, and individually to myself, one of the Jews of the older generation.

To begin with the collective subject, let me say that in my opinion the Jewish people is the most paradoxical in the world. It is not better than others, or worse, but unique and different—by virtue of its structure, history, destiny and character—from all other peoples, and paradoxical in its contradictions.

No other people in the world is so attached to its country of origin—Palestine—as the Jews, who are bound by feeling and religion, as well as by utterly mystical ties. But on the other hand, whereas almost any Jew can now return to Israel, it has not occurred to the vast majority to do so (less than twenty per cent of the world's Jews are inhabitants of Israel). And for two thousand years of its history the greater part of the Jewish people has lived outside Palestine. In fact Jewish history begins with the Egyptian Diaspora from which Moses rescued the Jews in order to guide them towards the Promised Land; a 'statist' period followed, to be concluded by the destruction of the first Temple and the Babylonian exile; after the return of the captives under Cyrus, and a period of thorough reorganization, the second

Temple and the kingdom of Judaea were wiped out by the Romans; that marked the beginning of a further Diaspora which has lasted for two thousand years and which shows no sign of coming to an end in the foreseeable future for the majority of Jews, despite the creation of the State of Israel in 1948.

There is another contradiction. The Jews are the most separatist people in the world. Their belief in the notion of the chosen people is the basis of their entire religion. All down the centuries the Jews have intensified their separation from the non-Jewish world; they have rejected, and still do reject, mixed marriages; they have put up one wall after another to protect their existence as a people apart, and have built their ghettos with their own hands, from the *shtetl* of Eastern Europe to the *mellah* of Morocco. Yet at the very same time they count as the most universalist people in the world on the level of religion: the grand, almost inconceivable, idea of a single God of all humanity is the inspired creation of Judaism. No other people had had the courage and the spiritual audacity to conceive such a revolutionary notion. Nor have the thinkers of any other religion proclaimed so passionately the equality of all races and all social classes, from master to slave, rich to poor, before God.

Lastly, while it is true that the Jewish people has always believed in its own superiority (expressed in the classic formulation, 'the chosen people'), I do not know any other community so fiercely self-critical: think of Moses' fulminations against the Jews after the incident of the golden calf, and the stands taken by some recent or present-day leaders such as Weininger and Tucholsky; only among us will you come across these true 'Jewish antisemites'—to use a paradoxical definition.

I shall cite one last proof of the unique character of the Jewish people by taking the example of those great Jewish statesmen active, after emancipation, among other peoples. Even if they will not admit it, there always remains a question of divided loyalties within them. I have had the privilege of knowing several Jewish statesmen personally—men like Léon Blum, Henry Kissinger, Pierre Mendès France, Bruno Kreisky and others—and good patriots as they have been and are in their respective countries, I am sure that their Jewishness does make them wonder about themselves, if only unconsciously. Disraeli himself, a Jew by origin and baptized in infancy, who was the true creator of the British Empire in the nineteenth century, was great enough to admit that the Jewish problem was a real one for him, and he showed it both in his novels and his actions.

So this accounts for the title of *The Jewish Paradox* as regards the Jewish people in general.

Now I come to myself. On the occasion of my eightieth birthday my friends in the World Jewish Congress gave a dinner for me in Geneva and made a series of speeches. In my reply I told them that I saw it as the greatest success of my life that I had been a fairly happy man, in spite of circumstances which ought to have driven me to the point of madness, or made me resemble some character out of Dostoievsky. Let me explain myself: I have devoted practically my whole life to Jewish politics despite having an ambivalent attitude towards both terms in that phrase — 'politics' and 'Jewish'.

I have no great admiration either for politics or diplomacy. I recently formulated my definition of diplomacy in an essay, when I called it 'the art of postponing inevitable decisions for as long as possible'. Politics always confirms situations which have been created by other causes—ecomonic, social, religious, etc. It is not truly creative, yet I have spent decades in the diplomatic sphere.

To be utterly frank, my attitude towards Jewry is equally ambivalent. The Jews being, as I say, a complex and exceptional people, it is not easy to have a clear and simple attitude towards them.

When I analyse myself I find that I have many characteristics not comparable with specifically Jewish traits. I do not want to go into philosophy here, but basically I agree with Schopenhauer when he says that life is only tolerable if one has an aesthetic attitude and takes it as a game, with the seriousness typical of children at play, and thoroughly aware that it is only a game.

I have always stated my reservations about present-day Jewish politics, and I have often been a nonconformist about Israeli political life; nevertheless, I have devoted the greater part of my existence, both quantitatively and qualitatively, to working for the Jewish people, and I do not regret it.

To sum up all these contradictions, I have occupied and still do occupy a rather odd position in the leadership of the Jewish people. I have been president of the most important Jewish organizations—the World Zionist Organization and the World Jewish Congress, to name only two—and I have always been quite critical of Jewish policies (sometimes including my own), particularly in recent years when I have been more an observer than an actor. One American journalist gave a good definition of my own role by saying that I had managed to be one of the leaders of the Jewish Establishment and simultaneously to be the leader of the opposition to that Establishment.

As a paradox myself, therefore, I believe that I am a good representative of the paradoxical fate of the Jewish people.

1 Portrait of a Wandering Jew

BEN GURION once reproached me with being a wandering Jew. I answered that some people had their roots in themselves, and had no need to put them down in any particular soil. It is undoubtedly a main characteristic of mine that wherever I go my roots go with me. I adapt at once, a talent which has never failed me as far back as I can remember. At the age of five I left Lithuania, where I was born in 1895, for Frankfurt, and there was no wrench at all.

True, I had a thoroughly happy childhood. After my birth in the little town of Visznevo, my parents left to study in Germany, because the Tsarist regime then in power in Lithuania only let a limited quota of Jews into the universities. My father and mother consequently went to Königsberg, and then to Heidelberg, before eventually settling in Frankfurt.

I spent those five years living with my paternal grandfather, a country doctor, and was brought up fondly by my grandmother and three aunts. Their main problem was getting me off to sleep. I would not go to bed early because the house was always full of visitors in the evening and I liked sitting up with the grown-ups. I had an independent mind, which I don't think I have lost since then. For instance, one night when my aunts wanted me to go to bed I stubbornly refused to say my evening prayer. You can make a child perform a particular action, but you cannot force him to pray. From that day onward I instinctively understood that religion had to be voluntary, or else it meant nothing.

In Visznevo I was leader of a gang of children who got up to all sorts of mischief and usually acted on my instructions, so it was logical for me to take the blame if ever we got caught and there was any question of punishment. What made me all the more willing to do this was that as a grandson of the doctor who often presided at the synagogue I was quite sure that there were no very dreadful reprisals in store.

My grandfather considered me a gifted child with no need to attend the *heder*, the religious primary school where Jewish children were usually enrolled. A rabbi taught me the Bible at home, and all the peace, kindness and attention that surrounded me gave me a feeling of great inner security which I still have today. In the course of my public life I have dealt with plenty of eminent people, but at no time have I ever felt any inferiority or weakness by comparison. There can be no doubt that I owe it to this exceptional upbringing.

Before the creation of the State of Israel the Jewish people never had any real power, either military, economic or political. Their fate was settled sometimes by friends, sometimes by enemies, but always by outside forces and wishes. Only Zionism has enabled the Jews to become more or less the masters of their own destiny. So when you analyse Jewish politics or the actions of this or that Jewish leader you often find a general feeling of inferiority: the top men are unsure of themselves, afraid of being snubbed, so they compensate by striking aggressive or rigid attitudes. Never having felt the slightest complex either of superiority or inferiority, I was more ready for compromise or concession when I thought it necessary.

You may wonder how that kind of character could be acquired in the midst of a Lithuanian Jewish community, and my answer is that the widely held opinion about the Jews of the *shtetls*, those little townships isolated in a sea of *goyim*, Gentiles, seems mistaken to me. It is commonly said that the Jews there led lives that were unhappy to the point of misery. That is not true: they certainly found themselves in an unenviable economic position, and with no political voice, but it is not the objective facts that determine a life, but the psychological reaction to those facts. And from that angle the Jews were generally a fairly happy people.

One of the great phenomena of Jewish psychology, which goes a long way towards explaining the extraordinary endurance of our people despite two thousand years of dispersion, lies in having created a thoroughly ingenious defence mechanism against the politico-economic situation acting upon them, against persecution and exile. This mechanism can be described in a few words: the Jews saw their persecutors as an inferior race. In the little township of Visznevo we lived in a rural setting, and most of my grandfather's patients were peasants. Every Jew felt ten or a hundred times the superior of these lowly tillers of the soil: he was cultured, learned Hebrew, knew the Bible, studied the Talmud—in other words he knew that he stood head and shoulders above these illiterates.

Of course the Jews were deprived of political rights, but even if they had had them they probably would not have used them. *Goy* politics were of no concern to them: it was a foreign world where they were only passing through; some day a Messiah would come and take them off to Israel, so the only thing that mattered was surviving until the coming of the Messiah, and not worrying too much about 'other people's' reality. It is through this ingenious reasoning, which is without parallel in history, that the Jews succeeded in overcoming what would have annihilated any other race. So the *shtetl* of Visznevo did not live a life of sadness or despair; it was happy to take part in the Sabbath and the religious holidays of the community from which it drew new vigour each time, since every Jew knew then that he would be going to Paradise. He did not believe: he knew!

On that subject, I recall staying a few weeks with my maternal grandfather before going to Frankfurt. This other grandfather was a *dayan*, a rabbinical judge, at Vilna, then nicknamed 'the Jerusalem of Lithuania'. The town's religious life was governed by seven judges, of whom my grandfather, a great Talmudist, was one. He spent his days and nights studying, while his wife kept a small shop which provided their living. Well, this grandmother told me that she knew just where she would sit in Paradise after she died: next to her husband, but on a slightly lower chair than his, because he was a great Talmudist . . .

At Visznevo my education was both religious and traditionalist. I went to the synagogue every Saturday and respected all the

Jewish customs, such as eating kosher—not that this was very unusual, since there could not have been a dozen Jews in the whole town who did otherwise. I have always retained a positive attitude, a blend of veneration and admiration, towards the Jewish religion. Without it there would be no Jewish people today. Yet in Israel the relations between state and religion constitute one of the great remaining unsolved problems. Ben Gurion has received a lot of blame for not having separated the two, but I understand him very well: such a separation might have had the effect of splitting the Jewish people into believers and non-believers. Even today it is hardly possible to lay down whether being Jewish basically means belonging to a race, practising a religion, or both together. On the other hand, what I detest is the use of the Jewish religion as a tool of policy. In Israel the religious party does not hesitate to do it, and that is a shame.

Personally I stopped being religious in the traditional sense at the age of seventeen, meaning that I stopped observing the laws, eating kosher, going to the synagogue and taking part in holy days—except of course for Yom Kippur, our Day of Atonement. But I have kept some roots, and mysticism is a part of my make-up. I studied it for many years, and even went as far as spending a month in a German monastery which was a great centre of Catholic mystical theology; if Hitler had not compelled me to involve myself in Jewish political life, I would probably have continued those studies.

Nevertheless, in spite of my attachment to the Jewish religion I do not like to talk about 'the chosen people'. Ben Gurion always used to refer to the Jews as 'God's chosen people'; I used to tell him: 'Leave that for non-Jews to say.' I will go into more detail when I come to explain my own conception of Zionism, but rather than 'chosen' I prefer the notion of a 'unique people'.

I had no problem adjusting to the move to Frankfurt even though the Jews of Eastern Europe lived on the fringe of the city's Jewish society, which was very Westernized compared to the environment I had experienced in Lithuania. I also discovered the existence of non-Jews. Some children may have gone through difficulties in the process, or even tragedies, but that did not happen to me, and for two reasons: first, owing to my great adaptability, and second, because my family happened to move in a circle of East European Jews. Frankfurt was then a great Jewish centre, both intellectual and financial. Most of the big Jewish bankers of France, Germany, New York and elsewhere come from there. My father, who was a well-known author, was in the confidence of these wealthy people, many of whom—like the Rothschilds—were public benefactors. He acted as intermediary between Jewish students turning up without a penny and these generous patrons. He distributed the bankers' cash, and the students, who came for the vacations, often ate at our house and sometimes slept there too.

A number of the men who became my closest companions, like Jacob Klatzkin, or who played major roles in Israel, like Moshe Glickson, founder of Israel's biggest daily paper, *Ha-Aretz*, were boyhood friends of mine. As well as that, thanks to my father's status in high Jewish financial circles, we were as much at home in the Jewish society of Eastern Europe as that of Germany, which was much more Western and unorthodox, although traditionalist.

I have said that my father was an author, but he also edited a Jewish weekly paper in Frankfurt, as well as teaching Hebrew language and literature at a Jewish teachers' training college run by the JCA, the Jewish Colonization Association, created by Baron Maurice de Hirsch with the purpose of founding Jewish farming settlements in Argentina. He wrote in Hebrew and German: in Hebrew mainly fables, but also poetry, and in German his weekly editorial. He was a traditionalist, and a convinced Zionist since his youth. That undoubtedly explains my own Zionism, which is a sort of inborn inheritance: I did not become a Zionist—I always was one.

My father's brother also devoted his life to literature. His name was Szalkowitz, and this calls for a brief explanation. In Tsarist Russia the worst thing for a Jew was joining the army: military service could last as long as seven years, during which you had to put up with a thousand and one annoyances, like not being able to eat kosher and practise your religion. Luckily there was a law exempting only sons from military service, and in Jewish communities it was the rabbi who kept the birth register. So when a father had three sons they were each entered under a different name; in my own family my grandfather was called Leibmann, my father Goldmann, and my uncle Szalkowitz!

This uncle, who unfortunately died quite young, was the first great publisher of modern Hebrew literature. He published Bialik, Pere:z and Mendele, founded the first modern Hebrew publishing house, in Warsaw, brought out an edition of the Talmud and was the true originator of the *Encyclopaedia Judaica* which I later brought to completion in Germany.

Before going to study in Germany, my father and uncle had attended a *yeshiva*, a seminary for Talmudic studies. As original Zionists, and even pre-Zionists, both had belonged to the Bnai Moshe (Sons of Moses) order founded by Ahad Ha-Am. Later my father was very active in the Misrahi, the Zionist religious movement, and attended several Zionist congresses as a delegate. So it was logical for me to be enrolled in a very religious Jewish school in Frankfurt, though I left it when I was nine years old for a German experimental school run by a famous educator. In the days of imperial Germany, schooling was very strict, but Frankfurt was quite different from, for example, Prussia, and school discipline was much more liberal there.

Frankfurt was a free town, independent and proud of it, and very much influenced by Jews; its biggest newspaper, the *Frankfurter Zeitung*, was founded by a Jew. And when I was six I used to play ball in the street like any other child—not a Jewish street, because ghettos were unknown in Frankfurt. A town like that was bound to reinforce my feeling of being equal, and later on it was a delight for me to assimilate German culture, which is still my basic culture to this day. I speak five languages fluently: English, French, Hebrew, Yiddish and German. I understand Italian and have just about forgotten Russian, for want of practice. I have travelled a lot, but my second native land is Germany.

I was about fifteen when I started to write for the *Frankfurter Zeitung* and made friends with a number of German intellectuals, in particular the Simon brothers, who published and edited the paper. So the synthesis between my very clear-cut and obvious Jewish identity and mainstream culture came about quite normally. I never had to debate the problem of whether or not I was a Jew, as many Jews did after their assimilation. I never grew away from Judaism only to return later on. I had no trouble at all in reconciling my feeling of being Jewish, and my duty to do my utmost to help the Jewish people, with my adaptation to German culture.

To revert to my schooldays, I was what is commonly called a brilliant pupil. On one holiday occasion I launched into a speech on the theme of 'Judaism and Hellenism', which took some nerve, seeing that I was barely fourteen and still in short pants. I also began to become familiar with French literature, and more particularly with the moralists and the encyclopaedists. La Rochefoucauld and La Bruyère were two of my favourite authors, and I used them shamelessly. For instance, in order to impress my French teacher I had no hesitation about trotting out my own thoughts preceded by the words: 'As La Rochefoucauld says . . .' This astounded the teacher. 'I can see how well you know the literature,' he would say admiringly.

So I was well thought of at school, in spite of the rather nonconformist views I expressed now and then. For example, I remember having to write a comparison of Joan of Arc and Cassandra for homework, and stating flatly that Joan of Arc seemed a little deranged to me, since she had wanted to live without a man and without love. The very irritated teacher sent for my mother and told her: 'Your son is oversexed!' I was not yet fifteen.

Running the children's gang in Visznevo and then becoming a star pupil at school served as a good apprenticeship for my future activities. A few years later I took on the responsibility for refugee Jews in Germany. Various Russian Jews who were taking the waters at different spa resorts in Germany were caught out by the outbreak of the First World War. They were all installed in the little health resort of Bad Nauheim, myself included, because of my Russian origins. We were considered as enemy nationals and placed under police surveillance.

That is where I learned Russian and was chosen to represent the Jews with the authorities. The Jews at Nauheim were free to do as they pleased, short of leaving town, but autumn came, and with it the Jewish New Year and Yom Kippur, both of them solemn occasions when orthodox Jews need to attend the *mikvah*, or ritual bath, beforehand. There was no *mikvah* at Nauheim, but there was one not far away, at Friedberg, where there was an old Jewish community. The Orthodox Jews appointed me to negotiate on their behalf with the police commissioner for permission to go there, even if it meant having a police escort. He heard me through, then burst out: 'Are you mad or what? Eighty thousand people come to the baths here every year, and you Jews have to go to Friedberg?' I tried to explain that it was a ritual bath, and nothing to do with hydrotherapy, but he would not listen.

Fortunately I knew von Eichhorn, the commanding general of the province, and I at once sent him a telegram quoting the specific paragraph of the Jewish legal code, the *Shulhan Arukh*, which requires orthodox Jews to take a ritual bath before great religious festivals. The Germany of Wilhelm II was based upon religion, so a few hours later our commissioner received a telegram ordering him to send them to Friedberg.

The war had interrupted my philosophy studies at Heidelberg University and I stayed for a while at Bad Nauheim, where I wrote a series of articles for the *Frankfurter Zeitung* under the general title of 'The Spirit of Militarism'. At the time of the First World War intellectuals tended on the whole to condemn Prussian militarism, but having been educated in Germany I was a German patriot. Besides, for Jews the whole world over it was a simple matter: Tsarist Russia was the worst enemy of Jews and Jewry, the Germans were against Russia, so we were pro-German. My personal background reinforced me in that attitude, and my articles tended to justify the German ideology. I would not write them today.

The owner of the *Frankfurter Zeitung*, Heinrich Simon, was highly impressed when he read them, and told me: 'This is too good for a newspaper.' There was a current series published under the heading 'The German War' in which the best-known German writers and politicians wrote in support of the German case. This collection was run by Dr Erno Jäckh, an important political economist who later held a chair at Columbia University. Although he was not a Jew, this great democrat left Germany when Hitler came to power.

So Heinrich Simon sent him my articles, which he brought out as a pamphlet produced in an edition of hundreds of thousands. Then Jäckh, who was head of a special section in the German Foreign Office producing German ideological propaganda abroad, summoned me to Berlin. I went at once, and a few weeks later found myself in quite an odd situation: on the one hand, I was regarded as an enemy alien and had to report to the police twice a week; on the other, I belonged to the Foreign Office and was issued with a German diplomatic passport.

To begin with I worked for the press office, but after six months I went to my superiors with a suggestion for setting up a section for Jewish problems. Remember that in those days the fate of the Jews basically depended on Germany: Lithuania and Poland, with nearly fourteen million Jews, were occupied by the Germans; Palestine was in Turkish hands, but Turkey was Germany's ally. So a Jewish section was created and I ran it till the end of the war, when I vacated it in favour of a learned archaeologist, Professor Moritz Sobernheim. So right up to the accession of Hitler, who closed it down immediately, Germany's was the only foreign ministry which had a Jewish section.

As for me, I returned to Heidelberg to complete my studies and submit my doctoral thesis. But after the defeat of Germany, the country suffered an unprecedented economic depression. Inflation was such that one American dollar was worth a billion, and then two or three billion marks. Nobody could grasp it who did not live through that period. And almost from one day to the next I found myself a multi-billionaire! This was thanks to my uncle Szalkowitz—he wrote under the pen-name of Ben Avigdor—who was in America at the time and got me a contract with the New York Yiddish newspaper *Der Tag* to write three articles a month at twenty-five dollars apiece, a fortune for anyone living in Germany.

Instead of buying up houses in Berlin I bought one in the Bavarian Alps, in Murnau. The painter Kandinsky lived in this little town for a long time, and my friend Jacob Klatzkin also moved there. When Hitler's attempted Munich putsch failed, he came to lie low with one of his friends near Murnau. His house was ten minutes from mine and I often used to see him out walking. It was said about him that he was *ein verkrachter Putschist*, a bankrupt putschist.

At Murnau I wrote articles, worked on books, extended my studies of philosophy and saw various friends, mostly writers, among them the great German Jewish author Arnold Zweig, who lived in Starnberg, half an hour from Murnau. I was with him when news came that the police had been to my house to interrogate me. My mother was there at the time, and I did not want her worried, so I returned to Murnau, where I found the assistant chief of police escorted by four officers. I asked him to what I owed his visit, and he answered: 'We have had a lot of information laid against you, coming from antisemites. There are three kinds: some say that you are not German though you claim to be; others that you are a leader of the Western European young communist movements, whose headquarters are in Murnau, thanks to you; and then there are some that claim you have no right to the title of "Doctor".'

The police searched my house and examined every book for signs of subversive literature: they were works of philosophy. Then they came in turn upon my naturalization certificate, my doctoral diplomas—one in jurisprudence the other in philosophy —and lastly on a letter from the German Chancellor assuring me of his gratitude for all I had done for the country during the war.

The day was very hot and the police were furious, grumbling about those 'antisemitic swine' who saddled them with so much extra duty. Finally their chief told them in my presence: 'This gentleman is a great patriot. Furthermore he is a person of importance, and if you bother him in future you'll have me to deal with.' I had become a protégé of the Munich police.

All the same, that was not the first warning, and my activities had brought me to the attention of some fascist groups. I had not foreseen Auschwitz, but I knew that there was serious persecution in store if ever Hitler should come to power.

After spending two years in Murnau I moved to Berlin to look after the *Encyclopaedia Judaica* and had some public clashes with a pre-Nazi antisemitic movement which called itself the 'Deutscher Völkischer Trutz- und Schutzbund'—which stands for something like 'German offensive and defensive racist union'. The members of this union interrupted Jewish conferences and caused brawling and police intervention; I was on their blacklist.

The idea for the *Encyclopaedia Judaica* had arisen because I had always felt that some such outline of Jewish learning was essential to strengthen the self-identification of every Jew, taken individually. And the work ought also to constitute a tool for researchers. I knew that there were several such projects in existence in the twenties, in particular the American *Jewish Encyclopedia*, partly financed by Jewish capitalists; it contained articles of an insuperably high standard—no one today can write like the great scholar Louis Ginsberg, for example. Then there was Baron Ginzbourg's Jewish encyclopaedia, written in Russian.

But the science of history develops very fast: none of these works mentioned Hitler, and the latest social and political developments. So it was my uncle Szalkowitz who first had the idea of a new encyclopaedia, and it straight away caught my imagination, and Klatzkin's too.

Szalkowitz was then making arrangements to move to Berlin, which was the great centre of Eastern European Jewry. The Weimar government was very liberal, so a good many Jewish artists and journalists were in more or less legal residence in the capital. Their main haunt was the *Romanisches Café*, which played an important part in contemporary German literature. I went there often with Klatzkin. Each group had its own table: there were the 'Yiddishists', 'Zionists', 'Bundists' and so on, all arguing among themselves from table to table. I particularly remember a man called Nomberg, not an outstanding journalist but full of humour, who boasted that he made love to three women every day. It was an invention, of course, to compensate for his ugliness and small stature. But one day I saw Nomberg sitting at a different table from usual.

'What's happened to you?' I asked him, 'Have you changed your views? Have you become a Zionist?'

'No, no,' he said, 'it's just that I've had a third letter of expulsion from the police, and I want to stay. So I've picked another table. This way they'll never find me.'

My uncle died just after launching this idea of a new encyclopaedia, and Klatzkin and I decided to take over the project and to print the *Encyclopaedia Judaica* in German, English and Hebrew. We had no financial backing, but I have always noticed that the less money you have, the more ambitious your plans: they, at least, cost nothing.

A friend provided five thousand marks—which we later returned, because he was not rich—and with that sum we published a sixty-four-page brochure containing a synopsis. This was to give an idea of the undertaking to the wealthy backers we wanted to interest. There was one article on the Cabbala, a second was geographical, a third literary. Then we began our collecting. I have been a big fund-raiser for a very long time, but that was my first campaign.

When I went to Frankfurt to see a Jewish banker called Dreyfus it was in the middle of a world crisis—unemployment in America, devaluation and so on.

'Dreyfus,' I told him, 'I am making a collection to finance my encyclopaedia. I would like you to open the subscription list.'

'Listen, Goldmann,' he answered, 'you know I'm a generous man, but with the crisis I'm losing millions of marks a day, and I can prove it to you. If I closed my bank I would make more money, but I have hundreds of employees with families, and I can't shut down, so I go on losing money.'

'I'll make you an offer then,' I replied. 'Let us change places. You be the publisher and I'll be the banker. And now, about that money, I offer double what you propose . . .'

He gave me double.

Another time I had an appointment in Karlsruhe, at the headquarters of the Homburger Bank, which Hitler later liquidated. I phoned from the railway station and Homburger said: 'Come here right away, because I have to leave: my wife is very ill and I'm going to join her in Baden-Baden. My suitcases are packed, but if you come at once we can talk for ten minutes. After that I'll be away for several weeks.' So I made haste and met a man whose mind was preoccupied by the bad news about his wife. He interrupted me after six minutes to say: 'I'll be frank, Mr Goldmann: I'm barely listening and I don't understand a thing about your plan. But you have been recommended by a friend, so [and here he glanced at his watch] you have been talking for six minutes, I'll give you a thousand marks a minute.' That was a lot of money at the time, but I insisted: 'It's very generous of you, Mr Homburger, and I readily accept your tariff—on condition that you let me talk for another six minutes.' He was a sportsman, and he did double his contribution. All the same, a point came when what with all the expenses involved in editing the encyclopaedia we had spent our last cent. We were employing eighty people, and the situation was becoming tragic.

So I went to see another banker, Schwartz by name. I spent twenty minutes describing our situation, at the end of which he promised me twenty thousand marks. Then a little later he said:

'How much had I in fact offered?'

'Twenty thousand marks, but if you don't want . . .'

'No, no, I shall keep my word. But I have a proposition to make: become a director of my bank and name your own salary!'

'What for?'

'You turn up here, you tell me about an undertaking which I didn't understand a word of, and after twenty minutes you take my twenty thousand marks. Imagine what your powers of persuasion could do with my clients!'

'Excuse me, Mr Schwartz,' I answered, 'but I can't accept. Even if I do have all the qualities to make a good banker, unfortunately I haven't got the defects!'

This Schwartz had had an associate, Jacob Goldschmidt, who had left him for a meteoric career in German high finance as head of the Darmstadt Bank. Although he was anti-Zionist, this very wealthy man, who collected Impressionist paintings and Chinese porcelain, helped us a lot, and it is mainly thanks to him that between 1928 and 1933 we managed to bring out ten volumes of the *Encyclopaedia Judaica*, as far as the letter 'L', to be precise. Then Hitler came to power.

On this subject, I often say that I am one of the living proofs that virtue not only has its reward in heaven but sometimes in this world too. Friends like Stephen Wise and Chaim Weizmann, very perturbed by the rise of the Nazi peril, had already advised me to leave Germany, but I could not leave all my collaborators out of a job.

After my mother's sudden death in Frankfurt I had bought my already sick father a flat in Tel Aviv, where he was looked after by a woman cousin and surrounded by friends like Bialik. A few weeks after Hitler's accession I received a telegram from Palestine informing me that my father was dying. I left at once with my fiancée, leaving Germany not by the main lines, because the SS were already manning the frontiers, but by a secondary line between Munich and Innsbruck. I was able to reach Palestine in time to see my father once more, and there I learned that four days after my departure the Gestapo had come to arrest me. My attachment to my father had just saved me.

The Nazis had twenty thousand copies of the *Encyclopaedia Judaica* burned at once: the articles on Hitler and on anti-semitism were not to their taste. But we still had our eight thousand subscribers.

In Switzerland, when I returned from Palestine, I wanted to resume publication, but we had no money left. Later on, German-speaking Jewry was just about annihilated, and it was not till after the war that I again began to edit a Jewish encyclopaedia, in English. It came out in Jerusalem in 1972 and cost nearly five million dollars to produce! At first we had thought it would only cost a million. There were four partners: myself, the Palestine Economic Corporation, which has invested a great deal in Israel, the Massada publishing house, which publishes the great *Universal Encyclopaedia* in Hebrew, and the Rassco building society.

The more I examined the project, the more I realized that we would be several million dollars short. I set up a sort of committee chaired by Joseph Schwartz, who had a good deal of finesse, but in vain. He told me: 'Listen, Nahum, it breaks my heart to admit it, but American Jews only give Israel money in order to make sure it survives.' I admit that the conflict with the Arabs was more important, but the American Jews had enough money to finance both.

To cut a long story short, in the sixties there was only one way to get the cash—borrow it from the American government itself. And it so happens that in the US there is an organization called AID, which lends money to poor countries. The loans are granted over twenty years, at an interest rate of two per cent, and are repayable in dollars. The sole condition is that they have to be guaranteed by a great banking institution or by a government.

I approached my friend Pinhas Sapir, then the Israeli Minister of Finance. He had the interest in the new *Encyclopaedia Judaica* of a man who suffered from not having been able to continue his own studies. So I said to him: 'There's no point me talking to you about cultural matters, since you're up to your neck in financial difficulties.' He literally sprang to his feet:

'What! You dare tell me, a lover of culture, that it does not interest me?'

'Fine,' I replied, 'in that case since you haven't got the money, give us a surety from your government.'

And he did it.

It only remained to interest the White House. One of Lyndon B. Johnson's friends was a Polish Jew called Jim Novy, who had come to Texas as a young man and settled in Austin, where Johnson was first elected to Congress. He was treasurer of the committee which financed his presidential campaign, and had a pass authorizing him to enter the White House day or night, and even to request a bed there, just like a hotel.

As chairman of the foundation to publish the encyclopaedia I therefore arranged the appointment of a man who very probably could not read a page of the Talmud, but who was very proud of his new title and obtained Johnson's recommendation. Thanks to him we were able to borrow two million dollars and publish the new *Encyclopaedia Judaica*, of which we have already sold twenty thousand copies at six hundred dollars each, which is not so bad.

My first attempt to resume the *Encyclopaedia Judaica* in Switzerland was not my only reason for moving there. This was in the early thirties and Stephen Wise had already written to me in Palestine: 'Get settled in Geneva to make the preparations for convoking the World Jewish Congress.' Later on, in America, he insisted: 'You are the only man who can organize it. I do not know European Jewry, whereas you can and must manage to pave the way for this congress.' Meanwhile I had taken the measure of the threat which Hitler represented and I wanted world-wide Jewish resistance against Nazism, so I agreed to take on the job.

In Geneva I represented not only the World Jewish Congress but also the Jewish Agency for Palestine with the Mandates Commission and the Council of the League of Nations. We had a semi-official position because, without being a state, we were still something more than a benevolent organization.

After the 1935 plebiscite which gave the Saar back to Germany the problem arose of the twenty thousand Jews then living in that province. They were threatened by the racist Nuremberg Laws, and addressed themselves to me to obtain the right to leave the Saar with everything they owned in French francs. Now the Saar Commission was chaired by Italy, that is to say by Mussolini. So I met the Duce, who, extraordinary as it may seem, was then pro-Jewish and anti-Nazi. After a very theatrical interview, which I have already related in my autobiography, he promised to help us, and kept his word by refusing to ratify the return of the Saar to Germany until the Germans accepted our conditions.

I also had occasion to talk to Count Ciano about the Palestinian problem. He received me at the Italian Foreign Ministry, and when I entered his office he asked me to sit down. He then stood up, and I made to do likewise, but again he said: 'Sit down.' Then, standing, and in a very ceremonious tone, he told me: 'I am to pass on a message in the Duce's name. The Duce asks me to tell you that he is pro-Jewish and will always remain so. The Duce is for the creation of a Jewish state and will not change his mind provided that Jewish state is independent and not a colony of England.' Ciano then sat down again and started talking normally ... Obviously this meeting came before the Ethiopia affair, that is, before the Allies drove Mussolini into Hitler's arms.

My work with the League of Nations essentially consisted in winning votes favourable to the future State of Israel and trying to improve the situation of the Jews in those countries where it was threatened. Before the Saar vote I sent a letter to Maxim Litvinov, the Soviet Foreign Minister, to inform him that I wished to discuss the problem on the League agenda. Litvinov agreed, and I went to the Hôtel Richemond, where he was staying.

He rose to greet me, cold as ice. He spoke very correct English, with an atrocious accent, and his first words were: 'You are a Zionist, sir?' spoken in the same tone as if he were saying: 'You are a known criminal.' I replied: 'Not only am I a Zionist, Mr Litvinov, but I am one of the eleven members of the Zionist world executive council. However, I have not come to see you about a Zionist problem, but about a Jewish problem.'

'Be seated, then,' he answered.

I began to explain my plan. He listened without losing his glacial air, then said: 'Yes, it is a reasonable proposal. I am ready to support it, but I cannot propose it.' I at once cried out: 'God protect us: if you propose it, everyone will be against. Be contented with voting for, but do not take any initiative.'

He then asked me: 'In your opinion, who might introduce the resolution?' I answered that I wanted the British minister, Mr Eden, to take it in hand.

'Ah yes,' said Litvinov. 'Do you know Mr Eden?'

'I know him very well.'

'And what has he said to you on the subject?'

'You know how it is with the English and their diplomacy: yes but, well perhaps ... It's never very clear.'

'Might I be allowed to give you some advice, Mr Goldmann?'

'Please do.'

'You should talk a lot more forcefully to Mr Eden.'

'What do you mean by "forcefully"?'

'You should not suggest but insist that he should put the proposal to the vote.'

'But after all, Mr Litvinov, Eden represents the British Empire, with its fleet and its army; I represent the Jewish people, with no army, no fleet, nothing. Then how am I supposed to insist?'

'You are wrong, Mr Goldmann. I have experience on my side: if your international Jewish organizations make strong demonstrations, the Western democracies have got to give way.'

'Mr Litvinov, two months ago I met the Vatican Secretary of State, Cardinal Pacelli [the future Pius xii], and Monsignor Pacelli talked to me about "the power of world Jewry". I didn't hold it against him—he is a Catholic, so what does he know about Jewish life? But for you, Mr Litvinov, with your Jewish intelligence, to talk such nonsense, that really annoys me.'

I shall never forget his reaction. He was quiet for half a minute, then he rose to his feet, came round the big table which was between us, and held out his hand: 'Let us shake hands, Mr Goldmann; I said something stupid, and I apologize.'

From then on we became great friends. When we walked in the corridors at the League of Nations the journalists would try to photograph us together, but Litvinov ran like a rabbit for fear of having his picture taken side by side with a Zionist leader.

Conversely, the Zionists themselves were anxious for contacts with Communist officials. They knew that the USSR could play a great part in the creation of the State of Israel, but it was all the more difficult because a great many Communists were themselves Jews and anti-Zionists. One day Litvinov turned up in Geneva with a delegation of fourteen members, eleven of whom were Jews. I asked the minister: 'What do you need a *minyan* for?' (The *minyan* is a prayer assembly consisting of at least ten believers.) Litvinov, who spoke excellent Yiddish, burst out laughing, then he explained: 'It's quite simple. I only need people who speak French, English and German, and in Russia it's only the Jews who speak foreign languages.' In 1978 that is no longer the case, but it was true then. In the thirties, it was the Jews who made up the International.

After the Munich agreement Litvinov delivered his famous

speech accusing the Western democracies of having betrayed Czechoslovakia and publicly predicting war. It was a magnificent speech. Litvinov was a poor orator, but what a text! He spoke in a frozen silence, and at the end only three people applauded: the Austrian delegate, I don't know why, the Albanian, and I. I was not in the chamber itself, but in a box, in accordance with my semi-official position. When Litvinov had finished I left my seat and went right across the chamber towards him. I told him: 'You have made an historic speech. Let me congratulate you.' He answered: 'Mr Goldmann, I shall never forget your gesture: it took courage. Come and see me tomorrow before I leave Geneva.'

So next day I went to see him. 'The League of Nations is finished,' he told me. 'I'm going back to Moscow this afternoon, and I won't be able to get in touch with you from there. So listen to this: if ever you read in the papers that I have resigned my position as Foreign Minister you will know that Stalin has decided to sign a pact with Hitler. As it happens I am in favour of such an alliance, because the democracies have betrayed the USSR and we cannot face the Nazis alone: until we have rearmed we shall be too weak. But it won't be me who signs the document, because Hitler won't go near a Jew. So if you find out that I have resigned you will understand that a Russo–German pact has been signed —which means that a few weeks afterwards there will be war, because Hitler will feel safe to the East.'

About three weeks later I heard that Litvinov had just resigned, and at once I cabled Stephen Wise, President of the World Jewish Congress, in New York: 'In a few months there will be war.'

Wise immediately went to see Sumner Welles, the US Assistant Secretary of State and friend of President Roosevelt. He told him: 'My friend Goldmann is very well informed and he tells me that war is imminent.' Welles replied: 'I'm sure your friend Goldmann is a very good fellow, but he's talking nonsense: there is no danger of war.' Soon after that, the war broke out.

After leaving Geneva because there was a threat of the Nazis occupying Switzerland, I moved to America, where I met Welles.

'I must express my admiration,' he told me. 'What foresight you had!'

I told him that although I had a pretty good opinion of myself, I could not lay claim to another man's credit, and I told him about Litvinov's confidences.

During the war I represented the Jewish Agency with the State Department. I was living with my family in New York, but every week I went to Washington, where I kept an office and a flat. Stephen Wise helped me a lot, and his support was all the more precious to me because the American Jews were very difficult. They were rich, and aware of their own power, but they were also jealous: few European Jewish leaders have managed to make themselves any permanent place in the United States. Out of these, the only men who managed to become popular were Chaim Weizmann, whom everybody admired, and Shmaryahu Levin, who was the best Yiddish orator of all, a great wit and a marvellous story-teller. Most of the others failed, and if I did eventually succeed after a few years it is because I was a sort of president of presidents, responsible for several important Jewish organizations. It was even said that I was the 'dictator of American Jewry', which is a bit too strong.

Be that as it may, Stephen Wise was one of the ten best-known Jews in America. He could not board a train without the ticket collector saying: 'Hey, it's Doctor Wise!' Impossible for him to go into a hotel without being recognized by the liftboy, or into a restaurant without the waiters coming to say hello. Wise could have been a senator, or even an ambassador—in fact the offer was made, but he turned down any public position in order to work for the Jews.

Nevertheless his influence was considerable. He was already a power behind the scenes when Roosevelt was governor of New York State. But his convictions were unshakable: for instance there was a point at which Roosevelt was cooperating a little with Tammany Hall, an organization with Mafia connections. Wise broke with him at once, but was reconciled when Roosevelt started to go after the mafiosi. He made a great contribution to Roosevelt's election as president.

One of Stephen Wise's principal qualities was courage. At the age of twenty-two he was already a famous rabbi when the rabbinate of the biggest American synagogue with the richest congregation fell vacant. The president of the congregation was an eminent jurist but also an anti-Zionist, the lawyer Louis Marshall. Marshall laid down one condition: that the rabbi appointed should submit his sermons for vetting. Wise straight away said: 'Me be censored? Not on your life!' And he gave up an appointment which would have multiplied his salary several times over as well as conferring considerable authority.

At the same time he was very naive politically, and used to confess that he always needed an oracle. This was originally Judge Louis Brandeis of the Supreme Court, then it was me. Wise had a habit of saying: 'I'm sure it's politically valid; my friend Nahum says so!' He often used to say that he loved me like his own sons, and he himself looked after my children's education, choice of schools and so on.

Wise only acted out of love. I have never met a man with so much love for others. He made no distinction between important and less important matters, and he could spend two days finding a family to adopt some orphan child. I would tell him: 'Doctor Wise, you have far more pressing business,' but he answered with the famous Talmudic saying: 'A single Jew is like all of Jewry.'

My basic job in the United States was to win acceptance for a partition of Palestine, but there might not have been a Jewish state had President Roosevelt lived. Having said that, Roosevelt was pro-Zionist as much out of personal sympathy as for reasons of domestic policy. In that he differed, for example, from Dean Rusk, who became director of the United Nations department around 1943 and was therefore my opposite number in the talks on the partition of Palestine and the establishment of the State of Israel. Rusk was a very honourable man, and very sensible, but he maintained that the American interest lay with the Arabs, not the Jews. And a majority of the State Department was anti-Zionist at that time.

Roosevelt for his part pursued a humanitarian policy: a hundred thousand Jews to populate Israel, okay. Helping refugees, okay. But building a Jewish state, not a chance! He was convinced that the Arabs would sooner or later destroy it.

One book has been published making the monstrous accusation that Roosevelt was an antisemite. This is unfair and repugnant: on the contrary, Roosevelt and Sumner Welles fought against the policy of the Congress, which was to refuse visas to émigrés. It is true that subsequently the President was afraid of the Congress.

Before Yalta Roosevelt came under pressure from American Jews who wanted him to accept the idea of partition. He agreed to put their case to Ibn Saud, who was then the most important figure in the Arab world. He described the meeting to Stephen Wise. Although he himself considered the idea of a Jewish state to be unrealistic, he had done his utmost to convince Ibn Saud, saying that in an under-developed Palestine the Jews would bring wealth and intellectual culture, and would make the soil productive. But Ibn Saud replied that he detested trees, universities and modern science, and that the Koran was the one necessity. 'So how could you live there as a tiny minority among Arab fanatics?' Roosevelt concluded. 'They would exterminate you.'

Wise was at a loss, and Roosevelt went on: 'Stephen, I'm going to ask you a personal question: you are a rabbi, with religious and moral obligations. Will you take the responsibility for getting millions of Jews killed if you do eventually get there?' Wise was shaken, but stated that he stood by the official programme of American Jewry. Then Roosevelt concluded: 'I agree that the majority of Jews want partition. But I'm warning you, you may be committing a crime.'

Our great stroke of luck was that Roosevelt was replaced by Harry Truman, who was a simple, upright man. He said: 'My friends are Jews, the Jews want partition, all right, they can have it.' He was not a calculating man, and his honesty was proverbial. He used to keep a supply of stamps for the letters he sent his mother: there was no question of using the White House stamps for his private correspondence! When he was not re-elected they were going to take him to the station in a White House car, but he protested: 'What does this mean? An official escort? What for?' And he called for a taxi.

Truman had one essential gift in addition: he knew his limits, and in many fields he leaned on his Secretary of State, Dean Acheson. The President had a Jewish childhood friend called Jacobson, his co-partner in a shop before he went into politics, and it is partly due to this man that we got the Negev.

After the United Nations vote on partition the Arabs threatened war, whereupon the American State Department changed its attitud e and wanted to postpone the creation of the State of Israel. It was Truman who decided, against all his advisers but one, who was Jewish, that the state must be set up as planned: he had promised his friends, and he always kept his word. So when the United Nations wanted to rule against the Negev belonging to the Jewish state, Weizmann tried to see Truman, but he refused, because he felt deluged by the endless flow of Jewish delegations. It was Jacobson who made himself Weizmann's go-between, and Truman said to him: 'Since it's you who ask me, I'll see him.' And following that interview he instructed the American delegation to insist on the Negev remaining with Israel.

Secretary of State Dean Acheson was a very different figure. He was a very cultured, aristocratic-looking man, not at all popular with the members of the Congress, who sensed his superiority. They used to say that there was nothing American about him, and he ought to be at Westminster. In fact he came over as a lot more British than Yankee. He had no trace of the provincial politician, and as a student of world history he always put problems in a universal framework. He was a friend of the Jews, but not of Zionism, and I am quite proud of having persuaded him to help us.

As I say, Truman was a modest man and left international policy to Acheson. If he had not consented to partition, Truman would never have given the go-ahead by himself. Now the Secretary of State's main argument was: 'For decades you will not have peace and you will be risking catastrophe, because the Americans will not be able to support you against the Arabs for ever.'

I replied: 'Listen, Mr Acheson, I'm talking to you now not as a Jew but as an American. I am an American citizen. Right, let's say you refuse partition. What will happen? Terrorism will gain ground in Israel. The Jews will not accept the immigration ban; I won't accept it myself. Half a million Jewish refugees who have survived Nazism are living in the accursed land of Germany. Their one wish is to leave that country where they are still living in camps. Are you ready to receive them in America? No. In other countries? No. Then Menahem Begin, the extreme rightist leader, will take power. I personally will not accede to his policy of terror, any more than Weizmann will, but the extremists will be dominant ... What will be your attitude then? When the Jewish terrorists are killing the British will you take a stand against the British? And when the British are killing Jews, where will you be?'

Acheson had heard me out without interrupting. 'Mr Goldmann,' he replied, 'you are the first Zionist leader to explain to me not only what is good for the Jews but what is good for America. It is for that reason that I appreciate you. I shall sleep on what you have said. Come tomorrow and I'll give you my reply. Come alone, not with a committee.'

Acheson's answer was crucial, because together with the Secretary of the Treasury, John Snyder, and the Secretary of War, Robert Patterson, he was a member of the committee appointed by Truman to settle the Palestine question. So I was feeling very anxious when I went back to see him at six o'clock the following night. His first words were: 'I accept.' And he went on: 'Now it's up to you to convince the other two. But you may tell them I'm with you.'

Snyder gave no trouble. 'If Acheson agrees, so do I,' he told me. 'I'll only try to work out how much the affair will cost us.' But that left Patterson, and like everybody in the Pentagon this much respected man was against partition. The military thought that it was a completely senseless venture. So how was Patterson to be convinced?

A large body of American Jewish opinion was also against partition—some because they wanted the whole of Palestine, others because they did not want a Jewish state at all. Among the champions of this second trend was the American Jewish Committee, which mattered not so much for the quantity as the quality of its membership—they were top-level financiers or prominent intellectuals who were either anti-Zionists or actual supporters of assimilation. The current chairman of the Committee was Judge Joseph Proskauer, a former colleague and close friend of Patterson's. All I knew about him was that he was a leading figure in the Democratic Party and that he had close ties with the very influential Cardinal Spellman.

As soon as I had got Dean Acheson's consent I had a call from Wise informing me that Proskauer had taken the train to Washington and was going to see Patterson to tell him that American Jews were against the State of Israel. My own appointment with Proskauer was not till a week later, so I took the very dangerous chance of picking up the phone and calling Proskauer. I have already described this conversation in my autobiography, but it was so important that it is worth recalling again.

'You have an appointment with Patterson the day after tomorrow,' I told him, going straight on to the offensive.

'How do you know that?' he asked me, taken by surprise.

'Stephen Wise tipped me off. I must speak to you before you meet Patterson.'

'Then come tonight.'

Wise and Proskauer, great adversaries in politics, had holiday homes on the same island and a friendly personal relationship, and it was undoubtedly for Wise's sake that I was able to get through to Proskauer so quickly.

The discussion went on for hours that night, with Proskauer soon asking me to call him Joe. I concluded a lengthy case like this:

'You are a good Jew and you've done a lot for Jewry. So you ought to understand what convinced Dean Acheson. I told him what a dilemma he would face if terrorism took hold in Israel. But it would be worse for you. If Begin and his Irgun friends take power, Moshe Sharett, Weizmann and I will resign, but there will be terror just the same: Jews will kill British and British kill Jews. So where will you stand, as an American Jew? With the Jews who kill the British, and consequently against your own government, or with the British who will be killing Jews two years after Auschwitz?'

He stood up with tears in his eyes, embraced me, and said:

'I am with you one hundred per cent. I'll take you with me to see Patterson, but before that I must resign the presidency of the American Jewish Committee, which is against the State of Israel.'

The vice-president of the Committee was Jacob Blaustein, a big oilman and notorious anti-Zionist who later became a friend of mine and a great friend of Israel. Proskauer reached for the phone and told me: 'Go into the next room and listen on the other phone.' It was nearly one o'clock in the morning, and Blaustein woke up with a start.

'What's the matter?' he said.

'I'm resigning as president as of now.'

'What's happened?'

'Nahum Goldmann is here with me; he has convinced me that the only solution from the viewpoint of American Jewry is partition and the creation of a Jewish state. So when I talk to Patterson on Monday I want to be a free man. So you have my resignation.'

'Joe, you've fallen into a trap,' Blaustein blurted out. 'Do you know who you're dealing with? Nahum Goldmann is the shrewdest operator in the world, let alone the shrewdest Jew. He's making a fool of you, you're ruining your career!'

Proskauer stood on his dignity: 'I'm older than you, and not more of a fool than you, if I may say so. It's an insult to tell me that Nahum has trapped me. He has convinced me, and that's different. I won't pursue this discussion. Call an emergency meeting for tomorrow morning and announce my resignation. If not I shall announce it to the newspapers myself.'

So on Monday we went to see Patterson together. Only Proskauer's name was announced when we arrived, and when Patterson saw us together he exclaimed: 'But Joe, you've come with Nahum Goldmann! I thought you were on opposite sides.' Proskauer answered: 'Listen, Robert, I'm not here to talk, I'm here to tell you that Goldmann has convinced me. We had a momentous talk two days ago. I've been wrong all my life, and he is right. Everything he says to you has my approval. Now listen to him.'

So I made my point once again, and Patterson replied: 'My advisers are against the partition idea, but I understand what you're saying. Since Joe Proskauer and Nahum Goldmann, who have been lifelong adversaries, have struck an agreement on this solution, I have no right to oppose it. So you can tell President Truman that I agree.'

All that remained now was for Truman to give his final endorsement. I talked it over with his assistant, David Niles, and he advised me to go and see the President myself.

'No,' I told him, 'somebody is going to have to talk the thing right through with Truman—not just talk about the American Jews, but also allay his doubts about the elections, the Democratic Party and so on. I'm an American citizen, but I'm still a foreigner, whereas you are his close adviser, David. So you go and see him.'

And I can tell you that it was a sacrifice for me to say No to going to see the President and being able to say afterwards: 'I was the one who won him over!'

2 *The Congress at Work*

THERE IS A PASSAGE in the Talmud which says that on the morrow of the day when all Jews are united, the Messiah will come. The basic idea of the World Jewish Congress is to provide an organ which can be a moral spokesman in the name of the Jewish people. In fact there can be no legal spokesman, because the Jewish people are not a legal entity.

The WJC does not speak in the name of all Jews but only in the name of the majority of them. That may seem simple, but if you remember that the Jews are spread around upwards of sixty countries, that they live under diametrically opposed regimes and speak different languages, the task looks fairly hazardous; in fact it looked impossible to many.

The unity of the Jewish people, without which there would be no Jewish people, has been maintained over centuries in which religion dominated Jewish life. In spite of certain differences of rites and traditions, the religion is unified and has hardly ever suffered schism, unlike Christianity for example. The one schism dates from ancient times and involves the Karaites, who still exist in Egypt. There used to be one or two Karaite sects in Russia, but I believe they have disappeared. The Karaites only recognize the Bible, and not the Talmud, the great legal commentary on it, which is accepted by other Jews all over the world.

Naturally there have been differences inside Judaism—Hasidism, for instance, which appeared in the eighteenth century and preaches a more passionate, perhaps even somewhat irrational concept of Judaism. But none of this has destroyed the principle of one and the same religion.

In the nineteenth century, when the Jews started organizing

against Polish, Romanian or Russian antisemitism, there arose the idea of giving Judaism a non-religious base. The first such attempt was the Alliance Israélite Universelle, created in Paris in 1860 by great French Jewish figures like Adolphe Crémieux, but it did not work out, because the masses were not yet active enough, especially in Eastern Europe, where they did not yet enjoy equal rights. Rich and influential people dealt with the problem as philanthropists, but they did not elect representatives of a Jewish community, be it local or general. Although it created some branches in other countries, the Alliance stagnated for years. A great deal more important today, after being chaired by the late lamented René Cassin, it does not know itself whether it is a political or a cultural organization. The Alliance has founded schools in North Africa, Iran and Palestine, with the help of the French government, which used to use it for propagating French culture, but it makes no effort to play any important role in Jewish international political life.

Then came the Zionist movement, firmly based on the idea of a unified people, but linked with a programme aiming at the creation of a national home which should eventually become a state. A lot of Jews were against this, especially at the start, and the Zionist movement was unable to bring about unity. Although it has the ideological approval of the great majority, to this day it is still dependent on a limited number of supporters who cannot numerically represent Jewry in its entirety.

In America my friend Stephen Wise then founded the American Jewish Congress, the first attempt to create a democratically representative Jewish organization. Other movements relied mainly on a few highly-placed and influential people—those who in Hebrew are called *shtadlanim*, protectors of Jewry. Consequently the American Jewish Committee owed its importance to the quality of its members and its considerable financial resources.

When I met Wise in the United States to talk to him about an English-language edition of the *Encyclopaedia Judaica*, which was then appearing in German, he in turn wanted to get me interested in the idea of a World Jewish Congress. As I have said, it was the Nazi menace above all that made up my mind: I had realized at first hand in Berlin that the policy of appeasement being practised by the democracies was only increasing the power of Hitler, and from 1935 onward I was convinced that war was coming. I had certainly not anticipated Auschwitz, but I had a foreboding that Hitler represented the gravest danger ever to have confronted the existence of the Jewish people. Consequently it was necessary to create an organization that spoke in the name of all the Jews in the world, that fought Hitler politically and followed through with concrete efforts to save the Jews.

After the First World War, Zionists and other representatives of communities had put forward the idea of national rights for the Jewish minorities of Eastern Europe. It was therefore a matter of including a statute on minorities in the documents settling the frontiers of Poland, Czechoslovakia, Romania, etc, which were gaining independence thanks to the Versailles treaties. We then created in Paris the Comité des Délégations Juives, which played a big part.

This committee was not founded democratically but it nevertheless represented the American Jewish Congress and several other organizations. Even institutions like the American Jewish Committee represented by Louis Marshall, which did not join it, cooperated with it. The committee sent a delegation to the Versailles congress to request the mandate on Palestine and the statute of minorities. It obtained satisfaction: in the Polish parliament, for example, a group officially represented the Jewish community. There were others in Czechoslovakia and Romania. Then, when these rights had been granted, the Comité des Délégations Juives lost much of its importance, despite the exemplary activities of its chairman, Leo Motzkin. Only the American Jewish Congress and the Zionist movement were still supporting it when I became chairman after Motzkin's death.

I was then laying the groundwork for the World Jewish Congress which was to absorb this Comité des Délégations Juives. In spite of the jealousy reigning among the various organizations I gained the agreement of the great majority of Zionist movements. The opposition came from the Bund, a Polish Jewish socialist organization, which carried some weight and would not recognize the unity of the Jewish people for ideological socialist reasons, but in general the Jews of Eastern Europe did not set too many problems.

In Germany opinion was divided: some of the Zionists were in favour of the WJC, but the rest were obsessed by the idea of Palestine and indifferent to the rights of the Jews of the Diaspora. My great friend Kurt Blumenfeld, the undisputed leader of the German Zionist movement, was against the WJC. Nevertheless at the time of the World Zionist Congress I succeeded in having a resolution passed calling on all Zionists to support the WJC.

In the rest of Western Europe it was very difficult. In France, the Alliance Israélite and the Consistoire Israélite de France were against. Their argument was that the principle of a reunified Jewish people would give credence to the myth of the 'Elders of Zion' and risk stirring up antisemitism, and that Jewry was not a political but a religious entity. In England the Board of Deputies of British Jews, recognized by the British parliament, was equally hostile to the WJC. The Anglo-Jewish Association, then an assimilationist group although pro-Israeli today, was chaired by one of the Montefiore brothers and composed of very rich and influential men. I knew this Montefiore personally and asked him to support the idea of the Congress. He replied: 'Sir, I am ready to give my support and advice to the Jews of Eastern Europe when I am asked, but I am not ready to ask or accept their advice.' So the English Jews did not take part.

As for the United States, only the American Jewish Congress and the Zionists were prepared to join, and this situation lasted twenty-five years. Today, at long last, the majority of American Jews are participants in the WJC.

Despite these various abstentions we organized three preliminary conferences, the first in 1932, the second in 1933, the third in 1935. The World Jewish Congress was not formally created till 1936, at a great gathering in Geneva.

At these preliminary conferences we mainly discussed the situation in Europe, and a re-reading of our speeches at the time shows that Wise and I were warning Jewry against Hitler. The majority of the Jewish people paid no attention, and when

Schopenhauer talks about 'the accursed optimism of the Jews' we are bound to recognize that the philosopher of pessimism is right: most Jews maintained that Hitler was a passing phase, and we never managed to gain unanimous support for our case.

But we did succeed in enlisting all the Jewish communities of South America and Canada into the WJC, and most of the European ones—England and France excepted. Delegations came from Italy, Yugoslavia, Greece, etc. But, paradoxically, we had more success with non-Jews than with Jews. Most foreign ministers were swamped and badgered by the horde of Jewish organizations that besieged them night and day. It was much more convenient for them to have the single address we were proposing.

Governments looked forward to the order and discipline which would be engendered by the existence of the WJC, and here I shall single out one revealing episode which took place in France. I have already said that the Consistoire Israélite and Alliance Israélite had refused to join the Congress. We therefore established a French section of the WJC, which included figures as important as the poet Edmond Fleg, Léonce Bernheim, who was killed by the Germans, and the newspaper publisher Charles Bollag, who had privileged relationships with all French ministers. On the occasion of the creation of this French section Louis Barthou, then the French Foreign Minister, sent a congratulatory telegram to Stephen Wise and me.

When I made his acquaintance some time later, Barthou told me how a delegation from the Consistoire and the Alliance had gone to see him to protest. 'Most French Jews reject the Congress,' these delegates told him, 'and here you are, the Foreign Minister, greeting it in the name of France!' Barthou, who was a very shrewd politician, replied: 'Gentlemen, your patriotism is not in doubt. So I have no special efforts to make in your regard. But I am paid—just as you say, as Foreign Minister—to create a climate of opinion favourable to France all over the world. It is therefore more important for me to win over Goldmann and Wise, who for their part can be either pro- or anti-French.' The delegates went off in great disappointment.

I met Louis Barthou for the first time in Switzerland in 1935. He was passing through Geneva, where I was then living, and asked me to see him, as he told me, so as to get to know me better. He then asked me to tell him a little about my life.

'You interest me,' he added. 'You have led an exceptional life. Do tell me.'

'I'm a wandering Jew,' I replied. 'Born in Lithuania, brought up in Germany, and living sometimes in France, sometimes in Switzerland. I have had four or five passports. The Nazis have de-naturalized me for high treason, so I am stateless.'

'Listen,' Barthou replied, 'I have a proposal to make. It generally requires five years' residence in our country to obtain French nationality but there is an old law which permits the President of the Republic to have somebody naturalized after three years if the Minister of Justice suggests it. You have had a Paris flat for three years. I'll arrange for you to become French.'

'I'm very grateful,' I told him, 'but I'll speak frankly: I have great admiration for France, its literature and its civilization; I enjoy life in Paris; but my love for France is not great enough for me to fight on its behalf. My duty is to fight for the Jewish people. Now, there'll be war three or four years from now, and in France people are called up to the age of fifty-five; as chairman of the executive of the WJC I could not desert, because the antisemites would exploit that action straight away. I therefore prefer not to run that risk, and not to become French.'

Barthou shook my hand and answered: 'I appreciate your frankness very much. But get yourself naturalized by some Latin American state: they never go to war, even when they declare it!' So he helped me to become the Honduran consul in Geneva and thereby have the benefit of a Honduran diplomatic passport.

With antisemitism developing all over the world, the WJC managed to intervene on some occasions, but not enough in my opinion. I can explain by taking three examples, which I have already cited in my autobiography.

The first involves Romania, which had a flourishing tradition of antisemitism. In 1935 there was in existence a fascist organization called the 'Iron Hand', whose leader was the historian and poet Octavian Goga. The more importance Hitler took on, the more arrogant did antisemites in all countries become. Thanks to the Versailles treaty the Romanian Jewish community was recognized as a national minority, but Goga and his supporters had already succeeded in having their equality of rights abolished. The WJC therefore addressed a petition to the League of Nations, but this had to be categorized as 'urgent' in order to prevent the affair dragging on for years. The United States were very helpful by intervening directly with King Carol. The English and French also gave us official support. At that time the League of Nations was still strong enough to impress Romania, if not Hitler's Germany. The King sent for Goga and told him that since he was unable to withstand Jewish pressure they must part company. Hundreds of journalists were awaiting the outcome of the interview, and when Goga left King Carol he faced them, lifted his arms and said: 'Israel, thou hast conquered.'

But the second example shows that against Hitler himself the WJC partly failed. It is an accusation which I shall always bring against my own generation: the Jews could not or would not pay heed to our warnings. So when the racist Nuremberg Laws were promulgated the President of Czechoslovakia, Eduard Benes, who happened to be in Geneva, asked to see me urgently at the Hôtel Richemond. He was usually a calm man—you could say a little bureaucratic—but that day I did not recognize him. He was like a lion. He at once started to storm and rail at me:

'How can you sit quietly in your apartment when the Nuremberg Laws have just been promulgated? Do you know what they mean for you? It is a declaration of war against every Jew in the world, the beginning of the end for you. You content yourselves with protesting in articles when you ought to be calling an international conference right now to launch a crusade against Hitler. He is still weak, he can be stopped . . .'

He was beside himself, but I was only too well aware that if we did organize a conference there would be plenty of absentees. From every side I had been hearing people say that the good relations between America and Hitler must not be disturbed; the

French were talking appeasement, and so on and on. So I dragged in all kinds of poor excuses. 'It's very difficult, you know,' I told Benes. 'Our members are dispersed across many countries, and then in two weeks' time there are the Jewish festivals ...' He broke in: 'Don't talk nonsense, Mr Goldmann; you are too clever for that. Just admit that the Jewish people has not the slightest sense of dignity.' That day, I felt terribly ashamed.

The third example involves Italy: when I moved to Geneva my wife and I were living in a pension in the rue de Lausanne, because the Germans had confiscated or sold all our furniture. Quite early one morning, when I was getting dressed, our landlady came in and told me that the chief rabbi of Rome was waiting downstairs to see me, apparently very agitated. This Doctor Sacerdote was a devoted friend and a member of the WJC executive. It had to mean something serious for him to visit me at this hour, and I immediately thought about a pogrom: even if Mussolini was not yet Hitler's ally, he was no less a fascist.

So I went straight downstairs, where Sacerdote greeted me with these words:

'Get dressed at once, we're catching the plane to Rome and it takes off at ten o'clock.'

'But why?'

'We are invited by the Duce.'

'What does he want?'

'It is very irksome for him to know that Jews the whole world over are fighting Hitler. Hitler is not his ally, but he considers him as a friend. He therefore wants to try to find a compromise to settle the Jewish problem, meet a leader of Jewry and arrange an interview for him with Adolf Hitler.'

'My dear chief rabbi,' I answered, 'you can inform Mussolini that I won't be coming.' This came as even more of a puzzle to him because the Duce was then at the height of his power. 'Mussolini will not be able to achieve the cancellation of the Nuremberg Laws,' I explained. 'They constitute the basis of the Nazi philosophy. Then what can he scrape up? A few minor improvements—to allow Jews to leave Germany, not to apply the Laws too rigorously. And that is in the best of cases. If the

Duce obtains those improvements without consulting me, that's fine. If Hitler relaxes his persecution of Jews, our struggle will be that much less fierce. But if Mussolini undertakes that approach to the Führer with my consent that means that I renounce the principle of equal rights and that I agree to compromise. What Hitler is doing today to seven hundred thousand Jews in Germany will be done tomorrow to three million of their brothers in Poland. No, I can't be associated with this move.'

I am not certain that I was right: had I been able to foresee Auschwitz, I might have agreed to the meeting, although I am certain that if Hitler had accepted a compromise in 1935 he would have scrapped it later on. In any case, when I met Mussolini the following year, he admitted: 'Your refusal annoyed me, but you were right. You are a statesman.'

A similar opportunity came up in London when the German ambassador, Doctor Hoesch, tried to put me in touch with Goering, who had already received a delegation of German Jews and asked them to intervene with the English Jews for them to cease their anti-Nazi campaign. Some German Jews did in fact take this step—which shed very little glory on them—but achieved nothing. As for me, I refused to see Goering.

In fact, the only tangible success we did achieve against Hitler's Germany consisted in bringing about its resignation from the League of Nations through having the Nazis' anti-Jewish policy condemned. It was at that point that Goebbels had me denaturalized for high treason. My father-in-law, who was still living in Germany, described his interview with a Gestapo bigwig who said to him: 'Do you realize what your son-in-law is costing Germany? Every day he moves around. We have given two agents the job of following him, but no sooner has he arrived in Brussels than he is leaving again for Rome, and from there to Warsaw or Paris ... And we have to pay for all those moves!'

Today the World Jewish Congress represents the great majority of Jews. There are now about fourteen million Jews in the world. Take away the three and a half million living in Eastern Europe, who apart from the Romanians and Yugoslavs who do have seats in the Congress are unable to join us, and the Czechs, Hungarians and East Berliners who have lately been allowed to send observers to WJC meetings but whose communities are very small, and that leaves about ten million. Now it is no exaggeration to state that we represent at least eight million Jews. There are the three and a half million Israeli Jews, most of American Jewry, nearly all the European Jews, plus those in Central and South America, Australia, Canada . . .

One of the main aims of the WJC is to represent every Jewish community wherever it may be, whenever it is not strong enough to act for itself. This means that the majority of our interventions have to remain secret. For example, if there is a wave of anti-semitism in some Latin American country, the Jews of that country immediately ask us to intervene. We then contact the American State Department and the country's embassies in Washington or Paris, and nobody—either the Americans or still less the government of the country in question—wants publicity about the matter: these are sovereign states, remember.

For the Zionist movement, things are more simple: it collects money, announces the number of trees planted or hospital beds created, and organizes big banquets in the course of which every-body gets a medal and feels generous. With us, the watchword is confidentiality.

We are therefore the only Jewish association to maintain contacts with the Communist countries; not only with Romania and Yugoslavia (I often meet Tito and Ceausescu), whose Jewish communities belong to the WJC, but with Hungary, which used to belong, then left after the fall of Nagy and is starting to get back in touch, and even with Soviet Russia, although it has no official relations with world Jewry. The Russians have permanent and principally personal relations with us: I have close ties with Dobrynin, the Russian ambassador to Washington, and I knew Gromyko well when he was in office.

The Russians are disposed, if not to negotiate openly, at least to discuss the Jewish problem. They want me to pay them a visit, but I will not go before finding out what concessions they are prepared to grant. They have a high opinion of the WJC but will not make a move as long as Israel is on a war footing. I shall return to this subject.

Another of the WJC's activities, at the request of the former Israeli Prime Minister Yitzhak Rabin, is to study the relations between the State of Israel and the Diaspora. World Jewry cannot be content with saying 'Amen' or shouting 'Hurray' each time Israel does anything. I explained this at length to Rabin, and he asked us to make proposals and to organize a system of communication between the sovereign state and Diaspora Jewry which does not call Israeli sovereignty in question but likewise does not expose the Jews of the whole world to the accusation of double loyalty.

Menahem Begin, now Prime Minister of Israel, then the leader of the opposition, took part by my invitation in the General Assembly of the WJC in February 1975, and suggested a very extended form of consultation between the Diaspora and the State of Israel, so the Congress is pursuing its plans with the present government of Israel.

But our most important—and less known—activities were undoubtedly our contacts with the liberation and independence movements of the new North African states, especially with Algeria and Morocco. In the days of French dominion there were more than a hundred thousand Jews in Algeria and more than two hundred thousand in Morocco, most of them very gallicized. In Algeria, thanks to the famous Crémieux Decrees, they even had automatic French citizenship, unlike the non-Jews. In Morocco the Jews were on such poor terms with the Arabs that they were nearly all pro-French—which brought them the hatred of those who aspired to independence.

The WJC had the foresight to realize in time that the process towards independence was irresistible. That being so, it was not hard to imagine some sort of retaliation against the Jews, with persecution perhaps going so far as pogroms. We therefore had to get in touch with the leaders of the independence movements, which required all the more discretion and secrecy because official French Jewry would have made violent protests. We took the precaution of confidentially informing the French government about the step we had taken, and I must say that we found them very sympathetic. Then we established our first contact in Tunisia, with Habib Bourguiba.

The political director of the WJC was then Alex Easterman, an English journalist who had given up his profession to work for us. Easterman had paid several visits to Bourguiba while he was in prison. I have always thought that the best moment for establishing links with revolutionary leaders is when they are in captivity: later on, when they are in power, they never forget who visited them in their darkest hours. In this way Bourguiba remained friends with Easterman, who went on seeing him once or twice a year when he was Prime Minister and then President.

I personally had very little to do with these contacts, but Easterman and an Israeli WJC official called Golan (who later became economic adviser to President Senghor) had talks not only with Bourguiba but also Ben Bella, Bouabid and other Algerian and Moroccan chiefs. They explained why it was that the Jews of North Africa were pro-French and asked for assurances that there would be no reprisals when independence came. It must be remembered that there was a great tide of panic flowing at that time, not only among the Jews in those countries but throughout world Jewry. I recall a big conference held in Israel at which everybody expressed the fear of a massacre of the Jewish populations of North Africa.

The WJC was the one organization that took a grip on the problem, because all the rest were openly pro-French. Not that we ourselves were anti-French, but we were certain that the independence movements would win the battle in the long run. History proved us right a few years later, and the action of de Gaulle retrospectively bore out our own. Our approaches probably saved tens of thousands of Jews: there were no pogroms, and in fact I believe that not a single Jew was killed after independence. It is true that many of them left Algeria for France, but that was their own decision.

As for the Moroccan Jews, most of them wanted to go to Israel after Morocco's independence, but naturally that country was pro-Arab, and its anti-Israeli position prevented it from negotiating the terms of this emigration with the Jewish Agency. The Congress, which maintained excellent relations with the Moroccan government, then acted as an intermediary—incognito of course. The Jewish Agency took charge of the immigrants' introduction to Israel, but emigration permission and the creation of transit camps—one of them, in Casablanca, on a grand scale —housing several thousand Jews waiting to leave the country was in our hands. I should add that Hassan II and his father Mohammed v before him had always behaved in exemplary fashion towards the Jews. During the war, King Mohammed v did not allow the Vichy government to interfere with his Jewish nationals, despite heavy pressure from the Pétainists and the Germans. He considered the Jews as coming under his special protection, and never let them down.

All the same, our activities were relatively simple at the time: finding that there was antisemitism in a given country, we would go there and try to reach a solution. Or else, if it involved a country like, for instance, Bolivia, we addressed ourselves to the State Department in Washington; if it involved the Congo, we dealt with the Belgians. Today the growing complexity of international politics makes our life much more difficult. I once remarked that the primary character of the WJC was to act like a statesman, whereas other Jewish organizations tend to work more like politicians: their perspective is from day to day; ours is in the longer term.

That is why the Congress is continually working to establish a dialogue with the Russians. Of course this has not yet produced very much, but at least the conversational ice is broken. And in any case I am an optimist: if there is peace in the Near East in a few years' time, as I hope, the life of the Russian Jews will be greatly improved as a result.

We are also the only Jewish organization with a department for the Third World. You may wonder whether this matters much, since apart from Brazil and Argentina these countries have no Jewish problem—there are next to no Jews in Black Africa and in Asia. Yet the Third World is interested. I once had a long talk with President Senghor in the course of which he said: 'Senegal has no Jewish nationals, but in the United Nations and all the international organizations we belong to, day and night we hear the Jewish problem talked about. Then what is happening? Why are they persecuted? Come and explain it to us. I'm prepared to invite you to hold a conference on the Jewish problem at the University of Dakar.' I answered that Israel was quite capable of explaining the question. 'Certainly,' he replied, 'Israel is certainly a great country [this was before the break], but like Senegal it is a selfish nation: the Israelis want to sell or buy arms, and to influence our voting at the UN. They are not objective. Whereas you in the WJC have no direct interests at stake, in terms of cash, profits or markets. So you send us somebody!'

This is a new and extremely important factor for the Jews, since the majority of Third World countries are represented in international proceedings. Without them, even the Arabs could not do very much. So it is up to us to inform the Third World of our problems. The security of the Jewish world is not exclusively assured by the sympathy of the democracies which dominate the planet. We need to win the understanding of the Communist bloc, and of the Third World bloc too.

We must stand in a privileged relationship with them. The Russians have told us clearly that after investigation they have decided that the World Jewish Congress is not dominated by any power as such. Their conclusion is therefore that: 'Since you are defending only the interests of Jews, and not those of a state, we are ready to discuss things with you.' Not that this means that they are ready to do what we would like, but they are open.

The same goes for the Third World. If an American Jewish organization sends a representative to Black Africa, the Africans will think that the American State Department is behind it, and they will be on their guard. The Congress does not put their backs up.

By seeking basically to inform, the WJC is changing a traditional, not to say arguable, Jewish policy. Because for two thousand years Jews have been protesting! As long as we were unrecognized and persecuted and deprived of all rights, the only thing to do in fact was to protest—or else to keep our lives intact and wait for the Messiah to come. But with the fall of Hitler we became a factor of world importance. We have a state which is recognized by most other countries, respected by many, detested by others, and occasionally admired. Even within the Diaspora we have never had such a good position: after Auschwitz, non-Jews had a bad conscience and tended to give us privileged treatment. That is why they voted in favour of the Jewish state.

So what are we doing with this new power? We are mainly continuing to protest. This is no great exaggeration. Jewish life has two elements: collecting money and protesting. Jews interrupt a David Oistrakh concert on the grounds that he is a Russian, they send telegrams all over the world, they demonstrate today against Brezhnev, tomorrow against Kissinger, next day against Romania . . . This is becoming absurd. First of all, when protests go on too long nobody can take them seriously. Some *New York Times* journalists have informed me that they would not publish any more letters agitating against the USSR unless they come from prominent personalities; they were getting snowed under by them.

And when six women—pretty ones, I hope—kick up a fuss at the Helsinki Conference, things are getting farcical. Brezhnev didn't even see them. They were arrested, then freed twenty-four hours later. Where does it get us? Quite simply, we have made people a little more irritated. I am not saying that all protesting should be stopped; I do say that it ought not to be the only way.

The Jews have better things to do, starting with consolidating their 'interior front'. The basis of our survival, the explanation of the miracle of that survival, is that the Jewish people has existed not through its exterior but its interior front. If our survival had depended on exterior policy we should have disappeared long ago; we have kept going because our interior front was our strong point. About ten years ago, Argentine Jewry was celebrating its hundredth anniversary, the centenary of Buenos Aires' first synagogue. I was invited to speak. 'A hundred years ago,' I said, 'supposing you had asked me to inaugurate this synagogue, what would I have said? I would have said that our people were in a terrible situation, I would have talked about pogroms, expulsions, misery, the refusal of equal rights, etc. But I would also have said that the interior front was marvellous, that there was no call for concern about the existence of the Jewish people, because the children were religious, they were being brought up to respect tradition, and there was then a Yiddish literature. You could certainly be afraid of Jews being murdered, but not of Jews ceasing to be Jews while still alive. Today the exterior front has all the marks of prosperity: we have equal rights, antisemitism is waning, and we are pretty well off. Even in Argentina, the Jews play a political role: there are Jewish ministers, Jewish MPs. But the interior front is looking terribly bad.'

I then quoted a precise example: a few years previously a big Jewish organization had had an opinion poll conducted at Harvard, the university of America's intellectual elite. Two questions were put to one or two thousand Jewish students. The first question was: 'Do you still feel Jewish?' The second was: 'Why?' A small majority, about fifty-five per cent, answered Yes to the first question, but the majority of that fifty-five per cent stated that they felt Jewish so as not to upset their parents. That meant that if their own children chose assimilation they them-selves would not oppose it. I advised against publishing those findings because they were too discouraging for the future of American Jewry.

So this is what I was getting at: a people may reckon to be stronger outside than inside, but in the long run that does not work. If the façade is sound and the interior rotten, the whole thing will perish. No people in history has been murdered. A lot of peoples have been wiped out by their enemies, but if you look closer you find that they were peoples which had given up the struggle. This is not murder, then, but suicide. That is why I am not always optimistic about the survival of the Jewish people: day by day I observe the crumbling of its interior front.

Inside the World Jewish Congress I have had my critics but my challengers have never amounted to much. They are nearly all members of the ultra-nationalist Zionist group Herut, and what they have mainly done is to make a noise, supported by a section of the Israeli press which dislikes me. In Israel a lot of newspapers are in the hands of old Herut supporters, and they play an important part, because the majority of Israelis consist of Eastern Jews for whom the printed word is practically holy writ. If something appears in *Maariv*, they all take it seriously straight away. This kind of rabble-rousing sensationalist press is rife all over the world, but a fair section of public opinion does not take it seriously, whereas in Israel every editorial is received like a revealed truth, and there is no state where the politicians are so terrorized by this kind of newspaper as they are in Israel. Personally, I know I'm not their special favourite, but I pay them no attention. Of course there are serious papers, like *Ha-Aretz* or *Davar*, but the afternoon press, which is at a low level, is more widespread and influential. I once told one of these journalists, who is very well-known in Israel and has been sniping at me for thirty years, that I didn't know what he was more in need of—education or talent. It is people like that who have been stoking up the so-called controversy.

In the World Jewish Congress there has never been any great opposition to me personally. The revisionists of Herut attack my policy, and that is quite natural, but they only represent a tiny minority of the Congress. I get on perfectly well with their leader, Menahem Begin, and I told him at the time of the February 1975 elections: 'If Herut was to vote for me, I would feel there was something amiss.'

Frankly, though, I had wanted to retire from the Congress for some time and did so at the end of 1977. I do think that it is abnormal for a president to remain in office for more than twenty years. Perhaps it is my own fault, because I had not trained a successor, but it must be realized that being president of the WJC is a very hard job. The man who has that title has to speak several languages fluently and know the situation of the Jews in every country in the world. He also has to keep up relations with a lot of governments and people of all shades of opinion. It is a very complicated business.

What it amounts to is nothing less than re-envisaging the whole of international politics through the Jewish prism. There are good

Jewish leaders in particular countries, but they do not know much about the problems of other Jews, say in the United States, Europe or Latin America. In addition there are Jewish intellectuals who have great qualities but who do not want to get mixed up in Jewish politics, which are not exactly appealing. If I had found somebody who not only suited me (I am not a dictator, and I cannot appoint my own successor) but had majority approval in the Congress, I would have retired earlier.

I had already given up my presidency of the World Zionist Organization, whose members have still not designated a new president. But it is less important for the WZO than for the Congress to have a president. The WZO has an executive of twenty prominent personalities who work full time. The WJC cannot possibly have that kind of executive, because there are not even as many as seven or eight great Jewish international experts permanently resident in towns like Geneva or New York. That being so, the president's task is essential. I wish the best success to Philip Klutznick in this position.

But coming back to this mythical opposition which my adversaries would like to see raised against me, the truth is that I myself see it as inadequate! I have never been in danger of not being re-elected. I have never struggled for any particular position. I am the only Jewish leader never to have had a party behind him (except for the Radical Party at one point, but that was a tiny formation) and never to have gone hunting for a government job. If I became president of the Zionist Organization it was because Ben Gurion as good as forced me into it, and it was only logical for me to become president of the WJC with Stephen Wise's death, since we had founded it together. In the same way, at the Claims Conference I several times wanted to be replaced, but unfortunately nobody else had my relations with the Germans.

So I have never wanted to capture a position, and in that respect my life has always been very easy to live. At the time of my first speech before the Zionist Congress there was in the chamber one of the most famous Zionist leaders, Shmaryahu Levin, a great friend of Weizmann. He was accompanied by Meyer Weisgal, later President of the Weizmann Institute in Israel, who was hearing me for the first time and told Levin: 'Young Goldmann will be a great Zionist leader.' Levin told him: 'He has plenty of talent, but also one huge defect: everything comes too easy for him.' There is some truth in that.

Why then, you may ask, does my personality give rise to so much criticism on the part of some Israelis? The first reason—which I hasten to say I understand—is that I have never settled in Israel. Ben Gurion often reproached me for it, and the Israeli press still does. The second reason is that I am too independent. Israel is a very conformist country, and a hotbed not of financial corruption but of the corruption of power. For a single party to have dominated political life for so long is demoralizing. I obviously prefer Mapai to Herut, since I am a man of the left (not a Marxist socialist), but the fact of not having changed its regime for twenty-nine years proves that Israel is one of the most conservative countries in the world. There are hardly any democracies, except until recently Sweden, where that is the case, but the fact is that the Jews are revolutionaries for other peoples but not for themselves.

Professionally and financially I am therefore altogether independent. If I had ever had to become a Jewish politician and be paid for it, I would rather have swept the streets. This profession of faith goes against the whole life-style of the Israelis.

Lastly, and this is obviously the most important point, my opinion of the Arab problem has always gone counter to the majority. I have never hesitated to express my view of the question when I thought it necessary, so I fully understand why I in my turn have my critics. I once told Maurice Couve de Murville that on that particular ground I felt more *goy* than Jew: unlike most Israelis I am neither fanatical, nor pig-headed, nor convinced that I am always right. I am tolerant, and do not exaggerate the importance either of problems or of my own activities.

The Israelis have the great weakness of thinking that the whole world revolves around them. Ex-President Shazar, a friend for upwards of fifty years, whose intimate political convictions were close to my own, once asked me:

'Where does your terrible wisdom come from? You always foresee what is going to happen. How do you do it?'

'I am no more shrewd or intelligent than a good many Israeli leaders,' I answered, 'but the difference between them and me is that I do not identify myself one hundred per cent with any idea or movement. I keep my distance, I have my doubts and reservations; that is why I see things without blinkers.'

During a pretty lively discussion I once told Ben Gurion that he considered problems from the viewpoint of Sde Boker, his little kibbutz, whereas I saw them from a plane flying twelve thousand metres high. It is a different approach.

The Israelis suffer from this short-term policy. They feel that every least thing is dreadfully important, and it makes them ill. Stomach ulcers are a typically Jewish complaint. They are always irritated, excited or in a passion. Their discussions are always exaggerated. None of that has any correspondence with my own temperament, and from that angle I am something of an odd man out.

As a man of the left, I have often blamed the Israelis for not being revolutionary enough. And yet some people have seen these opinions to be in contradiction with my own personal life and private fortune. But what ideological charter of the left lays it down that you have to be a beggar to be a progressive? On the contrary, I believe that it is more convincing to be well-off and left than poverty-stricken and left. What has anybody's personal wealth to do with the quest for social justice? Unless one is a Marxist, there is no necessity for believing that the economic situation is what determines the degree of ideological enlightenment. On the contrary, I would go as far as to say that if it were possible a political leader ought not to be paid for his public activities. For any minister or diplomat, resignation is no easy matter—next day he is on the bread line. A man like me is a lot more independent. Thanks to my financial position I have never felt any economic motivation for obtaining any paid job, either in the framework of the Zionist movement or inside the World Jewish Congress, and especially not in the government of Israel, where I have several times been offered posts as minister or ambassador.

Moshe Sharett, who was my best friend, used to say to me: 'Nahum, we have no hold on you. You have accounts in several countries, and you have the laugh on us.' That was an exaggeration, but I still think that material independence enables its possessor to act much more freely and serenely.

To return to the World Jewish Congress, our relations with the World Zionist Organization were formally and finally established at the meeting of the WJC in Israel in February 1975. But our cooperation dates even from before the foundation of the Congress. Stephen Wise and I had realized that those who would help us from the outset would be the Zionists, for the idea of the unification of the Jewish people lies at the root of their philosophy. Yet there was a certain amount of opposition from the Zionist Congress to our WJC plan. Not an opposition on the principle, but on the advisability of encouraging it to become a reality. One Zionist school of thought wanted Zionism to concentrate its efforts solely on obtaining a Jewish national homeland (there was no mention yet of a state), organizing Jewish immigration to Israel, colonization and so on. Another school argued that Zionism ought also to take an interest in the problems of the Diaspora so as to ensure a Jewish education for the new generations.

The Eastern European Zionists, who were fighting to achieve the status of minorities and for participation in the political life of their countries, were naturally in favour of what was called 'the work of the present', meaning the organization and intensification of Jewish life inside the communities. The German Zionists were opposed. They played a great ideological role because of their German cultural background, and they came mainly from assimilated environments. Their then leader, Kurt Blumenfeld, had invented the terms 'pre-assimilation Zionism' and 'post-assimilation Zionism'. I aligned myself with the Zionists of Eastern Europe, because the problems of the Diaspora have always interested me.

Finally, the Zionist Congress adopted, by a big majority, a resolution to create the WJC and appealed to all Zionist organizations to support us. But formally there was no relationship between the WJC and the World Zionist Organization—apart from the fact that for many years I was president of both. When there was a problem between the two organizations, people used to say: 'Goldmann is negotiating with Goldmann.'

During the last war there was little cooperation. The Zionist movement was very limited and its main concern was with maintaining a Jewish life in Palestine. After the war, when I was elected its president, relations naturally drew closer, and for the past ten years we have been trying to formalize them. One of the major difficulties was in the actual rules of the WJC, which provided only for membership by local, territorial or national bodies representing the Jewish communities, excluding all international organizations. It was impossible for the Zionist movement, which is essentially international, to join the Congress and to be heard there. So we changed the rules, and today the Zionists have a fixed number of representatives in all the institutions of the Congress.

All the same, if the Zionist movement has real influence in the WJC it is not a decisive influence. This arises mainly out of Zionism being based on political parties, which I see as a misfortune, and which explains why the Zionist Organization finds itself today in a very critical state. Certainly the Zionist parties, which have lost all importance, had their *raison d'être* as long as there was no Jewish state in existence. Theodor Herzl even said that the Zionist Organization was the Jewish state on the march. As long as the Zionist movement was deciding policy, it was consequently necessary for there to be parties. Some wanted an Orthodox Jewish state, others a socialist state; some opted for liberal capitalism, some for conservative capitalism. But once the state existed, once it was exerting its own authority and sovereignty, outside Israel the Zionist parties no longer counted. All they do today is help the Israeli political parties. The situation is absurd.

In Buenos Aires, for example, every three or four years there are democratic elections to the executive committee of the Jewish community. You can see posters and banners saying 'Vote Mapai for Ben Gurion' or 'Vote for Golda Meir'. What has that got to do with the Buenos Aires community? Or what reason does a Chicago Jew have for choosing Mapai or Misrahi? What does it have to do with him? He doesn't even know the difference!

These things do not exist in the World Jewish Congress. That is why at the time of our last meeting, when Herut tried to prevent my re-election by attacking me on the grounds of my alleged political conception of Zionism, its intervention was considered ridiculous. Our problems are education, youth, antisemitism, equal rights for Russian Jews, etc. There have been indirect attempts to introduce the party system into the Congress through the creation of 'international associates'. Naturally when there is a meeting the members of the various political tendencies get together, but it is not official. The WJC has no Mapai or Herut: it has an American or a French or any other national delegation, embracing Zionists and non-Zionists alike.

So much for official relations, but this leaves the division of labour. Everything that concerns Israel is naturally the province of the Zionist movement, although it occasionally asks us to stand in for it—for example in the Moroccan emigration case which I have already mentioned. In the field of Jewish education the Zionist movement does a sizable job which requires a lot of money. The World Zionist Movement and the Jewish Agency operate with an annual budget of four to five hundred million dollars, whereas ours is two million dollars. So it is out of the question for us to finance schools or teacher training colleges. But we work in close collaboration at community level.

As to the nature of our relations with the State of Israel, this problem goes beyond the WJC, because relations between Israel and the Diaspora concern all Jews.

As I have said, the Congress unofficially assists the Israeli government in certain precise circumstances—for example when it is a matter of having talks with a Communist state or one of the African states which have broken off relations with Jerusalem.

But this collaboration with Israel on specific points has never prevented me from making severe judgements on its policy and diplomatic methods.

Neither the Jewish people nor its representatives have yet acquired the difficult art of real negotiation. In politics, all good negotiating presupposes a certain equality between partners. One may be objectively stronger and the other weaker, but psychologically there has to be common ground, otherwise it is not a matter of negotiation, just of *diktat* or submission. For centuries it was not possible for there to be such a thing as Jewish diplomacy, because Jews were not recognized as equals either collectively or as individuals. All they could hope for was to live from one day to the next and put themselves in the hands of the *shtadlanim*, the philanthropists who intervened now and then to save the community. That was the case with Moses Montefiore and Adolphe Crémieux, in the Damascus affair or at the time of the decrees on the Jews of Algeria. But they were not acting because they represented the Jewish people but because they were very influential in their own right, either economically or politically. Since the governments they were dealing with respected them and sometimes wanted to gain their good will, they were able to achieve something for their co-religionists. Men like these, labelled 'Court Jews', have always existed within the Diaspora, but they cannot be called Jewish diplomats or statesmen.

True diplomacy and a true art of politics can only come about subject to the existence of a programme, an overall view, and long-term objectives. No policy based solely on the problematics of survival can be constructive. And in the ghettos of the Diaspora the Jews could not make plans. They did not know where they would be the following day—whether they were to be looted, expelled or destroyed. During the two thousand years of the Diaspora, the sole Jewish statesman was the Messiah. The Jews tried to survive, and some day the Messiah would appear and solve all their problems.

Everything has changed since the Jews have possessed equal rights, representative organizations, and *a fortiori* the State of Israel. Our generation is therefore the first to have the opportunity of laying down a Jewish policy, and it has everything to learn in this field.

First of all, the Jews are still not managing to consider their opponents' demands as being as important as their own. An Israeli diplomat visits a head of government and informs him about what is good for the Jews; if the other does not seem too interested, the diplomat pays no heed to what his opposite number may want. During a public debate with the greatest Zionist opponent I have ever had, Rabbi Silver, I once said that the difference between a statesman and a politician is that one only takes account of what his supporters want, whereas the other is concerned with his adversaries' requirements, because they are the people he must settle with. It is often hard to find a compromise with Jewish diplomats quite simply because they do not even perceive the other party's wants. So they still have to overcome this egocentricity, the outcome of two thousand years of persecution and feeling inferior.

On the other hand, by studying the Talmud century after century, the Jews have acquired an acute sense of logic and dialectics. In my opinion theirs is a far more refined culture than the one which gave rise to Roman jurisprudence, which is considered the great classic of logic. But the result is that they have developed two notions which are not very realistic in most cases.

The first notion is their belief that if they are right from the moral point of view they have won a battle. Now in politics this is of little account. I do not wish to appear cynical and say that it counts for nothing at all; it is certainly better to be right from the moral point of view than not to be right at all. But this is not a decisive factor.

The second notion is their parallel belief that if they are right from the logical point of view they have won. Yet in politics logic means nothing. I once served on a commission appointed by Weizmann to negotiate with the British government. It was in the days of the British Mandate, and the chairman of the British commission was R. A. Butler, a cultivated man, later to become Master of Trinity College Cambridge. During one of our clashes I put forward a whole series of very dense, impeccably logical arguments.

I was certain that he would be unable to reply, but he heard me through very politely before smiling and saying: 'My dear Doctor Goldmann, I readily admit that all the logic is on your side, but we have the Empire, and had we obeyed your logic we would never have had that Empire!' He was absolutely right. Logic was with me, it is true, but with him lay the reality of power.

What the Israeli negotiators have to learn is that no one is ever altogether right. Absolute situations do not exist, because the absolute is impossible to reach. When the Israelis negotiate they are so sure of their own rights that they overlook those of the Arabs, thereby weakening their own positions in the eyes of the world.

One last point before I finish these strictures: the Israelis over-estimate the importance of propaganda and 'public relations'. The Israeli press keeps saying: 'Our propaganda is badly handled, we have a poor image', and so forth. I am familiar with the subject, since the World Zionist Organization has spent millions of dollars on propaganda. Well, I regret that, because it is worth very little. The decisive factor to influence world opinion is the character of Israel's policies, and if those policies are criticized by the majority of states, the best propaganda is helpless. The Israelis have inherited this misjudgement and this wild infatuation for slogans from the Americans. In the United States, everything is sold by what they call 'Madison Avenue' methods, from the street where their biggest advertising firms are based. This technique may be terrific for launching a brand of soap or toothpaste, or even a new newspaper, but not when it comes to disseminating a political idea by distorting it. President Lincoln once said: 'You can fool all the people some of the time, and you can fool some of the people all the time, but you can't fool all the people all the time.' That ought to give our propaganda experts food for thought ...

3 The Will to be Jewish

THERE IS NO ONE DEFINITION of Judaism which is altogether satisfactory. The Germans are famous for their genius for formulation, yet in the German language alone you could collect a library of hundreds of books on the theme of 'What is Judaism?' I remember giving a lecture when I was a student during which I offered more than twenty definitions: Judaism is a religion, a people, a nation, a cultural community, etc. None of them was absolutely accurate. The Jewish people is something extraordinary and unique—which does not mean 'better'; only some Hebrew words will cover it, but they have no adequate translation. *Am* is generally translated by 'people', because there is no better word, but it is not quite that. If you translate *Uma* as 'nation' it is equally misleading, and 'religion' for *Dat* is totally wrong. *Dat* is a form of life, it is jurisprudence, law, and faith as well. So we have to do without concise definitions.

For me, a Jew is a man who is born Jewish or has become Jewish by conversion, and who feels Jewish. That's all. If a Jew no longer wants to be Jewish, if he denies Judaism, if he gives his children no Jewish education, or baptizes them, then he can cease to be a Jew. After all that is why so many Jews have disappeared throughout the centuries; otherwise there would be hundreds of millions today. So a Jew takes it upon himself to be a Jew—he feels a part of the Jewish people, he identifies himself with its history and with its destiny. For some, the keystone is religion. For others it is the glory of a people which has given the world monotheism, the prophets, Spinoza, Marx, Freud, Einstein and so many other geniuses. For others again it is their respect for Jewish sufferings past and present that cements their adhesion to the cause of Judaism: they would reckon it shameful and immoral to cut themselves off from a people which has suffered such martyrdom to preserve its identity.

So there are all sorts of motivations—just as there are all sorts of motivations for the fact that one man is another man's friend, or loves a woman, or likes this book and not that one. But what counts is the will to remain Jewish.

I reject Satrer's definition that a Jew is anybody whom other people designate as such. In fact even if the Messiah eventually arrives and antisemitism no longer exists, I hope that there will always be a Jewish people. Even if others forget that Jews exist, I hope that they will preserve themselves as a people. How could so extraordinarily creative a people appear or disappear according to how other people felt? I do not accept such a negative definition, which is very much like the one suggested by Max Frisch in his famous play *Andorra*—if he's a foreigner, he must be a Jew. Is that a basis for such a people, to exist only because others consider it as different?

It is a fundamental problem. Jewish philosophy, thought and ideology are made up of manifold contradictions. One of them is that we are at one and the same time the most separatist and the most universalist people in the world.

On the one hand, we have always refused to renounce our identity. Unlike other religions, Judaism has never proselytized. Some great theologians, both Jewish and non-Jewish, have claimed that if Judaism had wanted to become a universal religion it could easily have taken the place of Christianity. The historians show that in the first centuries after Jesus Christ Roman society contained a lot more converts to Judaism than to Christianity; the Empress Poppaea was Jewish, members of the imperial family and court dignitaries were Jewish. But the Talmud says that a *ger*, a convert, is as hard to bear as a sore. Here we are putting a finger on the dual religion/nation aspect of Judaism. In fact if Judaism had only been a religion it would have been in its interest to absorb most of those who were ready to become converts, but it was also a people invested with a special mission, chosen by God; that is why the Jews opposed proselytism. Even in our own day it is quite hard to become a Jew.

On the other hand, there are no moralists so universal as the prophets. Although he designated the Jews as 'his people', the Jewish God is universal, he is the God of all humanity. In the same way the Jewish Messiah has never been a national Messiah: he is each and everybody's Messiah. That is the great characteristic of our people: we are apart, and isolated from the rest, and at the same time destined to fulfil a mission which concerns the whole world, to be the servants of humanity.

If I had not had to throw myself into public affairs because of Hitler I would probably have become a historian and written a book on the Jews and other nations. No other people in the world has had so many contacts with different civilizations: encounters with the Greeks, the Romans, the Christians, the Arabs, even the Chinese. It is by the way interesting to observe that the worst of these encounters was with the Christians, not with the Muslims, and also to stress that the ghetto is historically a Jewish invention. It is wrong to say that the *goyim* forced the Jews to separate themselves from other societies. When the Christians defined the ghetto limits, Jews lived there already. Certainly there is a difference between choosing one's neighbours freely and being obliged to live in a particular place and forbidden to leave it at night; but even today Jews have a tendency to live in a neighbourhood of their own, in an environment that facilitates the life of their community.

Before emancipation things were cruel but simple: being at best tolerated, the Jews lived a life apart, without worrying about the laws or customs of others. I often quote that brilliant remark of Heinrich Heine's—who was a very good Jew at the end of his life and whose conversion to Christianity was only a formality, his entry fee into Western society. Heine asked: 'How are we to explain the mystery constituted by the survival of the Jews without a country, without a state, without anything?' And he gave an answer: 'It is because in the *Shulhan Arukh* [the summary of the Jewish laws and prescriptions] they have a veritable portable homeland.' It is true: when the Jews were driven out of one country they would go to another, but carrying the *Shulhan*

Arukh under their arms. On this foundation they very soon constituted themselves a new country.

Today, except for a small minority, the Jews no longer live according to the *Shulhan Arukh*. They are emancipated from a political point of view and on an equal footing with others. Economically they have played a considerable part, particularly since the Second World War, and intellectually the three geniuses who have had the greatest influence on modern civilization —Marx, Freud and Einstein—were Jews. The Jews are therefore fully integrated, and the difficulty is precisely to maintain their identity, their character 'apart'. Otherwise there will no longer be a Jewish people.

The adult generation has been through two shattering experiences: the first, a horrible one, was the Holocaust, which most of them had never foreseen. The second, a miraculous one, was the creation of the Jewish state in which so few people had believed.

But for the younger generation these two facts belong to the past. I have two sons; through me they know about the tragedy of the Holocaust and Zionism, because they know that I was very active in them. But Israel seems quite normal to them. It is a state like any other, where every week there is talk of some new ambassador or minister—the usual routine in fact. This no longer has anything to do with the miraculous realization of the great dream of two thousand years. For the young, the new Jewish state is a fact, nor do they have to fear a resurgence of Nazism.

So the problem consists in finding new challenges for them, and I am very ready to suggest one: to make Israel different from what it is today. To build an Israel which is not content with having the best army in the Near East, spending most of its resources on the acquisition of new armaments, and being proud of winning yet another war which solves nothing and in any case may end in disaster. To build an Israel which concentrates instead on religious, cultural and social creativity. The new Jewish youth must become revolutionary. World Jewry, inspired by an Israel of peace and justice, must become a revolutionary movement. Not with barricades, bombs and terrorists, but as a champion of the war against poverty, illiteracy and inequality, for the abolition of the sovereign state, and for peace.

That is what would give new meaning to the sufferings of the Jewish people. After all, the Jews could have lived quite happily if they had had themselves baptized and renounced their condition. If they did not do so, it was essentially in order to obey the ideal of their prophets and of Messianism, in order to serve humanity. Today Judaism is forgetting its obligations: Jews belong to many reactionary and capitalist parties. The new generations must learn to be revolutionaries—revolutionaries in so far as they are Jews. As Americans or French men and women too, of course, but first of all as Jews.

We are living in an age in which the existence of minorities is everywhere under threat. Contemporary civilization has a tendency to flatten everything out so as to arrive at what has been called 'machine man'. The entire world is reaching towards a kind of world civilization. A song written in New York is sung in Moscow and Shanghai next day, in spite of any iron or bamboo curtain. The great danger lies in the erosion of the difference between peoples—and, within peoples, between the majority and the minority. To my mind, civilization has always been created by minorities: even in politics, it is they who make revolutions. It was a minority that created Zionism. The majority is generally opposed to change, but it flocks to the help of victory once the minority has achieved a success.

Nor has culture ever been the prerogative of the masses: it is the creation of matchless individuals, geniuses, or a small number fanatically devoted to an ideal. The first Christians were a tiny minority; so were the first Protestants. When ideas are adopted by the majority they lose their profundity. Because of technology, the abolition of distances, the coming of the telephone, radio and television, our civilization is growing more and more uniform. After the First World War we founded the Minorities Congress to obtain rights written into the framework of the Versailles treaty, then with the Second World War it ceased to exist. Well, the Jews ought to recreate the Minorities Congress, not to win political rights this time, but simply to survive culturally.

The Jews would not take these initiatives alone, but for example in the United States together with the Blacks, in Catholic countries together with the Protestants, and in Protestant countries together with the Catholics—in other words, wherever discrimination exists. A minority, whatever it is, has the right to demand that its members should benefit from the wealth of the state within which it finds itself, and to have, for example, its own schools. Once again for the Jewish people this is a question of survival.

There are other minorities—German, Dutch, Italian and so on—but they are not so decisive for their mother countries. If all the Germans in America were to disappear as Germans, which will undoubtedly happen within one or two generations, the existence of the German people would not be in danger. If the few million Italians living in Latin America were to forget their Italian origins, the Italian Republic would remain. But if the Jewish minorities all over the world were to cease existing as minorities, there would no longer be a single chance of the Jewish people surviving or of Israel staying alive in the midst of a sea of Arabs.

If we recreate that great minorities movement it will be a long-term process because naturally governments will not help and may even oppose it. But we have a duty to struggle for this right of minorities to retain their cultural identity, and it is up to the Jews to take the lead because they are long accustomed to gauging whether or not a government respects the rights of man and of the citizen.

I have always kept in touch with youth, and I have a high regard for Jewish youth. At the time of the Zionist Congress in 1968, when I resigned from my position as president, there was a delegation of Zionist youth made up of students and non-students. They were all opposed to the Zionist leaders and their policy, and they demonstrated against the Congress. Then they sent me a letter which I still have, in which they told me: 'You are the one Jewish leader who has remained young.' Each time I visit America I spend hours with Jewish students, and I fully understand their problem: they are not attracted by the Jewish leadership because it is third-rate, especially in the United States, where it consists either of functionaries or 'fat cats'. And yet no Jewish generation has produced as many intellectuals as ours. But they can't stand the present-day rigmarole of Jewish life in the Diaspora: the collections, the banquets, the medals and so forth. They therefore steer clear of Judaism, except for a minority (but better a minority than none at all) who are drawn towards Israel. Yet Israel cannot possibly influence the young in the long run. Israel today is politics, war and national defence, not the embodiment of the ideals of young people whose dream is of socialism and life on the kibbutz.

There is a story about a pagan who wanted to become Jewish. He stops the great Talmudist Hillel in the street and asks him straight out: 'What is the essence of Judaism?' And Hillel at once replies: 'Do not do to others what you do not want them to do to you.' I am no Hillel, but if someone were to ask me the meaning of Judaism I would answer that it was nonconformism. We are history's nonconformist people *par excellence*. We began with Abraham, who left his country not to conquer others or to get rich, but simply because he could not bear the idolatrous religion which surrounded him. From Abraham to Einstein, nonconformism has remained our most basic feature. If the Jewish people has survived it is because it was nonconformist, because it rejected the notions of the greatest number.

Since emancipation we have been becoming a more and more conformist people. The Jews follow the opinion of the majority; they support dictatorships if they are not antisemitic; they have made Israel a state like all the rest. But a conformist people has nothing to offer to its young idealists; it must be contented with the sort of prosaic young generation whose only aims are to live well, make love and make money.

The big argument of the young people I frequently talk with runs as follows: 'We are on the side of the Blacks because we are progressives, and consequently for equality and peace and against social hardship. The Jewish Establishment is reactionary and we have nothing to say to it.' It is these young people who must be taught the nonconformist tradition of Judaism and see it proved that it is in their interest to adopt it. We have to explain to them:

'Be against the Jewish Establishment and create revolutionary Jewish youth organizations. That way you will be returning to the sources of Judaism.'

The great danger is isolationism, which would be the death-knell of Judaism. First of all for a pragmatic reason: why should the *goyim* help us if we do not help them? If we lose our interest in the great idealistic movements, why should the non-Jewish idealists support us?

I will tell you a story on this subject which I had from my father and which I quoted during a debate about the World Union of Jewish Students, which the leaders of the Jewish Establishment were then hesitating to recognize. In a little village there were two fools. One of them climbed on the synagogue roof one day and said: 'I'll jump.' His family came running, the whole community gathered round to plead with him; it was hopeless—the fool kept saying: 'If anyone goes into the synagogue I'll jump straight away.' Then along came the other fool and asked what was happening. 'Leave it to me,' he said, and shouted up: 'Chaim, Chaim, if you don't come down at once I'll pick up a scythe and cut the synagogue in two.' And Chaim came straight down. The moral of this story is that if a fool understands the language of another fool, a revolutionary ought to understand the language of another revolutionary—even one who is illogical and unrealistic.

So it seems to me that the only solution is to create a young generation which is nonconformist, revolutionary and Jewish all at once. The success of that synthesis depends very much on Israel, which is taking the opposite attitude today, but without which nothing can be done in the Diaspora. It is all a function of peace. War is ruinous: it ruins the economy of Israel, its policy and its culture. It is impossible to state whether the people responsible are the Jews or the Arabs. I am simply stating the facts of the disaster.

On the day when peace comes, the leftist movement will undoubtedly be very strong in Israel, and it will be anti-Orthodox. A great cultural battle will then break out which, like Ben Gurion, I want to avoid at this moment: as long as war prevails, that kind of internal struggle would be terribly dangerous. But after the hostilities the first thing to do will be to separate religion and state. Today we confine ourselves to telling the leftists: 'Don't make a fuss on this question, you will be obstructing our defence policy, which requires national unity'—and the leftists, being good patriots, give way. But after the peace they will resume the debate.

There is the theory that peace represents a certain danger by disuniting the Jews, who have always stood together in adversity. This idea was valid when we were living in ghettos and adversity concerned every Jew. That is not the case today, when the war only affects the State of Israel. How long do you think Jews who live elsewhere in good conditions are going to go on being influenced by the war in the Near East? The first signs of disaffection are already visible.

At the time of the Six Day War, for example, all French Jews were fired with enthusiasm. Everybody wanted to take up arms in defence of Israel and a committee was founded for that purpose. The conflict ended without any volunteers being taken. Some Zionists then proposed that those who had not been able to fight for Israel should settle there as immigrants. The volunteers did not follow up that suggestion. Reality proves that immigration to Israel has been decreasing a lot in recent years. Whereas about half those Jews who are authorized to leave the USSR prefer not to go to Israel, and immigration from Europe and America is decreasing, emigration—particularly by young Israelis—is on the increase. This is principally due to the economic and psychological difficulties created by the state of war, and it is one of the most convincing arguments why Israel should make concessions which will enable a lasting peace to be concluded.

That is what makes me say that adversity is not the ideal unifying agent of Judaism, and if it goes on too long then war itself will become a routine. You cannot live a life determined by a conflict which breaks out again every three years. So we have to concentrate on the interior front—which implies a radical change in Jewish policy. Demonstrating is fine—it salves people's consciences and doesn't cost much. But working in a school or university, and performing even a dull kind of daily labour, is a lot more important.

In Israel the new generation attends the universities but does not want to learn Yiddish. We may regret it, but we cannot force them. It is worse still in the Diaspora, where the children are cut off from Jewish culture. How can a young Jew remain a good Jew if he knows nothing of Jewish history, and does not know what Jews have achieved in terms of religion, philosophy, literature and art? The only solution is to create full-time Jewish schools, as the Catholics have Catholic schools. But a lot of Jews are opposed to that kind of school network on the grounds that it would mean a return to the ghetto, which is totally absurd. Only the Orthodox Jews defend this idea, and on this point I am with them. Why not devise a system of Jewish schools which would be subsidized by the state, which would obviously determine the main lines of education?

The institutions I am concerned with have been trying to encourage a new awareness on the cultural level. The most important of them, the Memorial Foundation, has been able to draw upon sizable amounts in connection with German reparations. The Claims Conference and the Memorial Foundation have made contributions to the creation of Jewish schools and community centres, something like the French *maisons des jeunes* and *maisons de la culture*, which have big attendances everywhere. After the war our aim was to rebuild the cultural and religious life of the Jewish people. Adenauer supported us. Some German ministers wanted the reparations money to be spent only on the victims of Nazism and on philanthropic works. Adenauer told the supporters of that argument: 'The Bible says that man does not live by bread alone. We must help to revive Jewish cultural life; it is no less important than feeding the poor.' So it is thanks to that money that we were able to put up buildings and then to establish scholarship funds for Jewish writers and scholars working on Jewish subjects, as well as creating departments of Judaism in the great universities, and so on.

On the subject of education through the classic media—the press, radio and television—we have to yield to the fact that the Yiddish newspapers, which are struggling for survival, belong to an already bygone world. That admission fills me with sadness, because Yiddish was the popular language of millions of Jews for centuries. I only hope that Hebrew may now become the second language of all Jews and a Jewish press written in Hebrew may be spread throughout the Diaspora.

In the immediate future it seems to me that the most important thing in every country where Jews are living is to re-establish a literature and press written in the language of the country but whose content is Jewish. That would involve literary works as well as books of research. The day we negotiate with the Russians I shall ask for the creation, or recreation, of that kind of press and literature in the USSR.

The way it looks at the moment, in the English language in particular, the Jewish press of the Diaspora is very poor and very provincial. There are a few exceptions, like the London *Jewish Chronicle*, but in general it makes its living off the small advertisements and most of the journalists who work in it are unknown. When I was in the United States I tried to start a Jewish weekly —it is intolerable for a community of six million people not to have a great newspaper. But I failed. There have been other attempts, such as the monthly *Opinion*, founded by Stephen Wise's son, but they have all ended in failure. Although the United States does have a number of monthly and quarterly reviews of a high intellectual standard, the weekly news press in particular represents petty private interests and rarely gives an objective image of Jewish life.

A weekly which provided regular analyses of Jewish problems would particularly appeal to those young people who do not read the mediocre local Jewish press. It is not the staff or the money which are lacking, but the understanding of the Jewish leadership for such an organ.

In the longer term I also have in mind a Jewish radio station broadcasting in the languages of the countries of the Diaspora. The ideal would be a big central station transmitting in English, French, Spanish and Hebrew. The World Jewish Congress once spent some time negotiating with Radio Monte Carlo, but there again the project fell through.

Obviously there is another way, which involves a policy of

'entryism' into pre-existent radio and TV stations, but it is fairly difficult to get a foothold in them. Buying the time is practically impossible: on American TV a minute costs two thousand dollars! And in any case the networks do not accept propaganda. The only possibility is to make programmes that interest them, but that is very expensive. Also these are necessarily private enterprises, very uneven in quality and interest. Among the best and the longest-lived I would cite Rabbi Josy Eisenberg's Sunday programme in France.

In the cinema field there has never been any consistent policy of creating, for example, a characteristically Jewish production company with access to international distribution. Israel has spent a lot of money on motion pictures, but mostly bad ones, crammed with propaganda.

Claude Lanzmann, who made the excellent *Why Israel?* has asked me to take part in a film he wants to make about the Holocaust. It will take him two or three years to assemble the documentation, visit the sites of the big concentration camps, and in particular to collect the evidence of the survivors of the Holocaust. I asked him what he wanted from me, and he replied: 'No other Jew can be the pivot of this film. You lived in Germany before Hitler, you fought against the Nazis for ten years, you got away during the war and did your utmost to save other Jews, you know about the Allies and their shameful attitude, after the war you were the negotiator for German reparations ... so who better than you to commentate on all that?' I have not replied yet, but if I find the time I shall cooperate.

To perpetuate the memory of the unique communities which vanished in the Holocaust I am working at the moment on setting up a project which is very dear to my heart—the creation of the Beth Hatefutsoth, a historical museum of the Diaspora on the campus of the University of Tel Aviv. It is expected to cost ten million dollars to complete. In Israel the Hebrew poet and writer Abba Kovner is working on the idea, and our artistic adviser is Karl Katz, one of the advisers of the New York Metropolitan Museum. The museum will be one of the biggest buildings in Tel Aviv, with a floor space of ten thousand square metres. Its aim will be to show the ways and means by which Judaism was able to survive. It will contain not so much objects as illustrations of the great themes: education, religion, family life, Messianic longings, nostalgia for Zion, antisemitism, etc. It will all be displayed by ultra-modern methods—electronics in the service of Judaism, you might say. By pressing a button, visitors will see for example the Jews of Jerusalem praying before the Wailing Wall; by pressing another, an illuminated map of all the great Jewish migrations in history. There will also be space for archives where visitors will be able to consult a comprehensive range of documentation on whatever questions are of interest to them. In other words, it will be a living monument to the memory of the Jews all over Eastern Europe who can never be restored to life.

Until the last century, art played no role in Judaism and the Jews had no painting or sculpture. This was because the third commandment forbade them to make graven images or likenesses of living creatures, for fear of them becoming pagans. But since the ideology of a people, in philosophy, politics and religion, is an expression of its character, I think this prohibition on creating anthropomorphic painting or sculpture stems from some specific feature of the Jewish character. I know of numerous theories on the subject. One of them derives from Ernest Renan, the great expert on the ancient history of the Jews, who held that their basic sense was hearing, not seeing. And in fact Jews do listen but they do not look very much. Which explains their answer when God laid down the Ten Commandments. They said: 'All that the Lord hath said will we do.' Not: 'We want to see', as the Greeks would have done. God is invisible.

Renan was a friend of Taine, who believed that a people's character depended on its environment, not its race. He pointed out that the Jews were a people of the desert; in the desert there is nothing to see, but the slightest noise can be heard kilometres away. Like any theory, this one is one-sided, but interesting. Martin Buber wrote a lot about it.

Be that as it may, it is clear that with rare exceptions Jewish painting did not amount to anything more than illustrations of the Bible or of rituals. Not that these do not include some very fine manuscripts, although the Arabs outdid the Jews in this art of illumination. As for architecture, we know nothing about it, since the old temples were all destroyed. The architecture of the few medieval synagogues is Moorish or Gothic—nothing very original.

Now, the strange thing is that when they did start painting in the nineteenth century the Jews became first-rate artists: Pissarro, Modigliani, Chagall and so on. It was the same with sculpture.

On the other hand it is understandable that they should have become great musicians, because the tradition of music has always existed in their communities. By the way, have you noticed that Jews tend to be violinists rather than pianists? There is Rubinstein, of course, but the greatest violinists in the world— David Oistrakh, Isaac Stern, Yehudi Menuhin—are Jewish. The violin has more soul than the piano and suits the Jewish character better. But there is another explanation: to escape from a pogrom with a violin is feasible; not with a piano . . .

Within Jewry, taken as a human group, there is a dichotomy between the Jewish people that live in the Diaspora and the people that live in the State of Israel. This has been seen as a big obstacle to any prospect of unity, but even if I had the power to abolish the Diaspora and concentrate all the Jews in Israel I would not do it. In fact I am convinced that the reason why there is still a Jewish people in existence has a lot more to do with the Diaspora than with Jewish states. If all the Jews had stayed in Palestine when the Romans destroyed the State and the Temple of Jerusalem in AD 70 there would probably be no Jews left today. This is not just a personal hypothesis of mine, but a historical fact.

Some commentators have drawn the conclusion that a Jewish state was unnecessary, and in any case when Zionism first appeared on the world scene most Jews opposed it and scoffed at it. Herzl was only supported by a small minority. The rest rallied round later on, after the creation of the state, but without actually joining the Zionist Organization, which officially represents only one or two million people, only a fraction of the Jewish people.

Certainly if there were no Jewish state existing today that in itself would not make me despair for the future of the Jewish people, but that has to do with a certain irrational element expressed by the Hebrew saying: '*Nezah Yisrael lo yeshakker*'—'the Strength of Israel will not lie'. From a rational viewpoint, as a sociologist or an ordinary observer of Jewish life, without the state I would have doubts about the survival of the Jewish people after a few generations. The forces of assimilation would lead to a slow, progressive, undramatic disintegration of our identity. The great majority would lose the awareness of being Jewish and all desire to do anything to remain Jewish. That is why the existence of the state is absolutely necessary.

There is also a solid link between the Holocaust and the State of Israel. I often say that the Jewish people has paid for its state not only with the thousands of young men who have fallen during Israel's four wars but also with the six million Jewish victims of Nazism.

The justification of Zionism and the state is that Israel probably represents the only way, and in any case the most effective way, of building new foundations for the existence of Jewry. All the more so because Eastern European Jewry, which was the great strong-hold of Jewish life in the eighteenth and nineteenth centuries, has disappeared. And my own view is that it is an illusion to believe that the American Jewry of today, with all its financial and intellectual resources, could eventually replace that European Jewry. I recall remarking during a conference in the United States that it was absurd to imagine that Broadway could take the place of Volozkin or Belz, the great *yeshivot* schools of Poland. When a student at a New York *yeshiva* comes out of his institute he sees a pornographic cinema to his right and a strip joint to his left. That does not compare with life in Poland where the town was permeated with spirituality, and people's daily lives bore a constant relationship to the education they received.

The fact that the existence of Israel is indispensable does not therefore mean that the state contains within itself all the values of Judaism, or that all Jews should go and join it. Besides, simply from the economic point of view Israel could not absorb such an influx of population without territorial expansion and consequently further wars, not to mention the terrible risk of an Arab victory over an Israel which contained all the world's Jews: it would mean the physical end of us.

The Diaspora is a kind of guarantee or reserve. Somebody once said to me: 'The Jews are the biggest speculators in the world. They always rush to settle where the centre of civilization is located. When the centre was in the Near East they were in Palestine, then Babylon, then Alexandria. When the Romans had conquered the Near East they went to Europe, Rome, the Rhineland. Now that the Near East has become an important centre again, back they come. They always go where history's blue chips are.' Naturally this was all expressed in a rather prosaic and vulgar manner.

In my opinion the life of the Jewish people is not uniquely in the Diaspora nor uniquely in Israel, but in both. Israel and the Diaspora should be interdependent. If eventually there is the Jewish school system I have suggested, every pupil in those schools will have to spend a year in Israel. Even now, a lot of universities accept this arrangement and give 'value units' or the equivalent for such a year of studies. This can only lead to permanent and beneficial exchanges between Israel and the Diaspora—the proviso being, I repeat, that Hebrew should become the second language of the whole Jewish people. In Switzerland, the great majority of children speak two or three languages from primary school onwards, so it is not inconceivable for a reasonably intelligent people, eighty or ninety per cent of whose children receive a secondary education, to be capable of learning Hebrew. The new Hebrew culture will thereby embrace a sort of universal civilization which will prevent Israel from becoming a provincially minded country.

Eighteen per cent of the Jewish people live in Israel and more than eighty per cent in other countries. Other peoples—the Armenians, for instance—have undergone a diaspora, but never on such a scale. The Jewish diaspora is unique. If the Jews of the Diaspora were to decide tomorrow that Israel was no business of theirs, the affair would be closed and Israel would cease to exist, economically as well as politically. Would America support Israel if American Jewry stopped caring? In order to establish our state, we were able to make use of the examples provided by other states. The same goes for our army. But for settling the problem of the Diaspora there is no precedent available: we have to invent our own.

I sometimes talk to historians who believe that a parallel to our situation is to be found in Antiquity, where the majority of Jews lived in the Diaspora twice over: in the Babylonian era, then under the Roman domination. But the comparison cannot be any use to us, because in those days the ties uniting the whole Jewish people were of a religious nature: Israel was the centre where everybody turned in order to determine the dates of festivals, settle legislative problems and consult the great masters of the Talmud. Today those ties apply only to a minority, and besides that the Jews will have acquired the basis of their cultural background in the countries where they live.

Under the Roman Empire they had complete autonomy. The Romans imposed taxes but allowed the Jews their own jurisdiction, and there were courts of justice in which Jewish law was applied. That kind of system is unthinkable today, and things are further complicated by the fact that Israel is a sovereign state and cannot allow other countries' citizens to determine its policy.

Inside the Zionist movement an activist called Grossmann, who in fact became a member of the Zionist executive, produced a plan for creating a dual parliament in Israel: a regular parliament representing Israeli citizens and a kind of senate where the leaders of world Jewry would sit. It was an absurd idea, for no loyal Jewish citizen of the United States or France would have accepted being made some sort of semi-citizen. And I repeat that Israel cannot share its sovereignty with Jews from elsewhere, who are not fighting a war. During one of our frequent debates, Ben Gurion once said to me: 'I'm going to make you a concrete proposition. Let all the Jews of the Diaspora pay taxes in Israel and be available for call-up when we need them, and they will have all the rights of Israeli citizens, including the vote.' Begin, when he was not yet Prime Minister, had another idea: to create a permanent commission made up of thirty representatives of the

Knesset, the Israeli parliament, and thirty dignitaries nominated by the great organizations of the Diaspora—this mixed commission to have powers of decision. This is clearly an unrealistic suggestion. How could such a commission decide whether or not to cede the Golan? How would the Israelis put up with that? They would rightly say: 'We are the ones who are suffering and fighting, it is our sons who are dying, yet you want to make the decisions when you don't take any of the risks.'

I can't claim to have found the answer. All I know is that the time has come to open the debate. Ben Gurion only delayed it, because he would not admit that the Diaspora had any rights at all. I once said to him: 'Since you don't recognize the right of the Jews of the Diaspora to interfere with your policies, how can you claim your own right to talk to them?' But for him it was not a problem. He thought what so many others think—that it was for Israel to give the orders and for the Diaspora to follow them. Even today that is where many Israeli politicians stand. They tell the Diaspora: 'Shut up and admire.' World Jewry is too intelligent to accept this authoritarianism, and it has a lot more doubts about the wisdom of the Israeli government than is generally recognized. Nobody wants to embarrass the state, but the unease goes on growing.

Let us take an example: there is a certain Jewish budget provided by the hundreds of millions of dollars worth of voluntary contributions collected each year. Israel demands the greater part today, to the detriment of the institutions of the Diaspora. More and more people are arguing in favour of creating a collective body, with no right of decision, to draw up the balance sheet of available funds and make recommendations on their distribution according to the needs of the moment. Levi Eshkol understood this problem well and wanted to see it resolved. When I was president of the World Zionist Organization he and I called the first world conference of Jewish leaders in Jerusalem, but it was a total flop because instead of applying themselves to serious questions those in attendance spent their time frantically applauding all the ministers. It was a 'conference of cheers'. Eshkol was very disappointed by the setback and tried to organize another meeting, this time with a precise programme, but he died prematurely.

Golda Meir had much the same ideas as Ben Gurion: she distrusted the Diaspora and did not want it meddling with Israel's affairs. Fortunately Rabin fully understood the importance of the issue. During his four years as ambassador to the United States he realized that many leaders of the Diaspora would not let themselves be controlled by some representative of Israel; at the very least they wanted to be consulted. Rabin therefore gave the World Jewish Congress the job of studying the question, and we are starting to examine it. We therefore intend to call a conference of about thirty Jewish intellectuals and statesmen, chosen half from Israel, half from the Diaspora, which will examine the juridical aspect—is it possible to create a permanent body on which the state and world Jewry are represented without violating national sovereignty or threatening the autonomy and civic loyalty of the Jews of the Diaspora? I have recently been thinking that it might be feasible to convoke an assembly composed of all the members of the Knesset and an equal number representing the Diaspora communities. This assembly would meet once a year, for about a week, to discuss all problems submitted to it concerning both Israel and the Diaspora, but without taking decisions committing either side. If a consensus was reached on a subject of debate, it could be formulated as a resolution. I understand that it is not easy to set up such an assembly, but eminent jurists have assured me that there would be no difficulties from the point of view of international law, especially if the idea is explained in advance to the various governments. The assembly I envisage would symbolize the unique character of the Jewish people and would represent the minority living in Israel as well as the majority living in other countries. With its help, we would at long last be kept regularly in touch with Israel's plans and be rid of the present policy of the *fait accompli*.

When I was 'president of presidents' of the Jewish organizations of the United States I was not informed of the launching of the Sinai campaign. Ben Gurion had not wanted to tell anybody about it, but without our support Israel would have suffered a terrible reverse. On the day the war broke out, Moshe Sharett, Israel's Foreign Minister, was visiting Nehru—who was very anti-Israeli and used to tell Sharett that Israel was a very aggressive state. The minister was arguing that on the contrary his country wanted peace right up to the point when Nehru showed him the telegram he had just received, informing him that Israel had sprung to arms and gone into Sinai. Imagine Sharett's humiliation. That sort of thing ought not to happen again, because everything Israel does has repercussions on world Jewry.

When we have decided on the scope and method, it will remain to explain the why and wherefore of our organization to the government of every country where Jews are living, because it must not be possible to say of such an assembly that it works against the civic loyalty of the Jews. All the same, I am sure that people will understand. If it is pointed out to non-Jews that the Diaspora cannot exist without a centre, that after two thousand years of persecution the non-Jewish world owes the Jews a little more than a simple UN vote in favour of the creation of the state, and that without the solidarity of world Jewry Israel could not exist in the midst of more than a hundred million Arabs, all people of good will will admit that we are a unique people in a unique situation, and that we have a right to some form of cooperation with an officially foreign state. Naturally the antisemites will not fail to use this argument against us, but it does not matter so long as the civilized world agrees.

All the same, let us consider what would happen if Israel were to follow a policy contrary for example to French or British interests. This kind of problem has to be studied csae by case, but generally speaking it does raise the question of divided loyalties whose existence most Jews refuse to recognize—this is the well-tried Jewish method which consists in not raising unpleasant topics, which is to say burying your head in the sand. I am one of those people who often do debate such topics in public, and that irritates many Jewish leaders. And yet there the question is: it cannot be ignored.

I shall start by saying that there is no single loyalty, and that no one's life is lived under a unique allegiance. A man has loyalty towards his country, his family, his religion and his social class, and there can be conflicts among all these loyalties. Comparisons are never altogether valid, but let us suppose that the Vatican is following a very hostile policy towards a given country; it is then up to each Catholic to decide which loyalty is to get priority. It is the same in private life: suppose you love your father and mother but they are divorced and hate the sight of one another. Are you then to choose one and reject the other? Can a man have a wife and a mistress and be loyal to them both, or must he sacrifice one for the sake of the other? This Hitlerian notion of loyalty to a single object—in this case the Great Reich for which every citizen had to betray family, friends and religion—is derived from Hegel and is profoundly undemocratic.

If, in order to be loyal to the state, I must sacrifice all my other loyalties, that is the end of democracy. Loyalty is one of the great human attributes, and that means that we have to be able to pay for it by facing conflicts squarely. Let us take an extreme situation: say Israel goes to war with France. Every French Jew must then decide whether he is primarily French—in which case he abandons Israel—or Jewish—in which case he must leave France. But the existence of contradictions does not automatically constitute a reason for casting off one's loyalties.

Or let us examine the case of an American Communist. For an entire era, particularly in the heyday of the notorious Senator McCarthy, all Communists were considered as traitors to the United States—a criminal simplification. A Communist should certainly have the right to renounce Communism, but he should also have the right to say: 'Communism is more important to me than the American way of life.' He may even believe in all loyalty that Communism would be better for America.

If Zionism has an ideological task, it is to create a spiritual centre within the State of Israel, then to proclaim to all the world that Jews must be loyal to the State of Israel unless there is a political conflict, in which case each is free to choose.

It is precisely in order to avoid this kind of wrench that I am in favour of the permanent neutralization of Israel. I wrote as much in an article printed by *Foreign Affairs*, and I say again: Israel ought to be a country (and if need be the only country) which keeps out of international politics. I was even against its joining the United Nations, because the UN is no longer a neutral institution, above the battle, but a conglomerate of contradictory political interests. In every session of the United Nations, Israel is obliged to adopt a set position—against the USSR, for America, for the Blacks, against South Africa, and so on. In every vote it may find itself harming the interests of such and such a Jewish community in the USSR, America or South Africa.

The majority of 'good Jews' in America, especially the intellectuals, were against Nixon and the Vietnam war; they were even among the leaders of the anti-escalation crusade. So a furious Nixon harangued their representatives: 'If you force me to be anti-war I will also be anti-Israel. Why should I betray my alliance with South Vietnam and not my alliance with Israel?' And the Israeli government (especially Rabin, whose policy during his Washington ambassadorship was deplorable) exhorted the Jews to support Nixon and his Vietnamese policy.

I remember a meeting between the WJC leadership and Golda Meir, when Golda gave a scolding to Rabbi Prinz, then president of the American Jewish Congress, for his personal stand against the war in Vietnam. Golda told him: 'You, a good Zionist, are damaging Israel. Because of you and people like you, there is a risk of Nixon becoming anti-Israeli.' But Prinz replied: 'Listen, Mrs Meir, I have been a Zionist from childhood on, I have worked all my life for Zionism. And not only am I a Zionist, but I am a Jew brought up in the spirit of the prophets. I am also a father who loves his children and is raising them. If I supported Nixon in this criminal, immoral war, I would be betraying the spirit of the prophets, which seems to me a lot more important than your politics; what's more I would be abandoned and rejected by my own children, who would quite rightly see me as a reactionary. So I'm not going to sacrifice my convictions to some momentary policy of Israel.'

That is an outstanding example of a Jew's behaviour when he disagrees with the options of Jerusalem. Likewise he has the right (as is happening more and more often in France) to approve of the Israeli government on numerous points and at the same time to oppose its Near East policy.

A Soviet ambassador once told me: 'Your friend Ben Gurion believes that he is Prime Minister of a sovereign state. That's ridiculous. Israel is the fifty-second state of America.' That remark shows how hard it is for a Russian Jew to be altogether pro-Israeli as long as Israel's American ties appear so strong. That is why I ask for Israel to become a neutral state, guaranteed not only by the great powers but by the whole world, Arabs included.

If I had met Nasser I would like to have told him this: 'You Arabs are a very generous people. Your relationship with the Jews in history has been better than ours with the Christians. You have persecuted us, but we have also been through wonderful periods of cooperation: in Spain, in Baghdad, and in Algeria ... So remain generous. Ours is an unfortunate people. I admit that Palestine belonged to you by international law. But we suffered so much for two thousand years. We have lost a third of our population because we had no territory. Then grant us at least one per cent of your own, and guarantee our existence. Stand with America, Russia and France as one of the guarantors of Israel's survival.' I am convinced that a speech of that kind would have had a great psychological effect on the Arabs, by giving them a feeling of pride and still more of equality. And in fact I have put it to several Arab leaders who were fascinated by the idea. Unhappily it seems that Israel chooses another way.

To conclude this discussion of the psychological differences between Israel and the Diaspora, I know of no example more striking than what I call the 'Masada complex'. Masada was a fortress whose Jewish defenders, after four years of resistance to the Romans, committed mass suicide in their hundreds rather than surrender. Whereas throughout its history Jewry has continually made compromises (except in the case of forcible conversion) to safeguard the physical life of its children, Israel has developed a whole Masada cult. Speaking very sincerely, Masada is an absolutely anti-Jewish phenomenon. The Jewish ideal is to stay alive, and had the Masada example been followed there would not be a single Jew left. Mass suicide is all very well for high drama and poetry, but not when it is built up into a political, quasi-religious ideal. In Israel, some really intelligent people will tell you: 'It's magnificent, it's our destiny: we shall be killed, but we shall be heroes!' That is a pagan ideal, the very essence of anti-Judaism.

I asked a rabbi who is one of the greatest authorities on Jewish law: 'Does religious law require keeping the old town of Jerusalem at all costs?' He shrugged and replied: 'It's an absurdity! The supreme law of Judaism is to respect one's own life except in two cases: if you are forced to deny God, or if you are compelled to kill another man, in which case rather you should die. But otherwise the priority is staying alive. To sacrifice the life of a single soldier for the sake of the conquest of Jerusalem is against Jewish law.'

4 *The Creation of Israel*

THE NOTION of political Zionism is less than a century old, but nostalgia for Zion, the hill of the Temple in Jerusalem, has accompanied the Jews in all their exiles, throughout the two millennia of their dispersal. Zionism may appear monolithic to an outside observer, but it is made up of very different, if very deeply Jewish, elements; among these is the Zionism of Theodor Herzl.

There have always been two conflicting conceptions of Zionism. According to Herzl it had to be political. Herzl was an assimilated Jew who knew next to nothing about Jewish history. For him it was a simple matter, and he put it in a famous and totally misleading saying: 'The problem of Zionism is one of means of transport: there is a people without a land, and a land without a people.' So it was just a matter of finding the ships to carry the people to the territory, and the problem was solved! This was a simplification of genius. I always say that the people of genius are the ones who do not understand the ifs and buts and who cut the Gordian knot. If Herzl had grasped the Jewish problem in all its complexity he would never have written *The Jewish State*. But he was ignorant on that subject, and that enabled him to utter a double falsehood: first, Palestine was not a country without a people, since there were hundreds of thousands of Arabs living there; and second, the Jews were not a landless people, for the assimilated Jews were good Frenchmen, Germans, Englishmen and so on.

But without Herzl's erroneous formulation, political Zionism would never have existed. In his eyes, Israel was going to be a state like any other. He did not even think that Hebrew would be its national language: he believed that it would be German, perhaps because he himself was an Austrian Jew. Israel would be a liberal state of Western Europe. Herzl had adopted the European concept of a sovereign state as expressed by Hegel, grafted on the old idea of the return to Zion, and in so doing had created the Zionist Organization.

Against him there was Ahad Ha-Am, a great thinker steeped in Jewish literature and philosophy, who held that the state was unimportant. What was necessary instead, he argued, was a spiritual centre of the Jews of the entire world. In the end, though, he accepted the idea of a state. Chaim Weizmann stood at the meeting point of the two theories, half Herzlite, half Ahad Ha-Amite. What has been achieved today is Herzl's half, and so long as Israel ignores the Ahad Ha-Am half, by not making the state a spiritual centre, Zionism will not fulfil its historic mission.

After all, the Zionist political idea is absolutely unique and fantastic. You may claim that it is senseless or that it is magnificent, but in either case it remains unique. Imagine for a moment what would happen if all the peoples in the world were to reclaim the lands they occupied two thousand years ago. Do you see the chaos? Yet here is a people which has had the audacity to act in that way, and the world said Yes! But when I say the world, I do not mean the masses, or even the diplomats, but only a few great statesmen. All through my life I have observed the same thing: the diplomats were against the resurrection of Israel, and the great statesmen were for it. Without Balfour, Lloyd George and Wilson, we would never have obtained the Balfour Declaration of 1917 and what ensued from it. All the ministerial machines were hostile to the project, and all the functionaries said: 'After two thousand years of exile a people wants to return to its land? It's unheard of. The Arabs will never agree, and they are in the majority. Furthermore it is contrary to all the rules of diplomacy.'

I have always told the Jews: 'Don't hold a grudge against the civil servants for being opposed; an ordinary diplomat ought to be opposed.' It took a Lloyd George, who was very attached to the Bible, to speak up for Zionism; a Lloyd George who told

Weizmann at their first meeting: 'When I was a boy I knew the streets of Jerusalem better than the streets of London.'

Zionism is one of the great ideas of the twentieth century. But whereas originally it was great statesmen who approached it by appropriately great means, it then became the business of government departments for the Near East. From broad geopolitics it fell into a dreary little routine. Yet if Zionism is viewed from its beginnings, it can only be seen as one of the great successes of this terrible century, which has known Hitler and Stalin, revolutions, and people massacred in their millions. So that in this, one of the most brutal centuries in history, Zionism is one of the rare ideals achieved by those who envisaged founding a new way of life.

In spite of that, I am not certain that without Auschwitz there would be a Jewish state today. If Ben Gurion was still alive he would protest vigorously, but I am sure that truth is on my side. When the facts about Auschwitz became known, the reality appeared incredible. Even in the American State Department, some officials blamed themselves for not having rescued some tens of thousands of Jews, and they started to give positive consideration to the project for a Jewish state which would save the United States from receiving the survivors of Nazism.

Remember that in 1937 the British had offered us a small autonomous territory in Palestine. If we had accepted then, we would have saved hundreds of thousands of Jews. There are broad grounds for complaint about the Zionist 'crime' of hesitating for a year before accepting that little scrap of Palestine: when we did finally accept, the British had already withdrawn their offer.

Later on, I gained my greatest political success by persuading Acheson of the necessity of the Jewish state; it was Acheson who persuaded the other American leaders, President Truman included. He agreed in 1945, and I then began negotiations with Ernest Bevin, Britain's Foreign Minister under the Attlee government. Fortunately those negotiations failed. If they had succeeded there would probably not be a Jewish state today.

In fact we were prepared to make enormous compromises. At

the crucial meeting were Ben Gurion, Stephen Wise and myself on the Israeli side, Bevin, the Colonial Minister and a number of top officials on the British. Ben Gurion proposed: 'Give us a hundred thousand immigration visas and administrative autonomy, and you won't hear further mention of any Jewish state for ten years at least.' As I say, fortunately Bevin refused.

In my opinion, if we eventually have a national portrait gallery in Israel, the first statue should be of the grand mufti, Haj Amin el Husseini, and the second of Bevin. Because if the mufti had accepted the idea of a binational state, it would have put paid to any Jewish state; and if Bevin had agreed to administrative autonomy and the proposed immigration figure, the idea of Israel would have been postponed for ten years. And ten years later, nobody would have voted for the Jewish state, because Auschwitz would have been forgotten and the Arabs would have become too influential.

I dealt with the negotiations in my autobiography, so I will not go into detail here, but I do want to recall two particularly significant episodes concerning the attitude of the USSR. Although official Communism was anti-Zionist, I had not lost hope of persuading the Russians to vote for the Jewish state—if only to eliminate the British from the Near East. As the Hebrew saying goes: 'Whether a thing happens for love of Mordecai or for hatred of Haman, the main thing is that it happens.' Those were the days when some Zionists were suggesting putting it to the British to create a Jewish state in Palestine which would be a member of the Commonwealth. The chairman of their committee was a great friend of Zionism, the English parliamentarian Wedgwood. Chaim Weizmann wanted to be on the committee, but I advised him against it for two reasons: first, because the British government would never accept the plan; second, because the Russians would never vote for us if the Jewish state was associated with the British Empire.

Weizmann therefore stayed out of the committee, and when Gromyko delivered his famous speech in the UN in favour of the creation of a Jewish state it came as a bolt from the blue. Moshe Sharett could not believe his ears, and I said to him:

'I've been telling you for years that the Russians would vote for us in the end.' As far as I was concerned, it was no amazing revelation.

During the war, Benes had been president of the Czech government in exile in London. Learning that he was about to visit Moscow, I went to see him with Weizmann and we asked him to raise the idea of a Jewish state with Stalin. In his very organized, perhaps even slightly bureaucratic way, Benes sorted through his various files and told us: 'Look, I have sixteen problems to discuss with Stalin. I'm only staying in Moscow for three days and I'm not sure there will be time to broach them all. I'm going to put your plan at number eleven on the list. If I get as far as eleven, I'll talk to Stalin about it.'

I saw Benes again when he got back. 'I didn't have time to discuss your problem,' he informed me, 'but I did pick up something. You know that after long sessions of work Stalin usually has a film show. It happens around midnight, and after the show there is a meal. It takes a while to get from the viewing room to the dining room, and when Stalin took my arm to take me there I thought it was an opportune moment. I told him: "I have the question of the Jewish state on my list. After Hitler, the Jews will need a state of their own." And Stalin replied: "Tell your Jewish friends that the Soviet Union knows how much they are suffering at present and that we will do our utmost to give them some amends." He did not say "a state", but still he did say "amends".'

At the Paris Peace Conference in 1946 Bevin delivered an ultimatum: we must attend a meeting with the Arabs. So we set one condition: that the partition of Palestine and the creation of the Jewish state should be the basis of the discussion. The Arabs refused. The occasion was especially serious because a number of Zionist leaders in Palestine, Sharett among them, were in English jails at the time. The message we got from Bevin was: 'If you don't attend this meeting, it's finished.' He could be very crude. I formulated a diplomatic 'No, but . . .' kind of answer and went to his apartment in the Hôtel George v to deliver it. He read it, then took hold of it again, explaining: 'This is quite complicated. Let me read it over again.' He re-read it, and told me at last:

'Mr Goldmann, if I strip your answer and remove your fine language, it amounts to a refusal.'

'Mr Bevin,' I replied, 'a respectable man doesn't strip either girls or answers.'

There was nothing affected about Bevin, and he immediately hurried off to the next-door apartment where his assistants were working and called out: 'Come on, all of you, and learn how to make a witty retort!'

A trade union leader of high calibre, Bevin was an unusually ignorant man. His powerful personality stood in stead of culture. On my visits to England I often used to meet his colleague, the socialist Aneurin Bevan, who heartily detested him. I was describing one of my conversations with Ernest Bevin to him when I said: 'I settled the question by suggesting a pragmatic solution to Bevin,' and at that point Bevan broke in:

'Nahum, you're a big liar!'

'Why?'

'You'll never get me to believe that Bevin understands the word "pragmatic"!'

'That's true,' I admitted, 'so the word I used was "practical".'

'Well in that case I believe you.'

One day in 1946, while I was negotiating in Paris, the papers carried a story that there had been a terrible pogrom in a Polish seaside town. I went to Bevin, showed him one of the headlines, and said, 'You see, the war is barely over and still they go on slaughtering Jews.' Bevin read the article and sighed: 'That's dreadful! A pogrom like that in such a big Mediterranean port!'

I shall say no more to recall the great stages of Zionism, because the rest belongs to history—the proclamation of the State of Israel on 14 May 1948, Chaim Weizmann's election as President on 16 February 1949, the formation of the first Israeli government by David Ben Gurion on 10 March 1949 . . . it is a well-known story.

Less well known are the personalities of some of the great modern leaders of Israel. Ben Gurion and I often clashed with one another, both in public and in private, but in spite of our differences, especially as regards Arab policy, we had close ties, and I always admired the statesman in Ben Gurion. When Kissinger was still a professor at Harvard and adviser to the American government, he once said to me: 'It's a pity his shoes are too small for him: he could have given his real measure in a bigger state than Israel.' There is a lot of truth in that remark.

One of the reasons why he respected me was that I had the courage to stand up to him. You know, for years and years Ben Gurion ruled Israel like a *de facto* dictator. Not formally, of course, because he was a democrat, but in day-to-day life nobody in his party dared to contradict him, because they all knew that their own positions depended on him. It was very hard to argue with Ben Gurion, and when it did happen he never let it influence him.

Until his later years—say up to the time of the Lavon affair, after which he lost a good deal of his political flair—he was not only a great statesman but also a very able and cunning diplomat and politician, really one of the best I have ever come across. A promise from him was quite worthless. He did not hesitate to promise one thing and then do the opposite. He was absolutely unscrupulous. He never pursued any objective other than realizing the Zionist ideal and satiating his immense ambition. Far from being fond of honours he actually detested them, but he never had his fill of power. The publicity about his person, compliments and kowtowing irritated him: he only wanted to dominate.

I have known a lot of statesmen, but hardly any of them had his sense of history. He was convinced that every word he spoke was for eternity. So he employed a method I have never seen used by anyone else: when he was having an important conversation, he would be writing all the time, while listening attentively to what the other man said and making careful replies. He must have left one or two hundred exercise books full of his dialogues. I hope that a selection will be published some day, because they contain all the necessary documentation for making judgements on his policy.

So he took himself seriously, and in that light at least he was the opposite of myself. Not only do I not take myself too seriously, but I have a tendency to be slightly sceptical: I do not exaggerate the importance of one man, and I do not believe that my every action has historic meaning. Some of the events I have lived through—like my approaches to the Americans on behalf of the partition of Palestine, or my negotiations with Adenauer over German reparations—undoubtedly belong to history, but they are limited. With Ben Gurion, he attached the same importance to every single thing.

If we were on opposite sides, it was mainly because of the Arab question. For the rest we felt fairly close to each other, and on matters such as the partition of Palestine and negotiations with post-Nazi Germany he was on my side. In his fundamental conception of the character of the Zionist movement and of the State of Israel, Ben Gurion and I were in full agreement: both of us were convinced that if Israel became a state like any other it would not survive.

We had a mutual friend—an extraordinary man who, if he had not died so young, would undoubtedly have become Prime Minister—called Giora Josephtal. He was a German Jew from an assimilated family, who officially represented Israel in the negotiations with Adenauer and then for some years was secretary general of Mapai, the Israeli Labour Party. A member of the Zionist executive when I was its president, Josephtal was very close to Ben Gurion, who much admired him, and he was quite determined that I should take on the presidency of the World Zionist Movement. I kept refusing and insisting that I didn't have much regard for titles and it was enough for me to be plain Nahum Goldmann. It was no good: he kept coming back to the charge, and eventually convinced Ben Gurion to use his influence.

So Ben Gurion asked me to see him in order to press me to accept this post of president. I was very taken aback at first, because I knew how critical he was of the Zionist Organization. 'On top of that, we have had public clashes,' I said to him, 'so I don't see what your interest is in pushing me forward like this. Isn't this some manoeuvre of yours?' Then all at once he replied: 'I'm going to ask you two things. The first is to let me speak for twenty minutes without interrupting; the second is to turn and face the wall—I want to have your back to me.' I thought he was losing his mind, and told him I didn't see what he was getting at, but he explained: 'I want to talk to you in confidence for twenty minutes, more frankly than I have ever done, but I'm going to have to say a lot of complimentary things about you. Well, you know me and you know that I don't like making compliments. I know you too, and I know you don't like hearing them. The situation will be very embarrassing for both of us if you are looking at me: so turn and face the wall.'

So I sat facing the wall like a dunce and he talked to my back for twenty minutes. And that was very characteristic of Ben Gurion: a man who could be very brutal, even cruel, was also capable of that sort of delicacy. I cannot give a full account here, but this is the gist of it:

'I am sure that in the bottom of your heart you have a reproach to make to me, and that reproach is justified. We have had terrible defeats; six million Jews were exterminated. But we have also brought off two huge historical successes: the creation of the State of Israel and the reparations we obtained from Germany. I was always convinced that some day we would have our state, but I was very doubtful about getting a penny out of the Germans. You were the architect of those reparations, and together we were the architects of the partition of Palestine and the creation of Israel. Your contribution to the two triumphs of our generation has been crucial. So you have the right to wonder why I don't put you in charge of the problem which will decide the future of the State of Israel: peace with the Arabs. I'm going to explain the reasons to you ... Why did you convince Acheson and the other members of the Committee for Palestine appointed by President Truman? Because you are another Acheson. You could perfectly well have been an American Secretary of State: you have the same talent, the same culture, the same charm and the same gifts of persuasion as Dean Acheson. Why did you convince Adenauer, becoming one of his friends, that there had to be reparations given to the Jewish people? Because you are another Adenauer and could have become a German Chancellor. You spoke to those men as an equal because you share the same qualities. But with the

Arabs, who are barbarians, all your gifts are worthless. Neither your culture, nor your charm, nor your arts of persuasion would make any impression on them. The only thing they understand is force, and the iron hand is me, not you. That is the explanation. You can turn round now.'

'I understand you perfectly,' I replied, 'and I even find a lot of truth in what you say. Nasser is certainly no Acheson or Adenauer. But why not use the policy of the iron hand in the velvet glove? You will be the hand, and I the glove?'

'The moment will certainly come when I shall call for you,' he admitted. 'But not yet, not straight away . . .'

For years, Ben Gurion pressed me to settle in Israel and organize the opposition against him. 'Nowadays I'm practically governing as a dictator,' he used to say. 'If you start up a real opposition I shall fight you and I hope I shall win, but then there will be true democracy in Israel.' That is the measure of a really great political personality.

In my numerous discussions with Ben Gurion I used to tell him that our analyses differed mainly because I myself was convinced that time was working against Israel. Since then, the oil crisis has reinforced my argument.

But Ben Gurion stuck to his guns. 'On the contrary,' he would say, 'the intellectual and technological gap between the Arabs and ourselves will grow even wider.' And his other constant theme was that the Arab generation which had suffered the defeats of the war of 1948-9 and then the Sinai Campaign was psychologically incapable of making peace with Israel. He maintained that the next generation would probably have forgotten these defeats, and with them the shame and humiliation which a little people had inflicted on Arab armies ten time more numerous than theirs. This was obviously a false analysis, since the younger generation of Arabs is more patriotic and extremist than its elders, though it is similarly less corrupt.

On one of my visits to him in Tel Aviv, Ben Gurion was reading Nasser's book *The Philosophy of the Revolution*, which had just come out. He used to read books with great attention, making notes in the margin—he did it as seriously as he did everything else. So he asked me if I had read Nasser's book, and what I thought of it. I replied that it was just a political tract and that it certainly did not have the importance of Kant, or *Faust*, or *Don Quixote* ... 'On the contrary,' he snapped, 'it is an essential work that proves how right I am and how wrong your appreciation of Nasser is. Look, on this page he writes: "All the Arabs in the world must unite to conquer Israel." And here he says: "All the Muslims in the world must be united in order to achieve victory." And in this chapter he talks about "the great humiliation of the defeat of 1948". It's clear: Nasser is suffering from a psychological injury; he is humiliated, and he will not make peace before he has healed his injury, in other words before scoring a victory over Israel.'

You know that in 1948, in fact, Nasser commanded an Egyptian unit which was encircled by the Israeli troops, and he narrowly avoided being taken prisoner by Yigael Allon. All the same I was not convinced, and I said to Ben Gurion: 'Listen, when I was at Heidelberg I took courses in psychology, but then I gave them up, being convinced that they were no use. I am sure I was right, because in my experience everybody judges others in terms of themselves. It so happens that what you are telling me today is valid for a man whom I know very well and whose name is David Ben Gurion. He is a man who wants to bring all Jews together, who never forgives a defeat, never forgets a humiliation, and always wants to exact revenge. And no one can argue with him. Do you sincerely think that Nasser is another Ben Gurion?'

Chaim Weizmann, who towards the end of his life was obsessed by his antipathy to Ben Gurion, used to say of him: 'Ben Gurion will create the State of Israel then ruin it by his policy.' And if Israel continues to follow Ben Gurion's political precepts I am afraid that Weizmann may turn out right in the end. I have often asked myself why this clever, brilliant man, who was not a petty provincial like so many Israeli leaders, who had a statesman's perspective, and the admiration of a man like de Gaulle—why a man like that failed to see that without an agreement with the Arabs, Israel would have no long-term future.

I can only explain that attitude by his character. In fact it has often seemed to me that where statesmen are concerned, character comes before intelligence. They often understand with their heads what ought to be done, but their character forbids them to bring it about. That behaviour is typical of Ben Gurion; I can give one example which I shall never forget.

One day, or rather night, in 1956 I sat up at his house till three in the morning. Our real conversations often used to take place in the kitchen, and as usual he wanted his wife Paula to go to bed. When she insisted on staying, Ben Gurion would tell me: 'Nahum, you're the only one she respects. If I ask her she won't go to bed, but if you ask, she will.' So I would tell Paula: 'Just to please me, go to sleep.' Then Ben Gurion made coffee and sandwiches.

That night, a beautiful summer night, we had a forthright discussion on the Arab problem. 'I don't understand your optimism,' Ben Gurion declared. 'Why should the Arabs make peace? If I was an Arab leader I would never make terms with Israel. That is natural: we have taken their country. Sure, God promised it to us, but what does that matter to them? Our God is not theirs. We come from Israel, it's true, but two thousand years ago, and what is that to them? There has been antisemitism, the Nazis, Hitler, Auschwitz, but was that their fault? They only see one thing: we have come here and stolen their country. Why should they accept that? They may perhaps forget in one or two generations' time, but for the moment there is no chance. So it's simple: we have to stay strong and maintain a powerful army. Our whole policy is there. Otherwise the Arabs will wipe us out.'

I was stunned by this pessimism, but he went on:

'I'll be seventy years old soon. Well, Nahum, if you asked me whether I shall die and be buried in a Jewish state I would tell you Yes; in ten years, fifteen years, I believe there will still be a Jewish state. But ask me whether my son Amos, who will be fifty at the end of this year, has a chance of dying and being buried in a Jewish state, and I would answer: fifty-fifty.'

'But how can you sleep with that prospect in mind,' I broke in, 'and be Prime Minister of Israel too?'

'Who says I sleep?' he answered simply.

That was Ben Gurion all over: he had told me that so as to

show me how well he knew in his heart that Israel could not exist without peace with the Arabs, but his stubborn, aggressive, unbending character prevented him from following what his own intelligence told him. The best proof of that is that having lost his grip on power his intelligence reasserted itself; he even became a 'Goldmannite', declaring that all the occupied territories except Jerusalem should be restored. On this point I am in agreement with him: Israel must keep Jerusalem.

That does not alter my opinion that Ben Gurion is the man principally responsible for the anti-Arab policy, because it was he who moulded the thinking of generations of Israelis. I said to him once:

'You have managed to do something that only God had done before you. Not only have you created the State of Israel, but you have modelled the new Israeli Jew in your own image.'

'Well, that's not bad, is it?' he exclaimed.

'Wait a bit,' I went on. 'I am not sure that God scored that great a success by creating man; so I am not sure you made a success by creating the Israeli.'

Nevertheless, it was only natural for this role to fall to him, so strong was his personality. A man's importance is not always reckoned by what he does, or succeeds in doing; that often depends on circumstances, chance, and time. What defines a man is his specific gravity, as with rare metals like gold or uranium. There are people who, even if they achieve nothing, have no luck, and end as failures, remain great personalities. They are born that way. Ben Gurion is the only Israeli who belonged to this category. Of all the Jewish leaders of my own generation, I do not know of any other with so great a specific gravity. The word which fits him best is 'presence'. As soon as he appeared in any gathering, he became its centre. He might not want to preside, but wherever he sat, even in the back row, there was the president's chair.

I have already said that many Israeli leaders have been provincials. Israel is a small country, but Ben Gurion had a global conception of international politics. He foresaw the power of China, admired de Gaulle from the start, and when the General turned anti-Israeli he continued to defend him. He was loyal to him till the end, for he knew that de Gaulle admired him too, and had a friendship for him, as between equals.

He had a very deep-seated desire for learning. Born in Poland, he had come to Palestine very young. All his life he suffered from having been unable to study. The First World War prevented him because instead of going to Constantinople, where he had intended to enrol at the University, he had to go to America, then join the Jewish Legion created by the British. The lack of degrees did not bother him; it was lack of erudition that disturbed him. As in everything else, he was extreme in this field: I have never known a politician with so little understanding of art, music, or even literature. Paintings did not interest him at all, and music bored him stiff. When he had to attend the inauguration of the Mann Auditorium in Tel Aviv, there were great artists like Artur Rubinstein and Leonard Bernstein present, and at the conclusion of the ceremony he greeted 'the great conductor Rubinstein', confusing him with Bernstein.

More than literature, he was fascinated by the exact sciences and the natural sciences. He confided to me that if he had it to do again, he would not become a politician but a biologist.

There were very touching sides to him. For instance he set about learning Greek in order to read Plato in the original, and on that account one of my great friends, the former British Labour Party minister Richard Crossman, who taught Greek philosophy in Cambridge for ten years, once said to me: 'Tell your friend Ben Gurion when he's talking to me about Plato not to give the impression of having unearthed the text out of some forgotten manuscript!'

But that was Ben Gurion's misfortune: his ambition was to be a thinker and a prophet, and he was neither. He wrote very badly and stiffly. He was a poor speaker, and his speeches made you yawn, but on the other hand he could be a formidable debater: in a discussion he had no equal in attacking and demolishing his opponent. The truth is that he had no consideration for anyone, friend or foe. He dragged his foes through the mud and made his friends his slaves. Among Ben Gurion's successors and con-temporaries in the leadership of Israel I must say a few words about Moshe Sharett who, especially in the last years of his life, was my closest friend, both personally and politically. In my funeral address I said of him that his vices might be an exaggeration of his virtues. He had a rare gift for languages, a thoroughgoing perfectionism, and total honesty and integrity, but he lacked the courage to face up to adversaries stronger than himself. He had always rejected Ben Gurion's Arab policy, and found himself sacked from the foreign ministry with Ben Gurion's characteristic brutality. Fortunately I was able to alleviate this personal tragedy by persuading him to become chairman of the executive of the World Zionist Organization, over which I myself presided, and that gave him a new aim in life.

As for Golda Meir, she has some of Ben Gurion's defects without his greatness. She has a very powerful personality, but lacks subtlety. The great weakness of intellectuals is that they are too intellectual to be strong, whereas primitivism engenders assurance and power. Golda was always thoroughly convinced that she was right, and she used to get furious when satirists guyed her by singing quite a well-known nightclub hit whose refrain went: 'I'm truly sorry, but I'm always right.' Yet it was true: Golda has never seen any shades of meaning; for her the world is black or white, good or bad, and that is that. Which does not stop her from having great abilities, first and foremost her indisputable natural authority.

In the course of a private conversation she asked me:

'Why are we so often at loggerheads? Basically we have respect for each other, and we have collaborated for a long time. So why these quarrels? What is the difference between us?'

'The difference is this,' I replied. 'You are convinced that you have the hundred-per-cent truth in your handbag. I, who am older than you, have never been convinced of being in possession of the absolute or of being altogether right.'

In fact, Golda Meir should never have become Prime Minister. The position belonged to Pinhas Sapir, but he always refused it, and even after Golda's departure he preferred to become chairman of the Jewish Agency. I believe he made a double mistake, first by not taking the premiership, second by choosing Golda to occupy it. Because it was Sapir who discovered her. She was certainly well known as secretary general of the Labour Party, and she did enjoy a certain authority, but no one would have dreamed that she might become Prime Minister. Sapir encouraged her for fear Moshe Dayan might get the job.

I also see this as a proof of the inconsistency of public opinion and the limitations of direct democracy: two or three months before the death of Eshkol, there was an opinion poll which showed that two per cent of electors were for Golda as Prime Minister and more than sixty per cent for Dayan. Three months after Golda's appointment, her score was over seventy per cent. It is true that she has an extraordinary sense of public relations, and she had no rival in her TV representation of herself as the prototype of the Jewish mother, the Yiddishe momma full of kindness and compassion. She believes it herself, which makes her all the more convincing in the part. And yet God knows she is intractable: she is the most masculine woman I have ever seen, and Ben Gurion hit the mark when he said: 'She's the only man in my government!'

On the subject of the Palestinians, Golda has always had a very clear-cut attitude, unlike Weizmann's, for example, when he used to say: 'The conflict between ourselves and the Palestinians is not a conflict of justice against injustice, but a conflict between two equal rights.' My opinion is that our own right is superior, for Palestine is a matter of life or death for the Jews, whereas for the Arabs it only represents one per cent of their vast territories. But Golda Meir did not bother about this kind of subtlety—which explains both her authority and her utter failure: throughout her four years as Prime Minister, Israeli policy did not budge; the Yom Kippur War and the complete isolation of Israel were the consequences of this rigidity.

Once again we missed the chance of a solution then. The government kept saying that there must be no concession, Israel must maintain its super-armament and not give the Arabs the impression of being weak and afraid. Everything springs from this theory: the informal alliance with the United States, Russian hostility, the danger of Russia playing the Arab card, and so on.

In politics one can never be sure, but I have a strong impression that on more than one occasion we might have obtained peace.

At the time of the negotiations for the first armistice with Egypt, on 24 February 1949, in Rhodes, some of the Israeli participants informed me that the armistice could have been transformed into genuine peace. I cannot swear to that, because I was not there, but what I am sure of is that we missed another opportunity in 1967, after the crushing Israeli victory which brought the Six Day War to an end. Two days before the attack, Levi Eshkol had solemnly declared: 'We have no territorial ambition.' So after that miraculous victory—which Dayan himself could not quite explain, as he has told me on several occasions—if Israel had said to the Arabs: 'Sign the peace tomorrow, and we will restore all territories except Jerusalem', there might perhaps have been peace. A lot of Arab experts confirm this supposition now, but no, people want to cling on to what they have won— that is human nature. And this false policy which consists in hanging on to the *status quo* and not giving an inch, which was Golda Meir's favourite technique, has led to the impasse of today.

Bear in mind, incidentally, that I lay the main blame for this situation on the United States even more than on Israel. The Yom Kippur War is the fault of the Americans, who, for reasons of domestic policy (Nixon, the American Jews, anti-Soviet opinion) which I shall not analyse in detail, had spent years doing nothing. When they did try something, they did it too timidly: the Israelis sabotaged the Rogers mission just as they put paid to the Jarring mission. The Egyptians were blamed at the time, but since then I have received information indicating that they were ready to negotiate. Israel meanwhile was insisting on talking to the Arabs directly, without any intermediary, and calling for face-to-face negotiations—which would have forestalled one of the Arab governments' notorious 'Khartum refusals'—but I am not so sure that it was not a pretext for not negotiating at all.

I have been asked if my criticisms of the state I helped to create are due to the fact that I have never been a leader of it. I don't think this is so, but the answer lies in the field of psychoanalysis. Now, I have doubts about psychoanalysis, and I detest poking about in people's intimate thoughts, conscious or not. But frankly, as far as I am concerned, I do not believe that I am motivated by jealousy. At the very worst, if I had never been offered any official position it could be argued that my point of view was dictated by some sort of rationalized resentment. But that cannot be the case, because the parties have been after me for years to become a minister—not only the small Liberal Party, but even Begin and Herut. But if I had been a minister in Ben Gurion's cabinet we would have made life pretty hard for each other, and I would undoubtedly have ended up by resigning, because I have insufficient taste for power to bicker night and day with Ben Gurion.

All the same, it is true that a lot of Israelis resent the fact that I have not taken part in the political life of the state and have not settled in the country. For them, it is next door to being unpatriotic. I understand them, and it is the only reproach I do accept—even if at the same time I can reproach them in my own turn for not understanding my independence of character.

But there is something further. You know that some schools of psychology, Adler's in particular, claim that power is a stronger drive than sex. It is a point on which Adler disagrees with Freud. For me, power is one of the most dangerous and diabolical temptations of all. Without it, no idea can be put into practice, but to my mind the true Messianic era will begin when ideas can be put into practice without one first having to be in power, without power even existing. Which is what Lenin was proposing with the notion of the abolition of the state, an absurd idea on his part, since it is his own disciples who have been the most brutal exponents of state power.

Power corrupts, and absolute power corrupts absolutely. My experience proves to me that it corrupts masses and peoples more than it does individuals. During a revolt or a revolution, when the people 'scent' power, they become hysterical and brutal, so that collective power is often more dangerous than individual power. A single individual is generally more susceptible to reason and rationalism, so he can be influenced. With the masses it is a more difficult matter. That is why the most cruel wars of all are civil wars. They are worse than foreign wars because they are directed not by a minister, a general, or a king, but by the masses themselves.

That being said, the great danger in modern politics has to do with the power in the hands of every politician. The twentieth century might be the worst in all history, because anybody can start a world-wide conflict. The wars of ancient times, the Middle Ages and even the nineteenth century were local. The Germans and the French, for example, have often clashed, but it had little to do with other countries, and nothing with other continents.

Today, military technology threatens the survival of the species. Because of science, humanity can be wiped out, and each time a local conflict breaks out there is a risk of it degenerating into world war. The proof is that when the Arabs and the Israelis fight, everybody raises the possibility of a planet-wide extension. In Vietnam, a world war was barely avoided; it was the same with Korea, and with Cuba.

There has been a terrifying growth of power of all states; that is why I am a deadly enemy of the notion of the state, and particularly of its modern conception. In the past it was not the state which dominated the citizen's life, but religion. It might be cruel and brutal, but at least it had a certain moral legitimacy; when it killed people, it was in the name of faith in God. Today we kill for the big banks, the arms manufacturers, and for the extension of the power of the state.

My ideal is for the state to become an ordinary instrument, a tool. Unfortunately it is hard to get rid of it, because modern life has become too complex for the citizen. Communications and collective technologies can only be conceived and realized by a centralized state. No little backwater region can handle technically sophisticated developments. The other side of the coin is that the more centralized the state becomes, the less does democracy express itself.

America is a democracy mainly in name—not only because Johnson was a neurotic and Nixon a crook, but by the nature of things. Perhaps the America of Jefferson was a democracy, as Switzerland is today because of its several cantons. In a small province it is possible to hold plebiscites, but in a country of two or three hundred million inhabitants, where power is concentrated in one capital and has to deal with military as well as social problems, how much sense would that make?

The extent and complexity of the jobs to be done, and the expenditure they represent, confer on the modern state a constantly expanding power. The corollary is the temptation to abuse this power. That is why it is impossible to have a modern democracy without corruption. When tens of thousands of civil servants can exercise so much power, how are they to resist it? In a small state the complement of public servants is controllable, but what about the United States, where they are numbered in millions?

In our own time, the state has become the absolute ideal. The Congo is a state, Zaire is a state. It is a misfortune that this deplorable fashion, born at the end of the nineteenth century, should continue to spread. I am convinced that fifty or a hundred years from now the notion of the sovereign state will have disappeared, so as to forestall the outbreak of world nuclear war, and with it the death of all civilization.

When the United Nations Organization was founded there ought to have been an attempt at least to abolish the sovereignty of states and to constitute a sort of world power. Remember that despite appearances the scale is beginning to tip that way. State sovereignty is only a dangerous theory, but the reality is the Common Market, the Warsaw Pact, the Organization of American States, the Organization of African Unity, and so on, proving that every state has to give up its vaunted sovereignty little by little because of the complexity of the threats that concern us all.

But do not misunderstand me: when I speak of abolishing the state I mean the political state, not the cultural entity it represents. For instance, I could not imagine a world state all of whose citizens spoke the same language. That would be the end of civilization: Shakespeare and the Psalms of David can exist in a national idiom, but not in Esperanto. So the trend should be towards the theoretical, ideological and practical rehabilitation of the nation at the expense of the state. Nations alone, not states, create civilizations. Of course a state can subsidize theatres or universities, but it is not creative, it is only a technical tool.

To speak more precisely of Israel, I believe that the worship of the state does Israel harm. After all, one of the greatest Talmudists of our own day has declared that the worship of the state in modern Israel is the equivalent of the idolatry of ancient times. In one or two generations this will undoubtedly pass away. For the time being, it amounts basically to the inevitable and natural reaction of a people deprived of statehood for two thousand years, while other peoples had it. But the Judaic ideal ought to mean taking the lead among those who struggle against the state. This seems to me to be the great revolutionary movement of tomorrow, and not a movement deriving from Marxism, which is in decline now and will have disappeared in fifty years' time. The struggle against the arrogance of the state takes precedence over all the rest. Fulbright has written a good book on the subject, *The Arrogance of Power*.

Anyway, the sovereign state is not an eternal notion: it stems from a theory of Hegel, who in my opinion was Hitler's precursor in this domain. From Hegel to Hitler there is a continuity, because once you allow Hegel to claim that 'the state is the summit of human evolution' how can you blame Hitler for proclaiming that 'the thousand-year Reich is the one important value'?

But as I have said, we appear at present to be witnessing a general tendency towards enrolling states into broader units. There are a few nostalgics left, especially in Israel and France, so that I was able to tell Ben Gurion: 'There are still two people in the world who believe in the sovereignty of the state; they are you and de Gaulle.' But from that point of view things have moved on: Pompidou was no de Gaulle, and Giscard is no Pompidou.

Right now, those most jealous of their own sovereignty are the young states, precisely because of their youth, but the virulence of some nationalist movements is a phenomenon borne out by history. An idea, a class or a people becomes most extremist at the moment that precedes its fall. If the bourgeoisie and the aristocracy had not been extremist before yielding their place, if they had known how to make concessions, there would never have been any revolutions. In a few generations' time, the sovereign states will have had their day and a system of supranational entities will have taken their place.

It is true that at present the United Nations Organization looks rather farcical, but the principle of its existence is important. Take the more modest example of the European Community. It is hardly surprising if it is taking time to organize. I have often explained to American friends surprised that the Europeans do not unite more quickly that Germany, France, Great Britain and Italy are heirs to a long history. For them to give up, not their identity, but their absolute sovereignty, is no easy matter. I am sure that fifteen years from now there will be a unified Western Europe, although like de Gaulle I have a preference for a Europe stretching from the Atlantic to the Urals. In the same way, within a generation or two there will be a UN with real powers.

In an organization of that kind, minorities—not just states—will have to be represented. The state is a good delegate for political and military questions, but the minorities will have to make themselves heard at the level of culture and education. Their identity and their particularity must both be assured: for the whole of human civilization the disappearance of the minorities would mean a great impoverishment; for the Jewish people it would mean the end.

Over the years I have personally had a certain amount of power; as president of the biggest Jewish organizations I have had hundreds of millions of dollars in funds under my control, and thousands of employees, though let me say again that this was within the framework of international Jewry, not of a state.

What pleasures have I derived from exercising this power? Well, being in political life seems to me a very ambivalent thing. There is naturally the satisfaction of succeeding, especially over important questions, but I am talking here about my attitude towards political life in general, irrespective of successes and failures—art for art's sake, so to speak. Basically I dislike politics. Unless God has made you a politician or a diplomat—which was not the case with me, because I came into politics more out of a sense of duty—the negative experiences are necessarily more numerous than the satisfactions.

The fact is that you can never be who you are or believe yourself to be, you always have to be playing a role; you can't say what you feel or think, and even if you do manage to master certain situations, you are more the plaything of circumstances than their master. There are only two satisfactions to be derived from political activity. One is the intellectual pleasure of living in a sphere which encompasses nearly all the currents and tendencies of the collective life of the world and its people. That is more and more true today, when a real world-politics is taking shape and everything that happens in one state affects all the rest; you have to allow for tens and hundreds of factors (interests, trends, passions) in order to arrive at a constructive solution. Determination and obstinacy, which can be qualities in other spheres, are rather a source of weakness in politics. For someone like myself, who have always detested one-sidedness and have never paid overmuch attention to experts (I like to quote the witty French definition of the polytechnician as someone who knows everything, and nothing else), this need to be involved in all sorts of matters is a real intellectual pleasure.

The second pleasure to be had is getting to know a lot of interesting people, and influencing or seducing them. Seduction can become a passion. When one seduces a woman the sensation may be more acute, but seducing a statesman comes close to it. When I convinced Dean Acheson to accept the partition of Palestine in spite of his anti-Zionist convictions I felt an almost sensual pleasure coupled with great satisfaction for my own vanity: a success of that sort makes you feel that you are cleverer than your opposite number. I enjoy this fighting in which the weapons are words and the intellect comes first.

Weizmann felt the same way, and did not give a damn about the elementary exercise of power. Better still, he did not understand it. Sometimes when we went to the headquarters of the Jewish Agency together he used to point to all the offices, typewriters and secretaries and ask me: 'What do all these people do? Why do they type so many letters?' He had a concept inherited from

Louis XIV: organization was a matter for the state, and the state was him: 'I, Weizmann, will go to see Churchill, I will go to see Daladier, and that settles it. What good is all the rest?'

In this, Weizmann was at the opposite pole from Ben Gurion, who got no pleasure from being persuasive, and furthermore did not try to be: he imposed. Our personal arguments entertained him a bit, but less than he claimed. He saw them more as a waste of time. His principle was: 'I am in command. I said do it, so do it, and let's hear no more about it!' That was in keeping with his un-intellectual character. Ben Gurion had a one-track mind, and could only deal with one thing at a time. The same was true of his private life—a year to read Plato, a year to discover *Don Quixote*, to the exclusion of any other book. From that angle he was the contrary of a Prime Minister. I often told him: 'A Prime Minister should take care of everything.' He would tell me: 'I take care of the Jewish army; the rest doesn't interest me.' That was his great strength, but also his weakness, because when you do only one thing it is to the detriment of all the rest.

Between Weizmann, most of whose motivations were of an intellectual nature, and Ben Gurion, who enjoyed nothing so much as command, lay the concept of a Roosevelt, at once a philanthropist and a wielder of power. He helped people, especially if they belonged to the underprivileged classes, but at the same time he practised one of the most subtle pleasures in the exercise of power: outwitting his interlocutors. I have done it myself, for the tactic, whether in terms of domestic or foreign policy, requires shrewdness. If you blurt out everything you want straight away, you will never succeed. You must only say part of it at the beginning, and the rest at the end. It is a great intellectual pleasure, I admit, provided it is not abused.

You have to know your own limitations and not underestimate other people's guile. The little politicians think themselves clever by deceiving everybody, but they soon gain reputations as liars. A professor of history once said: 'The difference between Metternich and Talleyrand is that Metternich lied to everybody and fooled nobody, whereas Talleyrand never told lies and fooled everybody.'

As for me, if I am able to have a certain degree of detachment about the exercise of power, it is mainly because I have never had to fight for it. When I won Acheson round, then when I got the better of Abba Hillel Silver at the power centre of American Jewry, it was a deep satisfaction. To have known Churchill, Acheson, Roosevelt, Adenauer and Ben Gurion has been a fulfilment for me, because unlike Stephen Wise I only like exceptional men and I prefer to sit alone with Plato than stand with the herd.

Yet socially I am not a snob. I have no great liking of the very rich, with a few exceptions, and I have never sought out their company, and American multimillionaires have complained about that more than once! Likewise, I rarely accept invitations from big public figures, and have never had myself invited to the White House, although I could easily have arranged it. To put it plainly, I like to help people, but that satisfaction is an amalgam of virtue and vanity. When I know that all it takes is a letter from me to get a job for someone, or a lifetime pension from the Germans for someone else, I do it as much out of altruism as for the pleasure of exerting a little of my power. It is an easy matter: I write a letter and it is done. If I had to work for three months for the same result, I don't suppose I would do it.

That is part of my character: I make up my mind fast, and I dislike long discussions, even if that means that I make mistakes. Patience is not one of my virtues. Certainly I can be patient when there is an outstanding objective involved—German reparations, for example. For them, I worked for twenty years, and Ben Gurion used to say: 'Haven't you had a bellyful? How can you keep going to Germany four times a year to ask for money? Nobody is that patient.' But in little things I am impatient.

Generally speaking I have a fairly high opinion of myself and I often give myself cause for it! But I have no vanity about my own ideas: I can be convinced. On my conception of Judaism, and on Zionism, I have never deviated, but on the tactical level I have often been blamed for not being consistent and for shifting my ground. My reply is that only fools and idiots do not vary.

But let us get to the heart of the matter: by nature, I am not a democrat. Churchill was unfortunately right when he said that democracy was the worst of all systems of government except for all the rest. I do not believe that parliamentary democracy as it exists today will last very much longer. The world has become too complex for its problems to be soluble by our good old democratic methods, in which considerations of domestic and local policy often count for more than external policy. That is why, from the point of view of this same external policy, the totalitarian states have a great advantage: there, five, ten, or at the most twenty people take the decisions.

In America, the very height of absurdity is achieved, when the representative of the cattle raisers of Wisconsin has a power of decision concerning arms for Thailand . . . Modern parliamentary government may just about work for a small country like Switzerland, but how can you expect a Milwaukee farm worker to think about anything other than the price of corn? What interests a Labour Party MP most is the wages of workers in his own constituency. How can he lay down the law about problems in the Near East, Laos or Cambodia?

I repeat that the two great experiences in my life were the partition of Palestine and the negotiations with post-Hitler Germany. And in both cases, if a plebiscite had been organized nothing would have been done. The majority of Zionists were for rejecting partition. And at the start of my negotiations with Adenauer I had to travel with a bodyguard for protection against extremists . . . Jewish extremists. It is concrete proof of the weakness of the parliamentary system that if the people had had the chance to vote there would have been no Israel, and no German billions.

A long time ago I found myself in Zurich with my friend Joseph Sprinzak, a great leader of Mapai and later first speaker of the Israeli parliament. We were going to have to face some very thorny problems during the Zionist Congress, and Sprinzak was nervous. One night, over coffee, I told him: 'Joseph, you're wrong. You're getting worked up about nothing. I can tell you in advance everything that the Congress will decide.'

'That's ridiculous!' he said.

'All right,' I replied, 'I'll make you a bet. You jot down the problems, and I'll write out the answers straight away on the same piece of paper. We'll compare them after the Congress.'

Ten days later we checked his list: out of the twenty-two questions he had asked, twenty of my answers agreed with the Congress decisions! He was stunned.

'But Nahum,' he said, 'this destroys all my confidence in democracy. A Congress like this costs us half a million dollars. Why spend all that money? Next time I'll write you a letter and you can send the solution by return.'

'You don't understand the meaning of what I did,' I told him. 'My talent has to do with knowing the psychology of the delegates. But your job is to give them the conviction that it is they who make the decisions. Otherwise there wouldn't be a Zionist movement.'

This anecdote does not compel any great respect for the masses, and in fact I believe that masses are stupid. One of the best books written on the subject is *The Psychology of Crowds*, by the French sociologist Gustave Le Bon, published in the late nineteenth century. I have read it several times, and what it shows is that crowds are nothing more than hysterical collectivities devoid of all logic.

So if I can I avoid consulting people and prefer to present my own organization with a *fait accompli*. It has often been said that Goldmann was the dictator of the World Jewish Congress, and there is a grain of truth there. But there it is, it so happens that I have never been afraid of responsibilities. That is why civil servants are fond of me: my attitude comes as a welcome change from the Israeli bureaucracy, where their boss dithers about making delicate decisions. 'Come back tomorrow,' they are told, 'I'll have to think it over.' So you wait for the boss, who waits for another boss, and nothing gets done. With me, you get an immediate decision, good or bad; the staff come to my office, describe their problem, and in ten minutes it is settled.

Ever since the days when I ran my gang of juvenile apple thieves in Visznevo, I have enjoyed responsibility. I have never said that any mistake made by the WJC was the fault of the executive; if I am the president, the responsibility is mine, although when I find myself at a gathering where it is obviously going to be impossible for me to convince the majority, I leave.

Which does not mean that I would prefer a totalitarian system. Israelis who do not approve of my policy of moderation towards the USSR often accuse me of being a pro-Communist living in plush hotels. That is idiotic! I am as anti-Communist as it is possible to be. By nature I detest police, the omnipresence of government and state absolutism. I dream of living in a society in which the state has been abolished and everybody acts by adapting to others. A totalitarian state in my view is the worst thing possible. All I say to my opponents is: 'Soviet power is considerable, so let's be careful and not try to force their hand.' As for the rigid Communist system, I reassure myself with the consideration that it will not last long. Inside a generation or two, Sakharov's forecasts will be proved right: capitalism will be half communist, and communism half capitalist.

In the case of the USSR, among others, I have been called a very pragmatic, very rational negotiator. Yet the irrational has often been the driving force of human progress, and has played an important part in the exercise of power. For great ideas, you have to be irrational, you have to try to reach the inaccessible, to want more than can ever be realized. It is the great utopias that create history, not the great realities. The Zionist idea, for example, is thoroughly irrational: for a people to wish to return to its former lands after two thousand years' absence goes against all reason. If Zionism had been rational it would have had to find another, more or less empty, country, which is just what the great English writer Israel Zangwill advocated.

The ideal of messianic peace is majestic, the ideal of eternal reconciliation for all is majestic, the ideal of equal justice for all is majestic, but none of that is realizable, even if human history lasts for millions of years more. Yet there must be a struggle for these ideals. Messianism is not possible, that is certain, but to want Messianism is crucial. The German poet Lessing said that the path that leads to the truth is more creative than the truth itself.

In lesser matters, on the other hand, it is necessary to be rational and not emotional. That is why I am critical of the attitude of Israel, which cannot tell the great objectives from the small. Everyone will lay down his life for the Golan. But when it comes to realizing a humanist Zionism, that can be left to utopian intellectuals like Goldmann.

There is, however, sometimes a danger of lapsing from pragmatism into opportunism. All politics is a question of degree and proportion, but the foremost danger is to believe that there are such things as eternal verities. I had a friend called Yitzhak Grünbaum, who was one of the leaders of the Zionist Radical Party, the only party I have ever belonged to. Grünbaum was an extremely brave man, with a character as pure as crystal: at the time of the creation of Israel he refused the post of interior minister because he did not want to run the police. 'The police are force,' he used to say, 'and force is immoral.' So he was an out-of-the-ordinary man, but unfortunately very dogmatic. During a rowdy meeting he once made a sad appeal:

'Can't we resume our old friendship and cooperate again?'

'My dear Grünbaum,' I replied, 'I can't respond to your appeal because you're much too young for me.'

'What do you mean? I'm fifteen years older than you!'

'That's easy enough: the opinions you profess today are the ones we both had twenty years ago. But I am twenty years older, while you have stayed at the same age. So you are too young for me.'

I believe that you must always know just how far concessions can go without violating or abandoning great principles. For example, I would never have agreed to give up the idea of a Jewish state, even at the time when I was fighting Vladimir Jabotinsky, who wanted to annex the whole of Palestine, Jordan included. Today I would make no concession over Jerusalem, whose value as myth and mystical symbol is undeniable. But to fight a war for the Golan, or Sharm el Sheikh, is the life of two thousand Jewish soldiers not worth more than all of Sharm el Sheikh?

In the heart of my pragmatism, which takes account of all the negative aspects of men and things, nevertheless I always remain an optimist. This is a great strength which always supported me when everybody was jeering at me about the German reparations. Even Ben Gurion, who was totally in favour, used to tell me: 'Nahum, I am with you, but you won't get anything.' And when I saw him again after signing the Luxembourg Agreement he cried: 'What you have obtained is a greater miracle than the creation of the state!'

As regards the Russians too, my optimism has never faltered. More than ten years ago I anticipated that we would see a great emigration of Russian Jews. The only one who believed me was Ben Gurion, and the emigration did happen. Besides, if I was not an optimist, do you think that I would be mixed up in Jewish politics—which are the most thankless pursuit there is? At the age of sixteen I kept a private diary in which I wrote: 'The Jews are a people who have to be admired but whom it is difficult to love.' In fact greatness—whether in individuals or in groups— always commands admiration; love often derives from different considerations.

The statesman often has something in common with the actor, except that the actor is only the interpreter of a part, while the statesman is both author and executant. What is my approach to these two parts which I have played for so long? Being the author means expressing one's ideas in speeches, articles or books. The difficulty, for a statesman, arises out of not always being able to tell the whole truth: it depends on timing. In politics, what is an excellent idea right now may become idiotic or harmful ten years —or even ten minutes—later.

On the occasion of one great debate inside the Zionist Congress, for instance, I utilized the support of Jabotinsky's revisionists to 'bring down' Weizmann, who was too pro-British in those days. Then I had to change alliances during the same meeting because the revisionists, consistently enough, were demanding a Palestine on both sides of the Jordan. Jabotinsky's friends never forgave me for that desertion, and in 1943, when Weizmann and I came out in favour of a State of Israel, they protested: 'We were proclaiming the necessity for the state ten years ago. Now you see how right we were!' But Weizmann answered with one of those little stories he had a knack of telling: 'There once was a Jew who lived in a little village near the town of Pinsk. This man had a twelve-year-old son who, like all Jewish boys of his age, had to prepare for his Bar Mitzvah. So the man sends him to Pinsk, and the boy makes his Bar Mitzvah there. When he gets back, the father exclaims: "You see how things are in a big town? In the village nothing has happened for twelve years, and after only a single year in Pinsk, already there's a Bar Mitzvah!" '

To return to where we began, the political author has to choose the moment that seems to him to correspond with reality. As for the actor, in public affairs he is mainly a speaker. Since my first speech, delivered when I was thirteen and a half, I have certainly made thousands, and yet I have a fairly low opinion of rhetoric, for in my opinion profound truths cannot be spoken in a speech, nor can the most personal truths: without appearing indelicate, it is hard to talk to two thousand people as you would talk to a friend.

Of course there are several types of orators. Vladimir Jabotinsky used to make marvellous speeches, but he worked them out carefully then learned them word by word, before delivering them in a manner which made it quite believable that he had only just thought them out. With some exceptions—for instance in the case of a political statement having to be translated into several languages—I never prepare a speech, and even in the case cited I do not consider myself under any obligation to respect the printed text. The *New York Times* threatened not to publish any more statements of mine unless I said everything I had put in the press hand-out. So in New York I have sometimes interrupted a speech to announce: 'Having forgotten to say what the *New York Times* is expecting, I'll say it now, just to please them.'

That was quite unlike the style of Jabotinsky, whom I once met in Chicago at half past eleven at night, much to my surprise. I asked him:

'But Jabo, what are you doing here?'

'I've been making a speech.'

'But I knew nothing about it. Who was it for?'

'For a group of students.'

'Zionist students? How many were there?'

'Twenty-five, thirty.'

'How long did you speak?'

'Two and a half hours.'

'Jabo, you're crazy! Speaking for two and a half hours to twenty-five students . . .'

So I asked him back to my apartment, where he sat up till two in the morning explaining his own art of rhetoric. 'Every speech of mine is prepared at length,' he told me. 'It's a work of art. Does it matter to the Mona Lisa whether she has one visitor or a thousand? It's the same thing with my speeches: whether they're heard by two thousand people or twenty-five, they don't change.'

Some orators deliver brilliant monologues, like Jabotinsky; the audience does not interest them. My own speeches are always dialogues: the public does not react by speaking, but it laughs, or finds other means to express itself; when I feel it getting bored I tell a story, or else I make cuts—which is always possible, since I hardly write anything down. But I detest demagogy and I try hard always to keep up a certain standard. I once had to speak in front of seventy thousand people, and that is dreadful: you can't say anything intelligent, just spout slogans.

But to be honest I am going to quote you one exception. The first concentration camp I visited with Wise after the war was between Frankfurt and Höchst; there were sixty thousand Jewish victims of Nazism in it. You can't imagine how much weeping, screaming and sobbing there was. The survivors thought: 'Wise and Goldmann are here, so the war is over. We've won.' But they did not know where to go. The British were not allowing immigration to Palestine and the Jewish state was not yet on the cards. So I made a speech, in Yiddish. Every three minutes, twenty or thirty thousand people would burst into tears. I told them: 'The war is won. You are no longer threatened with death, but you can't get out of this damned country yet, because the free countries won't take you. It is not broad daylight: we are in a tunnel several years longer yet. All the same, I tell you, not to comfort you but because it's true: at the end of the tunnel I see the light, and that light is the creation of a Jewish state.'

I cannot describe the ensuing scenes: women fainted, the weeping crowd chanted: 'Jewish state! Jewish state! . . .' When Stephen Wise and I drove away, he too was sobbing, and in the car he said to me through his tears:

'I understand you comforting those people, but now we're by ourselves, tell me: do you now believe in a Jewish state?'

'Yes,' I replied simply.

Then he fell into my arms. And subsequently, in every speech he made, Wise would say: 'Nobody believes that there will be a Jewish state in a few years' time. Well, I'm telling you that it will exist, because Nahum is convinced of it!'

5 'I, Chancellor Adenauer . . .'

THE OBTAINING of German reparations after the war was, for me, one of my crucial successes. After being thrown out of Germany by Adolf Hitler, I returned to speak to Konrad Adenauer almost as an equal. How those talks proceeded is a long story, and perhaps the one I am most attached to. I believe I have said that culturally I was still very German, at the same time as being a Jew and, in the 'universal' sense, a cosmopolitan. For one short century before Hitlerism, Germany gave Jews all civil rights, and in return the Jews enriched that country in every field: literature, philosophy, music, politics, finance . . . Certainly Hitlerism swept the German Jews away, but there was nothing it could do against that manifold, incomparable contribution.

I say again, the great mistake of the German Jews was the failure to weigh up the dreadful risks of the Nazi adventure in time. I have often said that if we had not belonged to the generation which created the State of Israel we would count among the worst in Jewish history because of our lack of foresight and absence of solidarity before the Nazi period. Together with a few friends, I personally never stopped sending out alarm calls, but could not or did not know how to make myself heard.

When I was representing the World Jewish Congress and the Jewish Agency in Geneva I had regular meetings with the leaders of German Jewry. The meetings were clandestine, because they were forbidden to have contacts with a man de-naturalized for high treason. We tried our utmost, but the Jewish people did not help us much. The democracies too were very much at fault, but before we accuse non-Jews, let us first accuse ourselves. Later, when the Jews started to understand the horror of the situation, Germany was already so powerful that there was no longer anything to be done.

Apart from my encounter with the survivors of the concentration camps after the liberation, I only returned officially to Germany in order to meet Chancellor Adenauer and open negotiations about reparations. These reparations constitute an extraordinary innovation in terms of international law. Until then, when a country lost a war it paid damages to the victor, but it was a matter between states, between governments. Now for the first time a nation was to give reparations either to ordinary individuals or to Israel, which did not legally exist at the time of Hitler's crimes. All the same I must admit that the idea did not come from me.

During the war the WJC had created an Institute of Jewish Affairs in New York (its headquarters are now in London). The directors were two great Lithuanian Jewish jurists, Jacob and Nehemiah Robinson. Thanks to them, the Institute worked out two completely revolutionary ideas: the Nuremberg tribunal and German reparations.

The importance of the tribunal which sat at Nuremberg has not been reckoned at its true worth. According to international law it was in fact impossible to punish soldiers who had been obeying orders. It was Jacob Robinson who had this extravagant, sensational idea. When he began to canvass it among the jurists of the American Supreme Court they took him for a fool. 'What did these Nazi officers do that was so unprecedented?' they asked. 'You can imagine Hitler standing trial, or maybe even Goering, but these are simple soldiers who carried out their orders and behaved as loyal soldiers.' We therefore had the utmost trouble in persuading the Allies; the British were fairly opposed, the French barely interested, and although they took part later they did not play any great part. The success came from Robinson managing to convince the Supreme Court judge, Robert Jackson.

The Institute's other idea was that Nazi Germany ought to pay after its defeat. That still required belief in the defeat, at a time when it seemed likely that the war in Europe was lost for the Allies, but like Churchill and de Gaulle I kept my faith. I never doubted for a moment, because I knew that Hitler would never manage to moderate himself and that his excesses would draw the Allies into the conflict. According to the Institute's conclusions, the German reparations would first have to be paid to people who had lost their belongings through the Nazis. Further, if, as we hoped, the Jewish state was created, the Germans would pay compensation to enable the survivors to settle there. The first time this idea was expressed was during the war, in the course of a conference in Baltimore.

Once the Nuremberg trials were over, this reparations problem received further consideration. Several Jewish leaders then attempted to establish relations with Adenauer, but their proposals were often ridiculous. One organization suggested a payment of twenty million Deutschmarks—and at the conclusion of the agreement I obtained, the Germans will have paid out a total of eighty billion!

Our 'contacts' were Walter Hallstein, then an under-secretary of state, and later president of the EEC, and the diplomat Herbert Blankenhorn, director of the political department of the German Foreign Ministry and Adenauer's right-hand man. These two have remained close friends of mine.

During a meeting of the World Jewish Congress in London, a Russian Jew called Noah Barou, a wonderful man and great idealist whose premature death was a severe blow, talked me into taking an active part by first of all meeting Adenauer. I was very hesitant at heart, because it was no easy matter for me to talk to the Germans again. And in fact it was eventually my head, and not my heart, which decided me to negotiate. But I laid down a pre-condition: before I would meet the Chancellor to open negotiations, Adenauer had to make a solemn statement to the Bundestag; he must say that although the Germany of those days was certainly not the Germany which had produced Auschwitz (Adenauer himself had been in prison under Hitler, and then had to hide in a monastery bacause the Gestapo were looking for him), it nevertheless inherited the Nazis' responsibilities, and reparations were its duty; he must add that material reparations could not erase the evil done to the Jews by the Germans.

There were several attempts to arrange an interview between us, but I refused to see the Chancellor until the speech was made. For instance, there was an occasion when my wife and I were on holiday by Lake Lucerne and Adenauer was half an hour away, in Bürgenstock. Blankenhorn came to see me and said: 'Look, Adenauer is on holiday near here; if you meet him, nobody will know. And he is very anxious for a visit from you.' I did not give way.

Not long afterwards, in Paris, to be precise at the Hôtel Raphaël, which was a very good establishment where Eisenhower also stayed (I always stay at hotels patronized by generals: they choose the best because they aren't paying!), a member of the first German parliament, a socialist Jew called Jacob Altmaier, came looking for me. He was one of Adenauer's advisers on Jewish questions. 'The Chancellor has decided to go your way,' he announced. 'He will be presenting a solemn declaration to the Bundestag in a day or two, and he wants you to read it first and make any remarks you may see fit.' I made a few corrections, which Adenauer did not always observe, and two days later he made his speech. The whole German parliament stood and observed a five-minute silence in memory of the Jewish victims of Nazism.

So from that angle things had gone as I wanted and preliminary talks could begin. But there was still a big problem: a huge majority of Jewish public opinion was hostile to any contact with the Germans. That is an attitude I understand very well, by the way, and I have often said that if the Jewish people had unanimously agreed to the idea of negotiating for cash reparations from the Germans I would be ashamed of being Jewish. The Jewish people were bound to display their opposition, but its leaders had to take no notice; that is politics.

Adenauer sent me a message declaring his readiness to negotiate with a single representative of the Jews of the Diaspora. For negotiations with Israel he wanted to deal with a separate delegation. Previously the Israeli government had sent diplomatic notes to the four Allies, the USSR, France, Great Britain and the US. It explained that the cost of absorbing half a million Jewish survivors of the concentration camps was a billion and a half dollars. Israel wanted West Germany to pay two-thirds of this sum and East Germany one-third. Tel Aviv had addressed itself to the Allies in order not to talk directly to the Germans.

To this day the Russians have not replied to that note, while the other three Allies said that they agreed to Germany paying but were unable to negotiate in the name of the Jews; they had their own problems with the Germans and were negotiating the questions of occupation and sovereignty. So the Israeli government was in a fix, and Ben Gurion and Moshe Sharett sent for me and said: 'The kernel of the negotiations has to be handled in the name of the Jewish people, because the Nazis' victims were victims as Jews, not as Israelis. We can't go too far out on a limb ourselves, because Herut has turned this business into a political hobby-horse.' In fact there had been big demonstrations in Israel, and stones had been thrown at Ben Gurion inside the Knesset itself.

Again, I understand that reaction; I understand anger and indignation coming from people who had suffered so greatly. Something like it happens today with the Russian Jews: the people who have been through Soviet prisons and work camps are the most anti-Russian. We owe them respect, admiration, but above all the refusal to do everything they ask. Without the German reparations that started coming through during its first ten years as a state, Israel would not have half of its present infrastructure: all the trains in Israel are German, the ships are German, and the same goes for electrical installations and a great deal of Israel's industry ... and that is setting aside the individual pensions paid to survivors. Israel today receives hundreds of millions of dollars in German currency each year. When Pinhas Sapir made a great speech in my defence to the WJC, he said: 'Goldmann has brought Israel eight billion dollars.' In some years the sums of money received by Israel from Germany have been as much as double or treble the contribution made by collections from international Jewry. Nowadays, there is no longer any opposition to the principle—even some members of Herut draw reparations.

So I convoked the Claims Conference in New York (to be precise, the 'Conference on Jewish Material Claims Against

Germany'), representing all the major Jewish organizations. There were angry demonstrations outside the hotel where we were staying, and I had to leave under police protection. On top of that, there were violent disputes within the Conference itself, because nobody could agree on the composition of the executive. The debate had already been going on for half a day without any conclusion when a member of the American Jewish Labour Committee got up and said: 'There's only one solution: we give Goldmann full powers to choose its members, and we appoint him president!' So I was unanimously appointed—which would be unimaginable either in the Zionist Congress or the WJC.

My first meeting with Adenauer had to be kept totally secret, and the time came when the Chancellor informed me that he was to visit London to deliver a lecture, and that he could meet me at Claridge's Hotel. He asked me to get in touch with Blankenhorn to make the arrangements and discuss procedure. I saw Blankenhorn together with Barou, and made the immediate stipulation that before opening the negotiations proper, Germany must accept the Israeli demand of one billion dollars not as a target but as a starting-point. Blankenhorn exclaimed: 'But that's quite impossible! How can the Chancellor make such a commitment without consulting the members of his government, especially his Finance Minister, Fritz Schaeffer, who is a very powerful personality? You'll have to wait.' Bear in mind that this scene occurred long before the famous German 'economic miracle', and that in the fifties Germany was very poor. But I refused to bend, and told him: 'Without such a promise I will not advise either my Claims Conference colleagues or Ben Gurion to accept the principle of negotiation.'

When the day came I arrived at Claridge's, and there I had one of the most impressive conversations in my whole political life. The atmosphere was glacial. Remember, I was face to face with Germany's first chancellor since Hitler. So I went straight to the point: 'Mr Chancellor, this moment is historic. Usually I dislike high-sounding talk, but the instant when the representative of the Jewish people meets the leader of the German nation which has murdered six million Jews is necessarily historic, and I am going to tell you why. I only ask you to allow me to speak for twenty minutes without interruption.' And Adenauer, who had the hieratic features of some medieval statue, never lost his poker face as he heard me out.

I finished like this: 'Mr Chancellor, I will not play the diplomat, because our problem is not one of diplomacy but of morality. If you decide to negotiate, you are committing yourself to a moral duty. If you decide to approach the question as a diplomat, it is better for us not to meet again. The Israelis are asking for a billion dollars, and I have asked for that amount to be considered as a starting-point. Mr Blankenhorn informed me that by the terms of your constitution that was quite impossible. My answer was that I could not wait, because the Jewish people is in uproar and the majority are opposed to any negotiation liable to wash Germany's hands of its crimes. But now that I have met you I think I can feel confident that you have a strong enough personality to momentarily ignore the strictures of your constitution—when such a subject is at stake.'

Adenauer looked at me before replying: 'Mr Goldmann, I have not had the pleasure of meeting you till now.' And in fact this had been a possibility, because he had been a member of the pro-Palestinian committee before Hitler's accession. 'So you have known me for half an hour,' he went on, 'and I must tell my friend Blankenhorn, who has known me for many years, that you understand me better than he does. If you will please go into the office next door I will send in my secretary. Dictate the letter to him, and I will sign it.'

I dictated the letter, and Adenauer made only one alteration— where I had written that the billion dollars was to be *die Basis*, the basis, he substituted *die Grundlage*, the foundation—which came to the same thing. And he ended the interview with these words: 'Send Herr Barou to see me this afternoon, and I will hand over the signed letter.'

No other statesman would have dared to do that. After signing, he had great difficulties with his cabinet, which accused him of behaving like a dictator by promising the billion dollars without consulting anyone. But he was Adenauer, a true leader, and they all came round in the end. That is often the way to run a democracy.

That conversation remained unknown for a long time, for we had decided that if the press got wind of it we would both deny ever having met. All the same, it was no use having stepped up my precautions and entered Claridge's by the service door; everybody felt that there was something going on, and even *The Times* hinted at it.

Armed with the letter, I then went to the Claims Conference, where the committee unanimously approved the opening of negotiations. At the same time Ben Gurion faced the Knesset, where opposition raged against the talks. The majority of the Mapai leaders were in favour, with the exception of Golda Meir and a few others, and so were the Liberals. But Herut and Mapam were against. If Israel had refused I would not have been able to negotiate: it was impossible to assume such responsibilities alone. Finally the Knesset designated a group under the leadership of Giora Josephtal and Felix Shinnar, so Israel and the Claims Conference each had their own delegation. It was agreed that the two delegations would take turns to negotiate with the German delegation, which was headed by two extraordinary men, the eminent jurist Otto Küster and Professor Franz Boehm, who recently died after his eightieth birthday. Ben Gurion once said in public that if Israel had ten men of Boehm's moral stature life would be better there. This is a typical Ben Gurion exaggeration, but it is true that Franz Boehm was a truly outstanding figure, both morally and intellectually.

So the Germans discussed collective reparations with the Israeli delegation in the morning, and individual rights with the Claims Conference delegation in the afternoon. When a difficulty cropped up I would be informed and I would sort it out with Adenauer. The negotiations took place near The Hague, and I never attended them in person. They went on for six months, and I cannot go into detail here—a three-volume book is in preparation on the question!

Once Adenauer had provided the famous letter, I then had to see the German Finance Minister, Fritz Schaeffer. This right-wing

Catholic and life-long anti-Nazi was a man of total integrity, and one of the best finance ministers Germany has ever had. He started by telling me: 'Listen, my dear Goldmann, there's no blackmail you can bring to bear on me. I was never a Nazi, and Hitler had me put in prison. So that leaves me free to stand up to you, which an ex-Nazi wouldn't dare to do.' And he went on: 'What you are asking for is fine, and you have every moral right in the world. But you see I am neither a moralist nor a rabbi, but the finance minister of a country which at present is poor. So, as they say in Yiddish, show me the bottom line of the bill right now. What will all this cost?'

'I don't know the details yet,' I told him, and it was true: I have only recently learned them. I always say that a president is a man who signs an agreement but who is not familiar with it. I am a wholesale dealer; I lack the patience for any clause-by-clause examination. Still, Schaeffer persisted.

'Our expert Robinson has calculated that it would come to about six billion marks,' I told him.

'But our own experts make it eight billion,' he replied, 'and that is far too much.'

In fact, Germany has paid sixty billion marks up to date, and the total will come to eighty billion—twelve to fourteen times more than we reckoned at the time ... So the Germans cannot be accused of being stingy and of not keeping their promises. On the contrary, as soon as the laws were passed Schaeffer released the funds at once, and on several occasions he even granted advances—which wasn't easy, as the following anecdote shows.

Germany had contracted colossal debts, inherited both from Hitler and from the Weimar Republic. In order to rehabilitate itself in the eyes of the world, and to start doing business again, it therefore had to settle these debts. In that field the chief negotiator was Germany's leading financier, Hermann Abs, the director of the Deutsche Bank. He argued the repayment terms with the Allies point by point, and claimed that Germany could only pay a small amount. Learning of our own negotiations with the German government he went and complained to Adenauer: 'At the moment when I'm telling the Allies that we are bankrupt, you are offering Goldmann millions without any legal obligation. My situation is untenable. Adjourn negotiations with the Jews while I finish with the Allies.' Adenauer accepted in principle and had Blankenhorn telephone me to ask me to meet Abs in London. This is how Abs explained his position:

'Mr Goldmann, I accept your demands in principle. Nevertheless you must wait for six months, because knowing what your own requirements are, the Allies are making my life impossible. I have therefore suggested to the Chancellor that you should be paid an advance of two or three hundred million marks. In six months' time you can resume your negotiations.'

'I'm sorry, but that's impossible,' I replied. 'It is an emotional problem we're dealing with here. The Jewish people are troubled to the depths of their soul. We can't put the question in cold storage and say to the victims of Nazism: "Postpone your troubles. In six months you can start protesting again." Either we settle the problem now, or it will never be settled.'

I heard later that Abs was very annoyed by my answer, but some years afterwards he came round to believing that I was absolutely right. All the same, Adenauer was at his wits' end: the whole of Germany's industry and high finance was opposed to our claims. At the same time Schaeffer was arguing that the government of Israel would take a lot less than I was asking. In fact he had the Israeli budget at his fingertips, and at that time it was totally in the red. When I was president of the Zionist Executive in New York, the Israeli financial representative, Martin Rosenblueth, often used to look in on me around ten o'clock in the morning to tell me: 'Nahum, what are you doing sitting there resting when the banks close at one o'clock and we have a bill to pay?' Then I would have to put in emergency calls to the Zionist organizations to find a hundred thousand dollars on the spot. Schaeffer was acquainted with this situation, and he used to tell both Adenauer and me: 'What, you claim that Israel would refuse half or even a third of that amount? A bankrupt country?' I can now reveal for the first time that it was he who was right.

When Adenauer finally informed us that for the time being

Germany could only offer us two or three hundred million marks, I wrote him a letter breaking off the negotiations. I then received a telegram from Ben Gurion urging me to go to see him in Israel. I have already said that I was then travelling with a bodyguard provided by Israeli security, a young man of Turkish origin, who did his best but protested to his superiors: 'It's impossible to protect Goldmann. He makes appointments and doesn't tell me. He goes to the theatre without letting me know, and so forth.' In fact I was a very bad client.

When I arrived in Israel no one was allowed out of the plane before me and there was a car waiting at the foot of the steps to drive me straight to Ben Gurion, who broke into an immediate lecture:

'Nahum, don't be too ambitious. I'm told you can get three hundred million dollars right now. Israel has been asking for a billion, but you know what the position is . . .'

'Listen, Ben Gurion,' I replied. 'If the Germans stick at three hundred million, I won't sign. But I do advise you to sign in that case.'

'What's the difference between you and me?'

'It's simple: I represent the Jewish people, which is too rich for my liking. But you represent a bankrupt state. I can take the liberty of refusing. You can't.'

'So you'll be the hero and me the coward!' he retorted. 'All right, since you're not signing, I'm not signing either.'

Then he asked me what was my minimum. I said that for anything less than five hundred million dollars I would not accept any arrangement, but that I was hoping for between six and seven hundred. I finally got three billion marks, or about 823 million dollars: starting from a basis of a billion, eighty-two per cent was a pretty good deal.

I recall the circumstances very well. I was in Paris at the time, and when I returned to my hotel after an evening at the theatre there was a note waiting for me: 'Mr John McCloy, the American High Commissioner in Bonn, has telephoned twice and wants you to call him back, even if it's night-time.' So I woke up McCloy, whom I knew very well. 'Stay in your hotel tomorrow,' he told me. 'Professor Boehm will be coming to see you with some interesting proposals. I can't tell you any more.' I must point out that at the moment when the Germans stated that they would pay an advance of two or three hundred million, Boehm and Küster resigned at once; the fact that top German representatives protested against their own government on behalf of the Jews made a great stir in Germany, where most of the press was on our side.

After hearing from McCloy I informed Shinnar and Josephtal and asked them to join me when I saw Boehm. Next morning Boehm phoned me:

'Professor Boehm here.'

'Yes, I've been expecting you.'

'You've a good three-quarters of an hour to wait.'

'Why's that?'

'I've got to come on foot: I haven't a centime.'

'What? A man who comes to talk about billions hasn't a centime on him?'

'Adenauer sent for me yesterday to submit some fresh proposals to you. I had no money and the banks and administrative offices were closed; I have turned up with twenty marks in my pocket and not a single French franc.'

This candour was quite typical of Boehm. I told him to take a taxi and I would have the hotel reception settle it. It was in the course of the ensuing conversation that Boehm made a first offer of seven hundred million dollars and that I managed to step it up to eight hundred and twenty-three.

I am now going to tell you about two episodes which belong to the chapter entitled 'How to make millions by telling stories'!

When the two parties reached agreement to grant Israel three billion marks, the Germans argued that they had no liquid assets, which was true. Adenauer then announced: 'We'll pay you in power stations, factories, etc.' I nodded, and he went on:

'We also have a big butter surplus.'

'We don't want any butter,' I replied.

He looked surprised: 'And why not?' I had a good grasp of the Chancellor's psychology, so I explained: 'Israel is a poor country which has to make do with margarine.' There were several people present, among them Boehm, Walter Hallstein and Blankenhorn. Adenauer was very impressed, and turned to say to them:

'You see, my friends, what a courageous country Israel is. They will not eat butter! That is why we must help them!'

'On the other hand we need oil,' I added.

'But Mr Goldmann, there is no oil in Germany!'

'Mr Chancellor, is it the fault of the Jews if the good Lord has given oil to Kuwait and Saudi Arabia but not to Germany or Israel? It is very straightforward. The British companies have oil. Buy it from them and give it to us. For my country it is a question of life or death.'

He agreed.

Towards the end of the negotiations, Hallstein, Blankenhorn and I had to settle the final details. It was agreed that all the problems which came up but which we were unable to solve would be submitted to Adenauer, who would decide. Having obtained the three billion marks for Israel I asked for five hundred million dollars for the Claims Conference so that it could rebuild the synagogues, schools and libraries destroyed in Europe by the Nazis. Hallstein was furious. 'What!' he complained, 'You've been negotiating for four months and you've never said a word on that subject?' Yet it was obvious that if I had mentioned it at the start of the negotiations, there would have been less given to Israel. But Hallstein went on:

'We had the impression that what you were asking was for Israel, and suddenly you demand half a billion for installations outside Israeli territory. Impossible!'

'I can't go back to the US and talk to my colleagues without having settled this problem,' I replied. 'The Germans destroyed; the Germans must pay.'

Hallstein was a very good man, and a great jurist, but a bit of a bureaucrat too. He asked me for two days to check his figures and to find a legal basis.

'Find it or not,' I told him, 'what I want is the money, not the basis.'

We stopped there, and two days later Hallstein produced his figure:

'I have made an estimate. Synagogues, schools, etc. can be valued at three hundred and fifty million dollars.'

'My minimum is five hundred million.'

It was impossible to agree, and we decided to leave it to Adenauer to decide. Hallstein was the rapporteur, and he said: 'There is a problem. Goldmann is being stubborn and I think he's wrong. My estimate comes out at three hundred and fifty million, but he insists on a minimum of five hundred.' The Chancellor asked me for an answer, and I told him this Jewish story: One Israeli asks another: 'Why has Israel asked the Germans for a billion dollars? How does the government know that it costs exactly a billion to integrate five hundred thousand refugees? Actually it might cost ten million less or twenty million more. So why this figure of a billion?' And the other man replies: 'In my village there used to be a grocer with a stammer. One day an old Jew comes into his shop and asks him: "Moshe, how much for a kilo of potatoes?"—"Twenty kopeks."—"And a quarter of butter?"—"Twenty kopeks." And he answers "Twenty kopeks" every time. So the old man is surprised and asks: "Moshe, how is it possible for everything to cost twenty kopeks?" And Moshe replies: "Because it's easier to say." '

Adenauer smiled, but without seeing what I was getting at.

'Imagine me returning to New York after six months of negotiations with three hundred and fifty million dollars,' I concluded. 'That won't catch anyone's attention. But five hundred million is a good round figure that nobody will argue with.'

'Then half a billion it will be,' the Chancellor decided.

The second episode in the 'How to make money by telling stories' chapter occurred a few years later on, when Israel was urgently in need of twenty million marks for a shipment of oil. The tanker was in Haifa harbour, but it was refusing to unload its barrels without cash down, so the Israelis asked me to fix it. Schaeffer was then in Paris, where he was chairing the finance ministers' commission of the European Coal and Steel Community. When I phoned him he told me: 'I have to chair a meeting at the Quai d'Orsay at nine o'clock tomorrow morning. If you come for breakfast at eight, I can give you coffee and twenty minutes, no longer.'

I felt able to make this intrusion because I knew that he liked me. Every time he saw me he used to say: 'Here's my friend Goldmann, the man who stole half a billion dollars from us. Still, you'll take a cigar won't you?'

So next morning I went to see him thinking about the twenty minutes he was allowing me, and I told him a story: 'One day a beggar comes to see the famous Baron Amschel Rothschild. The butler tells him that the Baron can't see him. "Tell the Baron I only want a single word. You stand behind me, and if I speak another word, throw me out." So the butler passes on the message, and the highly intrigued baron has the beggar brought in. He steps forward and says "GeMaRa". "What does that mean?" the baron asks. "*Guten Morgen, Reb Amschel.*" (Good morning, Master Amschel.) The baron starts to feel amused. "What do you want?" he asks. "GeMaRa." "And that means?" "*Gibt Münze, Reb Amschel.*" (Give money, Master Amschel.) The baron bursts out laughing, and gives him a hundred marks, but the other man doesn't budge. "Is there something else?" the baron asks. "GeMaRa." "And how does that translate?" "*Gibt Mehr, Reb Amschel.*" (Give more, Master Amschel.) Well,' I told Schaeffer, 'that's all I want from you.' The laughing minister took out his notebook: 'I'll make a note of your story to tell it at the ministry, and rest assured, you'll get your twenty million.'

Before leaving this reparations question, it is worth recalling that even today the Germans spend one billion two hundred million marks under that heading. The public thinks that the greater proportion goes to the State of Israel, but it's the other way round: Israel has officially received the equivalent of three billion marks, although the real value is higher because the prices of the products concerned were fixed at a time when the world rates were at rock bottom. But the individual Jewish victims have received twenty times as much. Obviously, because hundreds of thousands of survivors have settled in Israel, a considerable fraction of these individual payments reverts indirectly to the state: there are thousands of Israelis whose living is provided by the German payments.

Still, the negotiations are not over yet: the Russians have never replied to our requests, and there has been no reaction from East Germany. Of all the Communist states, the GDR is certainly the most hostile to Israel, and its press is ferocious. Eventually this led to my telling Adenauer: 'You claim that you represent the whole of Germany and you do not recognize the GDR. In that case, be consistent and pay its share!' After months of negotiations he accepted, and now a Jew from Leipzig receives the same pension as a Jew from Frankfurt. We have therefore lost our main ground for asking East Germany for individual reparations. Only the GFR could ask for its contribution to be repaid, but that is its own business. Of course there is the question of communal assets nationalized by the GDR, but it must be admitted that the returns are paid to the Jewish community. This has three thousand members and a satisfactory budget, which explains why I have never been very active about East Germany. Nevertheless, a state which wanted to be respected all over the world might make a gesture by helping the thousands of victims of Nazism who have not received their full entitlement of reparations. As a matter of fact I have been told through a mutual friend that Erich Honecker, the Secretary General of the East German Communist Party, would like to meet me. I would be happy to meet him, but I have heard nothing from him as yet, and I am doubtful whether he has the will to do anything worthwhile. Yet in my opinion a gesture of that sort would be of far greater benefit morally to the GDR than financially to the East-German-born Jewish victims of Nazism.

Obtaining reparations from Austria was a different matter altogether. When a committee was set up to negotiate with Austria I refused to chair it at first: I felt in advance that the Austrian government would have a very difficult attitude. But the Jewish victims of Austria insisted, and I took a delegation to Vienna, which was then occupied by the Allies. As it happens my first contact with the town was very pleasant: because we had come from the United States with the approval of the American government, and I was an American citizen, I was allocated a suite at the Hotel Bristol which belonged to the American commander, who was on holiday. It was a magnificent apartment equipped with a red telephone, and I was informed that this had priority over all the networks in the world, just like the US president's telephone. 'You can get Buenos Aires in two minutes,' somebody said. So I took the opportunity to call friends all over the world—it was costing me nothing. Still, after three days the switchboard operator got suspicious and said: 'I suppose all these calls are official, Mr President?' Not wanting to tell a lie, I confined myself to saying: 'What do you think, Fräulein?' She blushed and apologized.

The difficulties I encountered with the Austrians, and more particularly with Chancellor Raab, were not altogether their fault, because after the war the Allies actually issued a joint statement saying that Austria should be considered as a democratic victim of Nazism. Some months later my friend Sharett publicly stated that Israel had no claim to make against Austria. This was a twofold error, and I had no leverage at all when I went to see Chancellor Raab, who in any case had nothing to reproach himself for, because he himself had been in a concentration camp.

At that first meeting at the Chancellery he told me that he was very honoured to make my acquaintance, plied me with compliments, but added:

'Actually you and I both find ourselves in the same situation: we are both victims of Nazism.'

'That's just it, Mr Chancellor,' I replied. 'I'm here to ask you how much the Jewish people is to pay you ...'

Fortunately he had a liking for irony, which is one of the elements in Viennese charm, but he remained immovable. 'We cannot give any undertaking on our own,' he said. 'We can only pay if the Germans help us.' Now the Germans would not pay a penny for Austria, because their argument was that Hitler was Austrian and Nazism had come from Austria.

After a few days I told Raab:

'Mr Chancellor, I am stopping our talks here, because

these negotiations lack dignity. I'm leaving for New York tomorrow, and in a week's time I'll be back in Vienna, but not to meet you. I intend to ask the Germans to send me that film of Hitler's entry into Vienna, where he had a warmer welcome than he did in any other town. Then I shall hire the Musikverein hall, which has two thousand seats, and I shall show the film for nothing.'

'Are you sure you won't stay?' he then asked.

'Not unless you change your tune.'

I had just got back to the hotel, at half past twelve, when I was called to the telephone. It was Chancellor Raab. 'Listen, my dear friend,' he told me, 'these negotiations are absurd. I am surrounded by six ministers and you have your American colleagues in tow. So come on your own: we'll eat Viennese sausage and settle the whole business.' I returned by myself, and we did in fact settle the business: Austria paid thirty million dollars, cash.

All the same, some years later Austria had still not improved its legislation in favour of the Jews. I took advantage of a visit to Washington by Chancellor Raab to meet him and ask him to double the sum already paid.

'My dear Doctor Goldmann,' he replied, 'we are gentlemen, men of honour. We came to an arrangement: how can you go back on it?'

'Mr Chancellor,' I said, 'I read in the *New York Times*, which is a very serious newspaper, that you are to go to Moscow to ask the Russians to reduce the reparations you owe them. Khrushchev will then tell you: "How can you ask me that, Herr Raab? We are gentlemen, men of honour, and an agreement is an agreement." '

'It's impossible to negotiate with you, Mr Goldmann,' Raab concluded. 'You're too clever a man.'

And he paid thirty million dollars extra.

More recently I had talks with Chancellor Kreisky to obtain a further sum of thirty million, which has since been approved by the Austrian parliament, thanks particularly to the attitude of Kreisky and his Finance Minister Androsch, but in spite of these efforts the Austrian Jewish survivors of deportation are receiving only a tiny fraction of what the German Jews are paid. Fortunately the Austrian Jewish community has a lot of property.

To return to Germany, Konrad Adenauer's career was utterly extraordinary, because it did not really start till he was seventy years old. Up to the last war he was known in his role as mayor of Cologne, but his reputation was limited. He had never sat in the Bundestag; once or twice the Catholic Party, then called the Zentrum, considered making a chancellor out of him, but he refused because he did not expect to win a good majority. During the war he was threatened by the Nazis, who retired him from the mayoralty of Cologne and put him in jail. Yet he was not a man of the left but a conservative, with strict views about the respect due to the constitution. His great career began after the liberation: he was elected Chancellor in 1949 and hoped to remain at his post till he was ninety. He often told me: 'Gladstone was prime minister till he was eighty-five. Why shouldn't I do better?'

He was first of all a Catholic, and kept up a close friendship with the cardinal of Cologne. When he made his first visit to the Pope as Chancellor, German protocol required him not to kneel: a German Chancellor may not kneel, even before the Pope. Adenauer promised not to, but he told me later: 'When they opened the doors and I saw His Holiness in all his glory, without realizing it I found myself on my knees!'

Yet this man could be very hard. His capacity for hatred was limitless, and his absolutism legendary. At one point he had considered becoming President of the Republic, but since the German constitution confers no real authority on the President, he decided against it. I have heard that during his cabinet meetings there was hardly ever a vote. He used to sum up, then conclude: 'This is the final decision', even if the majority was against him, and no one had the nerve to request a vote. That natural authority served us well, especially in the case of the three billion marks, whichw e would never have obtained if it had had to be put to the vote.

His reputation as a shrewd and fearsome politician was such that his socialist opponents, Schumacher and others, had warned

me: 'He will promise you everything, but keep to nothing.' They
were wrong: he kept to ten times more than he had promised,
basically because he felt a moral obligation towards Israel and the
Jewish people.

My long conversations with Adenauer (which often had to do
with music, when he would defend Palestrina, for example, and
I Bach) convinced me of the importance of the place of personal
relationships in politics. The Israelis have a lot of trouble in
understanding this, and are seldom able to establish a flow of
friendship and trust. Ben Gurion managed that with de Gaulle,
but in general the Israelis complain, criticize, demand and
vehemently insist. No offence to the Marxists, but a sense of
psychology is nevertheless a more determinant factor than
economics or so-called historical objectivity.

It is true that I enjoyed a very privileged relationship with the
Chancellor. He was fond of talking to me about music and
painting, great interests of his, as well as about questions of
international politics. I always had my doubts about his rigid,
negative policy towards the Communist bloc, and I argued in
favour of a more understanding relationship which might make
life better for the Germans in the GDR. I am also convinced that
had he remained in power longer, he would have modified his
policy a little, as he implied in one of his last speeches, when he
caused a general stir by declaring that Russia wanted peace.

When Adenauer went to Israel, he was no longer Chancellor.
He had telephoned beforehand to make sure that I would be
there, and I invited him to a big official dinner, then to a reception
at my house. On the first day he was to be awarded an honorary
doctorate by the Weizmann Institute, and he asked for me to
preside at the ceremony as a 'colleague', because I held the same
degree. The flight from Bonn to Tel Aviv was rough, because of
a heavy thunderstorm, but Adenauer had insisted on continuing,
against the pilot's advice. The President of the Institute, Meyer
Weisgal, had put his own house at the disposal of the Chancellor,
and I was sleeping in the house reserved for guests. I was on my
way to bed when Weisgal phoned: 'The old man has had a bath,
then came downstairs. He seems in great form and wants to see

you.' I threw some clothes on, thinking it was something urgent, but I had hardly laid eyes on Adenauer before he said: 'I have a question to ask you. A few weeks ago I attended a reception in Cologne where there were a lot of intellectuals.' He pronounced this word 'intellectuals' just as he might have said 'criminals', so greatly did he detest them, for he himself was singleminded almost to the point of being naive—as many great and powerful personalities are, in my experience.

'The discussion,' he went on, 'was concerned with defining the difference between wisdom and intelligence. All sorts of definitions were given, but none of them satisfied me. So I promised myself to ask your opinion.'

'Mr Chancellor,' I replied, 'intelligence is a matte rof brains and wisdom above all a question of character. To be wise you have to be tolerant, understanding and liberal, ignore your own vanity, and not believe that the truth is all yours. It is possible to be intelligent and at the same time to behave like a perfect imbecile.'

He liked my answer a lot, and noted it down, in his customary way, in a small notebook.

This scene happened on a Monday. The following Wednesday we all met at a dinner for twelve given by Levi Eshkol, who was then Prime Minister. During the dinner Eshkol suddenly stood up to make a speech, which was unnecessary at such a private gathering. The speech had been drafted by a civil servant, and Eshkol had not even read it through in advance. But it contained a sentence which went something like: 'Mr Chancellor, we are convinced that under your leadership the German people will rejoin the family of civilized peoples.'

This was quite simply an insult. I was sitting to Adenauer's right, and knowing him as I did I at once realized that he was furious. He had total control of himself, and his wooden face never allowed any emotion to show through. He stood up, said a few words, then sat down, and only then did he tell the German ambassador: 'Send for my plane, I'm leaving tomorrow. There has been an insult here to the German people which I represent, and I will not stay a day longer in Israel.' The incident was taking on all the proportions of a political scandal which would be all the greater because it came on the eve of the launching of a big Israeli loan in Germany. All the dinner-guests were dumbfounded, Levi Eshkol tried to excuse himself to Adenauer by saying: 'Mr Chancellor, I meant to pay you a great compliment,' but Adenauer replied: 'Mr Prime Minister, I do not care what you think, and your opinion of me does not interest me in the slightest. I represent the German people. You have insulted it, so I am leaving tomorrow morning.' In the meantime about a hundred assorted personalities had arrived for coffee. Eshkol had stayed in the dining room with his foreign minister, Abba Eban, the German ambassador and Felix Shinnar, all of them in search of a solution, and the Prime Minister asked me:

'Stay here, you have a lot of influence with him.'

'Do your best,' I replied, 'and call me in as a last resort if you can't find a way out.'

In the salon all the guests were standing around wondering what had become of Adenauer, and since raised voices could be heard coming from the room next door they could tell that there was something unusual going on. After a few minutes Eshkol's secretary came looking for me: 'The Chancellor is getting more and more furious; you've got to intervene.' When I came in you could have cut the atmosphere with a knife. I sat down by Adenauer and said to him: 'Mr Chancellor, do you recall our conversation the other day about the difference between wisdom and intelligence? Well, understand what has happened. Many people in Israel were against your being invited: the victims of Nazism, Herut and so on, and that is understandable. So the official who drafted the text thought he would appease the opposition by slipping that wretched sentence in. Eshkol had not read the text in advance, so he must be excused. So prove that, not content with being intelligent, you are also wise.' He smiled as he replied: 'Yes, I understand, but an acceptable way out will have to be found.' I asked Eshkol whether his speech had been distributed to the press. As it was midnight and the Tel Aviv papers go to press at about two in the morning, it had already been done. So I advised the Prime Minister's secretary to phone all the editorial offices and inform them that the crucial sentence might have been in the manuscript but that Eshkol had crossed it out, and it had never been spoken. 'That is a solution I accept,' Adenauer said, and the incident was closed.

During the same visit he had to go to Yad Vashem, the site of the monument to the memory of the six million Jewish dead. I was busy, and had not meant to accompany him on this occasion, but once again he phoned me: 'This will be a distressing moment for me. Do me the service of coming with me and holding my arm during the visit.' So we went there together, and as we entered the crypt he almost wept. He held back his tears while I grasped his arm. At the end of the ceremony he thanked me with these words: 'Without you, I could not have borne it.'

I also knew Willy Brandt, but our relations were all the more cordial because he is an intellectual and his moral stand was exemplary. No other German could have prostrated himself as he did before the memorial to the defenders of the Warsaw ghetto.

He very much enjoyed the stories I told on my visits to him, and once he told me:

'I've made my preparations for meeting you. Each time we meet, you tell me two or three stories that have me fascinated, and I don't give you anything in exchange. Do you know who the first socialist was?'

'No.'

'Christopher Columbus! Because when he left Europe he didn't know where he was going. When he reached America he didn't know where he was. And right through the voyage he was financed by other people.'

Brandt has his strong points and his weaknesses. His strength lies in his ethical position. He is a brave, honest, generous man who left Germany with the advent of Nazism, and his concern for the underprivileged classes comes not so much from political reflection (he is not a Marxist) as from the bottom of his heart. He is a man very much to be trusted, and a leader whose views are generally just. As a statesman he is gifted with a sense of historic perspective and with courage. But his weakness lies in the way he puts these views into practice; it is the effect of his virtues—

because you pay for your virtues as well as for your vices. He is not tough enough, and when he puts his trust in his assistants he often does not know them as individuals. Nevertheless he keeps faith with them—which has done him harm. He also has that inherent weakness of intellectuals which consists in not making quick decisions. You know Goethe's famous saying that the man of action must be blind. Well, Brandt is not blind enough. He is slow to make his mind up, which is fine in ordinary times but troublesome in time of crisis.

Though he has sometimes been very critical of Israeli policy he is a friend of the Jewish state. As for me, I almost blush to recall his kindness towards me. When Germany's most popular illustrated paper, *Der Stern*, published an eight-page feature on a day in the life of Willy Brandt, he sent the photographer away at eleven o'clock at night saying: 'Now, before going to sleep I'm going to read a few pages of Nahum Goldmann's autobiography.'

Helmut Schmidt is a very different personality. He is also a personal friend, and three months before his election I predicted that he would be Chancellor when he himself did not believe it. He has the mind of a leader, and basically sees himself as an economist, so his decisions are very firm, with no room for wavering. Today he is one of those statesmen who have acquired a worldwide reputation. Taking initiatives with Ford, Kissinger, Callaghan and Giscard, he is the moving force in the present crisis. He is an expert who has a pragmatic sense of economics and doesn't care much about theory. He does not admit it openly, but a concept like Marxism means nothing to him. If he is a social democrat it is because he genuinely wants better distribution of wealth, but he will never sacrifice the daily necessities to any ideology of any shade.

Having said that, and in spite of the fact that a man like Willy Brandt managed to become its head of state, I am not sure whether the problem posed by Hitler has really been solved in Germany. The Germans are the most complex people in the world; compared with them, the French appear harmonious, elegant, logical and straightforward. For me, Hitlerism remains an enigma.

The Germans have paid an enormous debt, so enormous that no one—neither they nor I—had dreamt that it would reach the approximate figure of eighty billion marks. They have made several attempts to alter our agreements, but I quoted a remark which Adenauer noted down: 'The Talmud says that if you start a good work you must finish it, otherwise it is a sin to have undertaken it.' Now that debt is almost settled, and the younger generation have promptly lost all feeling of responsibility for the past. The notion of a special relationship with the Jews was very strong in Adenauer's time, and it survived under Brandt, then with Schmidt, but not in the new generation of Germans, and especially not among the intellectuals who, because they tend to the left, are hostile to the policy of Israel.

A German leader once told me: 'I am a friend of Israel, but do you know that half our oil comes from Libya? If Kadhafi, who doesn't need money and is in a position to do without an income for six months, stops supplying us, our industry is finished.' And it is true: if Germany is a great power today it is thanks to its industry, not because of the literature, the philosophy and the music to which Jews gave so much, and where their absence is felt in every field.

6 *The Uncles from America*

As a former American citizen, who lived for some time in the United States, my opinion of Americans and American Jewry is very mixed. I must explain this view by turning the clock back a few years. I remember that when Hitler came on to the political scene the American Jews did not take the matter seriously. Someone once remarked: 'Stupidity in politics is worse than immorality.' The Jews were short-sighted: they thought that Hitlerism was an ephemeral matter and made no protest about the appeasement orders put about by the democracies. But my reproach goes further than that, because the American Jews did not help the refugees.

When the Hitlerite threat began to make itself felt, a conference of the main Jewish organizations was convoked in London; it appointed a small committee consisting of Chaim Weizmann, Norman Bentwich (an eminent London lawyer and director of the Department of Justice in British Palestine) and myself. The Council of the League of Nations had reached its own decision, which was to appoint a high commissioner for German Jewish refugees, who would keep in touch with government representatives on the one hand and the big Jewish and non-Jewish organizations on the other. I had put forward the name of Lord Robert Cecil for the post, a very liberal and progressive British statesman, and a friend of Zionism and the Jews, but unfortunately he declined. The Council chose James McDonald, director general of the Foreign Policy Association, a typical American, brimming with good will and optimism, who later became America's first ambassador to Israel. At first he did not understand the complexity of the problem. When Weizmann and I went to see him at his Geneva office, McDonald told us: 'Gentlemen, the matter is not as difficult as all that. There are seven hundred thousand Jews in Germany; I shall get visas from England for half of them, who will then be able to go to Palestine. We'll take the rest in America, and the whole thing will be settled two or three years from now.' I did not want to discourage him, and contented myself with warning him that in my view the question was a little more complex. This irritated him, and he replied: 'No, I assure you: in a few years we'll have the problem solved.' There was a popular film on show at the time called *Sonny Boy*, and after leaving McDonald I said to Weizmann: 'From now on I'm going to call him Sunny Goy.' The name stuck.

Later on, in 1938, Roosevelt called another conference, at Evian, in order to make a show of being an active ally of the Jews. Assaults, looting and expropriation, in fact all the hardships then being endured by the German Jews, were forcing him to make some sort of effort. All shades of opinion were represented: the trade unions, Catholics, Protestants, Jews, Quakers, etc. We, the Jews, made up a delegation of ten people, including Golda Meir, but from our viewpoint Evian was a fiasco. The British had sent Lord Winterton, who was such a thoroughgoing reactionary that it was almost a provocation.

During the four or five days I spent at the Hôtel Royal in Evian, where the conference was held, I got next to nothing except geography lessons. Country X would be announced, for instance, and its representative would talk about the climate, too hot or too cold, or about troubles with steel production, or the price of raw materials—in other words, he was ticking off all the reasons why there was definitely no room for Jewish refugees in his country. It was a frightening display of indifference.

Around then I received thousands of letters from Jews who were putting all their hopes into that conference. I kept one sent by a German Jew who said the opposite: 'I follow politics very closely and I am convinced that nothing will emerge from the Evian conference. Everybody has the best possible reasons for not letting the Jews into his country. Nevertheless I am hopeful that, thanks to this conclave formed by representatives from thirty

governments, you may achieve one result at least: a visa for me.'
I obtained that visa, but not without difficulty. More should be
written about the Evian conference, because it highlighted the
immoral attitude adopted by the great powers towards the Jews.

It wasn't much better during the war. The World Jewish
Congress had good contacts with the Polish Jewish resistance,
which sent messages to London asking the Allies to bomb
Auschwitz, which would have meant the camp being unable to
function, at least for a few months. When I raised this question
with the British they replied:

'Can't be done—we'd be killing Jews!'

'Don't be more royalist than the king,' I replied. 'Do it, since it
is Jews who are asking you. What difference is there for them
between being gassed by the Nazis and bombed by you?'

They would not hear of it: they needed all their planes and all
their bombs to fight the war, they said; their only aim was to win.
For a better grasp of how absurd that refusal was, you need to
remember that at that time the British were often bombing
factories located only a few kilometres from Auschwitz.

Now Roosevelt never intervened in this debate. Looking back,
I sometimes blame myself for not having gone to see Eisenhower,
who might have been able to do something; but he was very hard
to reach, because that excellent strategist was mainly concerned
with preserving a united front among Allies who used to quarrel
like madmen.

Another example was the occasion when I received a phone call
at my office from Under-Secretary of State Stettinius. 'Come and
see me at once,' he said, and I went straight to his office.

'What's going on?'

'I'm going to let you in on something which has to remain a
secret,' he told me. 'Promise me not to mention it to anyone.'

'Except Stephen Wise,' I replied. 'I can't have any secrets from
him, and if, as is likely, you're asking me to do something, he has
far more influence than me in America.'

Then he handed me a very long dispatch and told me to read it
on the spot. It concerned Joel Brand, one of the leaders of the
Hungarian Jewish community. Eichmann had sent for him and

told him: 'If you get us ten thousand trucks we will release a hundred thousand Jews bound for Auschwitz. You can take them and ship them to Palestine.'

'Consult Wise before I communicate with the British,' Stettinius said, 'because they're the ones who have to give their consent about Palestine. Give me your answer in two days' time.'

'There's no time to lose,' I replied. 'I guarantee that Stephen Wise will agree: accept.'

'But do you know what ten thousand trucks would mean?'

'I'm no soldier, but I imagine that it's a great gift for the Germans, otherwise they wouldn't have asked. But be realistic: you can't walk into a shop and ask for ten thousand trucks as if they were herrings. There are delivery hold-ups, transport difficulties, production limitations and so forth. For the moment, the main thing is to save a hundred thousand Jews. Then we'll drag our feet; we'll say that we can only give them five hundred trucks to start with, because we can't produce more—we'll invent a pile of excuses. But meanwhile, at least the deportation of those Jews must be stopped.'

'And what about the British?'

'Promise them everything they want! It's only a matter of gaining a few months, and by then the Germans will have lost the war.'

Maybe Stettinius was ready to close the deal, but the British sabotaged it. Joel Brand went to Egypt to see Lord Moyne, the top British representative there, to inform him about the German offer, but he was arrested. Weizmann got nothing in London either. The United States did not put enough pressure on the British, and the American Jews bear a heavy responsibility, but the main blame for that failure lies with the British.

The Polish government in exile in London once sent us a message from the Jewish resistance in Poland. The Polish Jews were asking us to send twenty leaders to the White House, to go on hunger strike until there was a decision to bomb Auschwitz. We did not do it, and had I gone there myself I would not have succeeded in enlisting the others. The Establishment is very hard to shift.

Stephen Wise and I were the revolutionary minority of the WJC, which was far from having the authority it possesses today, and in fact most Jewish organizations were openly opposed to the Congress. The following tragic story is a good illustration of this conflict behind the scenes.

I received a cable from Gerhart Riegner, head of the WJC office in Geneva, saying that the Hungarians, then allied to the Germans, were prepared to release some thousands of children for a payment of three million dollars. The World Jewish Congress did not have that kind of money available, but the Joint Distribution Committee did. The separation between politics and philanthropy in wartime is one of the greatest absurdities of American Jewry; the JDC could have allied itself with the WJC, but its leadership refused on the grounds that philanthropy is a pure thing, whereas politics is dirty!

We called a meeting of several American Jewish leaders— whom I would rather not name even now—to explain the situation, and they all chorused: 'What! Send money to the enemy? But we can't risk that without authorization.' I told them that Roosevelt was sure to authorize the payment and they should go and ask him.

'How can we, Jews, suggest to Roosevelt that financial assistance should be given to the Germans?'

'But what do you think Hitler wants with three million dollars? It's certain to be some official working on his own account or for an undercover organization.'

But they still refused to see Roosevelt and left the job to Stephen Wise and me.

We went to see Mrs Roosevelt, a marvellous woman who generally acted as a go-between in delicate matters. She informed us that the President would not oppose the transfer of funds if Secretary of State Cordell Hull agreed. We therefore had to negotiate with Hull, who had mixed feelings about us. The Secretary of the Treasury, Henry Morgenthau, volunteered to talk to him, but there was nothing he could do: for three months, the State Department sabotaged the affair by using every kind of bureaucratic argument to delay the decision. When, finally, he agreed, it was too late: the children had already been deported. Once more the American Jews had taken a typical line: they were ready to give money, but refused to involve themselves politically.

There may be an historical explanation for this. Right up to the Second World War the American people retained an isolationist mentality. Without the impetus given by the 1939-45 conflict (and to a lesser extent by the war of 1914-18), America's accession to power would have taken several decades, perhaps as much as a century, and it would then have learned the art of diplomacy and politics step by step. But the war thrust the USA brutally into becoming the topmost power in the world, which is why it has displayed so many weaknesses and errors, often aggravated by the lack of genius of its chiefs of state. When England became the leading world power in the course of the nineteenth century it had had two hundred years to prepare. It was the same with France. America, which still has a certain provincial spirit, has not had time to serve its apprenticeship. The rest of the world has to be patient and wait for it to acquire the sense of international politics which is so essential in this century, the most complex and intractable era in all human history.

The same goes for the American Jews. They certainly had fellow-feeling for their brothers in Europe, but on the level of Jewish survival, spiritual creativity and even of responsibility for the future, American Jewry amounted to a reserve army for a long time. The fighting role, exposed to fire but also exploring new paths for Judaism, had devolved on the communities of Europe, and particularly of Eastern Europe. Once Hitler had smashed the Jewish 'front' in Europe, destiny forced the American Jews into the front line. This new situation put to test a leadership which was in no way prepared to assume so many responsibilities. Even today the Jewish leaders of the United States often have little idea of what to do. Their political background is weak, because it has not absorbed the great tradition of European Jewry, and the hopes harboured by some American Jews seem to me to be illusory.

According to a widespread theory in the United States there are two Jewish centres in the world: Israel and American Jewry. Thus there is a well-worn parallel drawn with Israel and Babylon. But like nearly all temporal comparisons this one is meaningless. In ancient times, religion was the great unifying force, and at some moments in history Babylonian Judaism was much more constructive than Palestinian Judaism. The best proof of that is that the Talmud of Babylon played a much more important part in Jewish life than the Talmud of Jerusalem.

Another feature characteristic of Americans in general, and therefore Jews in particular, is the influence wielded by finance in the United States. In Jewish life, the leaders of the Diaspora have tended to be intellectuals—first rabbis, later journalists, writers, great orators, in other words ideologists who expressed themselves through literature, in whatever form. In America Jewish life is dominated by the rich. I was only half joking when I said once that the reign of American Jewry was due to three factors: the multimillionaires who give money and understand nothing; the women who have nothing else to do but 'politicking'; and lastly the functionaries, who are overpaid. The result is over-organized chaos: there are too many societies, too many movements, too many charity directors who dominate the life of the Jews because they are professionals, and they know their business.

The 'money men' concentrate on consolidating their social position: it costs plenty to become president of a big community organization. But there are also hundreds of thousands of Jewish intellectuals in the United States who will not play any part inside Judaism because they are alienated by this millionaire ascendancy. To be objective, I must admit that things are starting to improve and that the intellectuals are finally beginning to take an interest in Jewish life.

This transfer of the Jewish 'centre' from Europe to America has had one primary consequence: the prevalence of philanthropy over politics. Since the American Jews are rich, they have helped the needy, donating their money to build hospitals and old people's homes. But they have neglected cultural life. To understand this, you have to know how much the American institutional system differs from the European. In Europe, the social and cultural organizations are mainly paid for by the state. In the

United States it is private donations which finance the entire infrastructure, pension funds and theatres alike.

So here I find myself back on one of my hobby-horses: that politics and philanthropy ought not to be two separate things. Instead of concentrating their efforts on the intellectual development indispensable to the survival of Judaism, the American Jews have channelled their funds into welfare work, by building hospitals or helping the European Jews who were poor. Before the war they supported their Russian or Romanian brothers, and since then, all those who were ruined by the Nazis.

Before the last world war I was in touch with the Polish government, which made no bones of its antisemitism, and in particular with its foreign minister, Joseph Beck. When I told him that Poland ought to grant its Jews greater economic freedom, his reply was cynical: 'On the contrary, we are actually thinking of maybe introducing the equivalent of the Nuremberg Laws.' And he explained himself as follows: 'We need foreign currency—dollars, for instance. Well, since there has been persecution of the Jews in Germany your organizations have been sending big sums of money. We have three million Jews in Poland: Germany only has seven hundred and fifty thousand. So we should be getting three or four times as much money!' So the Joint Distribution Committee paid a sort of premium for the persecution of the Jews. Up against executioners, it was wrong to say: 'We protest, but we'll pay up.'

Another example occurred after the war, when a few tens of thousands of Jewish survivors of the concentration camps went to Sweden. Thanks to Hillel Storch, our representative in Stockholm, who was a personal friend of Prime Minister Tage Erlander, the WJC had good relations with the Swedish government. The JDC offered to cover all the expenses of looking after these refugees. We intervened, and the Swedes recognized that they had a moral obligation—considering how much they had benefited from their neutrality—to take these expenses on themselves. In that way we saved American Jewry some tens of millions of dollars.

As I say, the situation is now beginning to change, and the

most convinced philanthropists (even those who remain anti-Zionists) understand that it is more important to create a Jewish school than a hospital. This may sound brutal, especially coming from a man of my age, but people do die, and it is the young who carry on the life of Jewry.

Finally, there is one recent phenomenon which American Jewry must take into account, and that is the absolutely extraordinary blossoming of a generation of American Jewish writers. Twenty years ago the Jews played hardly any part in American literary life, and now they are promising to regain the importance they had in Germany under the Weimar Republic. But the point is that they are nonconformists, even progressives, and like young Jews almost everywhere they are highly critical of Israeli policy. American Jewry's 'guardians of the temple' ought to think about that.

Roosevelt was the first American I had to deal with at the highest level but, unlike what happened with Chancellor Adenauer, I was never close to him. It was Stephen Wise who was friendly with him, because he had been a lot of help to Roosevelt in the days when he was still governor of New York State. Wise and Roosevelt were such friends that Roosevelt once announced: 'I'm going to send you as ambassador to Hitler!'

'But Hitler will never accept me,' Wise said.

'In that case he'll have no ambassador at all,' was Roosevelt's reply.

Roosevelt was a fascinating blend of statesman and politician. The statesman had a tremendously broad and lofty vision of the world. The politician had the tricks, the shifts, and even the sharp practice. Charm was Roosevelt's great quality. Operating on some very exalted figures, he sometimes used it as a method. When he did not want to give straight answers he would be charming for half an hour and the other party would take his leave, very impressed, but without knowing precisely what he had meant. Einstein described his first talk with him, when Roosevelt produced his usual performance, not giving either a Yes or a No to any precise question. But with Einstein, who politically was very simple-minded, it did not work. 'Mr President,' he said brusquely, 'you have been talking for ten minutes and I know English well enough to have understood every word. But could you formulate your answer in only one word: is it Yes or No?'

Before I met Roosevelt in 1938 I had heard that for a good story he would readily sell half the United States. I very often judge people by the way they laugh, and the two men with the most massive laughs I have ever heard were Roosevelt and Aneurin Bevan: when they laughed the room shook and you felt like hugging them. Stephen Wise, who arranged my meeting with the President, had told me: 'If you want to win Roosevelt round, tell him one of your Jewish stories.'

When I came into the drawing-room where we were to take tea, Roosevelt said to me:

'Mr Goldmann, my friend Stephen Wise tells me that you are familiar with all the chancelleries of Europe. The Europeans have problems which I find myself unable to understand. Since you are not a diplomat and have no protocol to observe, you can speak candidly. Let's begin with Chamberlain: what is going on in his head? He signed the Munich pact and he is practising a policy of appeasement towards Germany; does he really believe that that will prevent war?'

'Mr President,' I replied, 'if you will permit me I shall tell you a Talmudic story which will give you the answer.'

'Oh, fine!' he said.

'It goes like this: the Bible says that if a man owns a bull that turns vicious and injures somebody, the owner must be warned, not punished; but if the bull does it again the owner is to be penalized and told: "You knew that your bull was dangerous, so you should have kept him enclosed." In the Talmud there is a big debate around the question of what the bull was thinking about on the second occasion—did it remember having already wounded someone? And Rashi, the great commentator on the Talmud, replied that the discussion was absurd, because according to him a bull is a bull and does not think.'

Roosevelt burst out laughing, then asked if I knew Georges Bonnet, the French foreign minister, a signatory of the Munich pact and rather pro-German, with a hard, unattractive face. 'I'm going to tell you another story,' I replied, 'but this one doesn't come from ancient times. There was a big Jewish banker in Berlin called Fürstenberg, who went to the Stock Exchange one day and asked his secretary: "Who is that young man? I like his face." "He's a con-man who has just completed a three-year stretch in jail." "That's all right," said Fürstenberg: "the man's face fits his character, so he's an honest man!" '

Not content with enjoying humour, Roosevelt was also a practitioner. This example occurred in particularly tragic circumstances. One day in the summer of 1943 we received an appalling message from Gerhart Riegner giving the details of the workings of the Nazis' 'Final Solution' for the extermination of the Jews. It was a Saturday, and I immediately phoned Stephen Wise to ask his advice. President Roosevelt seldom remained in Washington at weekends, and preferred to relax in his house in the country, Hyde Park. I suggested waiting till he returned on Monday morning before informing him of these horrible revelations, but Wise considered the news grave enough to warrant going straight to the President's adviser, Sam Rosenman, who had rented a house near Roosevelt's so as to be available in emergencies.

Alerted by Wise, Rosenman asked us to join him at his place. It was a sweltering day, and we were all in our shirtsleeves on the verandah when we heard the blare of a car horn and Roosevelt's car drew up in front of us. When he saw us together the President said: 'Oh, oh! Rosenman, Stephen Wise and Nahum Goldmann conferring together. Carry on, boys. Sam will tell me what I'm supposed to do on Monday.' The car was drawing away when Roosevelt stopped it and called out: 'Imagine what Goebbels would pay for a photo of this scene: the President of the United States taking his instructions from the three Elders of Zion.'

In the last few years the key figure in American foreign policy was not the President but Henry Kissinger, who is a very controversial figure in Israel. Before giving my own opinion of him, let me say that for Israel he was without doubt the best imaginable

Secretary of State; the school of opinion that thinks another man would be better is talking nonsense.

Kissinger is very complicated, but he is a quite extraordinary man: it took something extraordinary to turn a German Jew into an American Secretary of State. Yet he never played a big part in the Harvard pecking order—he was not a life professor, the highest position there, and few people at Harvard recognized his exceptional personality, which did not become generally apparent until he took up an official position and began his involvement with foreign affairs.

With Kissinger, as with most interesting men, it is once again the question of the difference between intelligence and character that has to be considered. Kissinger has an unusually high level of intelligence, because he has an overall grasp of situations together with great political skill in arriving at solutions for the everyday problems which relate to the underlying problem. He never isolates any given event from its historical context, which is understandable, after all, on the part of a Jew who lived through the Holocaust and had to leave Germany when he was sixteen. So when he says that the world oil crisis may lead to a new fascism he knows what he is talking about: he saw Germany when it had the six million unemployed without whom Hitler would never have become Hitler.

His personal experience has influenced him enormously. I have told him that the reason for his having always been severe and critical towards Europe is that he unconsciously detested the Europe which drove him out. It was Hitler who committed that action, of course, but then Hitler was Europe too. At the beginning, the democracies could easily have stamped out Nazism, but they did not dare: Flandin, Chamberlain and company were hoping that Hitler would put an end to the Soviet regime, and that is one of the reasons for their policy of appeasement towards Nazi Germany and their consequent indifference to the Jewish tragedy. Kissinger has never forgiven them.

He once made the very misguided statement that the difference between Europe and America has to do with America's interests being global, whereas Europe's are regional. This was a gratuitous insult, and my own belief is that Europe will unite itself. De Gaulle managed to delay this union, and that was his great political sin, in spite of all his merits. But de Gaulle himself was incapable of preventing Pompidou from being more European than him, and Giscard from being more European than Pompidou. It will take another generation, but the idea will come to term, and economically as well as politically Europe will be one of the three or four great centres of the world.

All the same, Kissinger's contempt for the Europeans was also his lucky break, because he was made to fit the dimensions of America. A woman friend of mine, a top Israeli journalist, once wrote a humorous piece on the theme of what would have happened if Kissinger's parents had gone to Israel—which Henry's father did in fact consider at one point. I sent the article to Kissinger, who had it translated and greatly enjoyed it. The theme was that in Israel he would probably have become a third-level civil servant in the foreign ministry, because he is good at languages. Since he is always having new ideas he would have sent bold memos to his superiors, and finally somebody would have said: 'This Kissinger who keeps suggesting crazy schemes, why don't we dump him somewhere where he'll stay quiet? Consul in Milwaukee, for instance . . .' And that would have been the end of Henry Kissinger.

There is a good deal of truth in this scenario: Kissinger could not have made a career in Israel. First of all, he would never have been on the side of Mapai, the party in power, and worst of all he is not 'plain' enough to make an Israeli politician. Churchill remained in the shade for years because he had too much genius, and that was in England, a more tolerant country than Israel.

Now that the generation of the great statesmen—men like Woodrow Wilson, Lloyd George, Balfour and Churchill—is gone, Europe and America are generally governed by ordinary men, and that is what gives Kissinger his exceptional position. There may be plenty to be said against him, but no one will accuse him of being ordinary.

Nevertheless, his liking for putting everything into perspective and making frequent references to history also has a negative side.

The basic book to read in order to understand him is his study of
the Congress of Vienna. He once quoted me something he had
written about nuclear arms, on which he is an expert.

'Listen, Kissinger,' I told him in reply, 'we are good enough
friends for me to take the liberty of being frank: I haven't read
your book on the subject, because what interests me about your
books is not the bombs, although the fate of the world depends on
them, but the author. And to know Kissinger it's enough to read
your first book. I have read it twice, and I may say that you have
a false ideal—Metternich.'

In fact he has two ideals—Metternich and Bismarck—and the
second means more to him than the first.

'Explain that.'

'You have a tendency to compare yourself with Metternich,
but what did Metternich do? He had a fabulous life style, lived
like a lord, kept mistresses, bought journalists, and his one real
success—and one which Kissinger, who is no great progressive
in domestic policy, admires the most—is that for thirty years he
stabilized the worst period of reaction that Europe had experienced. It was only the revolution of 1848 that succeeded in getting
rid of him, and if he had not left Vienna he would have been
killed, so bitterly was he hated. For more than thirty years the
man halted progress in Europe. Your Metternich was a practitioner of "kitchen politics". He was a very artful politician and a
very good diplomat who did his sums—What is the strength of
Saxony? What can I get from a Prussia–Russia combination?
That was the work of a great official, not of a statesman, who
could venture to sketch out a political line on paper, irrespective
of the reality. In the twentieth century that is impossible, yet that
is just what you yourself are inclined to do. You know that the
Russians have so many missiles and so many nuclear weapons, so
you do your sums, but you forget one thing: when Metternich
was using that approach, there was no public opinion alarmed by
social distress. That two million people should die of hunger did
not interest him in the slightest. What threat did it pose to his
regime? Whereas your are living in the twentieth century, when
there are the Blacks, the poor, the underprivileged nations, the

young leftists. You can't work out your equations by ignoring them. So it is a bankrupt policy to attempt to imitate Metternich today.'

'But after all, I'm already working an eighteen-hour day,' said Kissinger. 'How am I supposed to become an expert on problems with the Blacks, young people and the poor countries as well?'

'Of course, but before presenting your conclusions to the President you should consult the experts on those questions. For Metternich, that was pointless—the peasants are suffering? Very well, let them go on suffering! That was within the logic of a reactionary and totalitarian regime.'

But what makes Kissinger a complex figure is not so much his intelligence, which remains impressive despite his errors of appreciation, as his character. As I said about Ben Gurion, character often prevents a man from winning the successes earned by his intelligence. Vanity, the desire to achieve little personal victories, these are the limitations of many statesmen, and to some extent that is the case with Henry Kissinger. He is very egocentric, and believes that he can handle everything himself, feeling nothing but distrust for anybody else. 'To make peace in the Near East you're trying to eliminate the USSR,' I once said to him. 'But you won't succeed, because without the USSR a lasting peace is impossible.' I have often thought that if he could he would also eliminate the United States: he wanted to be the sole architect of peace in the world, and all he really wanted was to be left alone to get on with it. Unfortunately, as an American Secretary of State he could not altogether do without the United States!

Kissinger thinks himself above the rest, and he is often right, but he was wrong to show it. Most members of Congress, as well as most senators and high officials, are just not up to his level. That is why he bypassed them and gathered a little group of brilliant young people around himself. The rest—which is to say the three to five thousand functionaries in the secretariat—were there simply as executants, in his view, so they were very unhappy under his orders and often detested him. The truly great men are also modest—a quality which Kissinger lacks.

Often, when I went to Washington, he would ask me:

'What did you do this morning?'

'I saw so-and-so.'

'So-and-so? But he's an idiot! Why waste your time like that?'

'But I also saw so-and-so.'

'What use is that? The man's a cretin!'

'Listen,' I once replied, 'when I was a student in Berlin there was a professor renowned for his harshness and arrogance. When he was examining somebody he would take a sheet of paper, and each time the candidate gave a poor answer he would tear a strip off. By the end there was just a tiny scrap of paper, and he would hand that over and say: "Sir, I won't waste my time on you. Here is a piece of paper. Write down eveything you know on it, and bring it to me in my office ..." Well, it's the same with you, Kissinger: you would only need a scrap of paper to write down the names of the people worth visiting in your opinion.'

He burst out laughing, and replied: 'A scrap would be a tight squeeze; there'd have to be room for a few names!' His feeling of superiority is obvious to everyone, and it is one of the reasons why so many people dislike him.

Perhaps I should describe a very historic scene which Stephen Wise told me about. During the First World War, when things were looking very bad for them, the British sent an envoy to President Wilson. They chose Lord Reading, who was Jewish, a future viceroy of India, and one of the most brilliant British legal minds of the day. There was a lot he wanted out of Wilson, arms in particular, but this terribly influential man was also terribly conceited. So Wilson told Wise: 'As soon as he came into the office I decided not to concede him a thing. He took an insufferably condescending tone with me, playing the proud English aristocrat. He left Washington empty-handed, and the British must have understood why, because they then sent Balfour. He adopted a very modest approach by saying: "Who are the British? Citizens of a doomed nation if you do not intervene. You are the great leader, you can save us." He got everything he wanted!'

So pride is Kissinger's main weakness, unless it is his impatience. He grasps matters very quickly, and has an extraordinary gift for formulation. Once he told me: 'I can state a very complex international problem in one or two pages so clearly that even an ordinary high school pupil would understand.' What makes that a particularly valuable gift is that a president of the United States does not have time to go into detail. Eisenhower is supposed not to have read any memorandum more than two pages long, and Roosevelt himself required notes not to exceed a page. But Kissinger expects this kind of concision from everybody, and when he can't obtain it, he gets annoyed. Or else this same impatience leads him to make concessions he ought not to make. It is true that this also has to do with a certain lack of security.

Fortunately his sense of humour often saves him. A very excited CIA official once rushed to see him and said:

'Mr Kissinger, we have just heard from a reliable source that the North Koreans are going to make a penetration into South Korea on Wednesday. This could start a world war!'

'What day did you say?' Kissinger asked, picking up his diary.

'Wednesday.'

'Wednesday is impossible! See for yourself, I have appointments all day. There isn't room for that problem!'

Kissinger belongs to a very traditionalist Jewish family. His parents are devout, eat kosher, and don't travel on the sabbath; his father even refused to attend his wedding because he was marrying a non-Jewish woman and the ceremony was to take place on the sabbath day, which religion forbids. His mother didn't dare come for fear of angering her husband.

I have been asked whether Kissinger has managed to establish any special relationship between Jewry and the American government. When I first met him, back in the mid-sixties, his Jewish sympathies were very slight, although he had spent a year at an Orthodox Jewish school—but since the Germans had thrown him out of the state system, that was the only place possible. His attitude towards Zionism was guarded, and at Harvard he took no interest whatever in Jewry. He used to say: 'Given that there is a state, it would be immoral to allow it to be destroyed, but if I had been asked for my opinion before it existed, I would have said that it was not a solution to the Jewish problem.'

Since he has had responsibility for this Jewish problem, he has become much more Jewish himself. His new-found acquaintance-ship with the Jewish question in all its singularity and universality has developed his own Judaism, even though he may not admit it. 'You are much more Jewish unconsciously than consciously,' I once told him. This is quite apparent in his attitude to Israel, but he will never recognize it. He wants no quarrels with Jeru-salem, and yet his duty is to defend American interests, not Jewish: he is not the Israeli foreign minister.

He explained himself to me by analysing his own position. He understood the criticism of his step-by-step policy, he said, but if he insisted on total evacuation of the occupied territories to achieve peace, relations with Israel and the American Jews would get very difficult. He would then have to state that the Israeli policy, backed by the American Jews, is contrary to the interests of the United States, and it would be really tragic if in that way the first Jew to become an American Secretary of State were the cause of a new wave of antisemitism.

I answered that I respected his scruples but that his analysis was incomplete. In fact, any Jewish agitation against him would last no longer than a few months, whereas if he achieved peace he would become the big hero, not only in America but also in Jewish history. On the other hand, if he was not certain that Sadat wanted to end the war, I would advise him not to force the Israelis to give up the Sinai passes.

In conclusion, I will say that in any event Kissinger will remain an historical figure of our time. It was he who pioneered détente with the USSR, and he who established the first relations with China. Even if it was Nixon who thought of it first, that is not fundamental: in philosophy it may be important to determine who first hit upon a given concept, but politics is not philosophy. Kissinger has put key ideas into practice with a dynamism and capacity for work beyond belief. Taking every problem upon himself, he is naturally overstretched: the best minds have their limits, and in fact he does neglect certain questions. But in the gallery of American foreign ministers, he remains the most gifted. I know no one else who could have exerted such an influence. Of course it is easier to keep a hold on Gerald Ford than on Wilson or Roosevelt, but that ought not to belittle Kissinger's role. As regards the American policy in the Near East I have often attempted to modify his analyses. Only the future will show to what extent I may have succeeded . . .

7 The Sickle, the Hammer, and the Star

THE SITUATION of the Russian Jews is very ambiguous, because they constitute the only minority in the Soviet Union to have no territory of its own. But if they are classified as 'Jew' on their domestic passports it is because after the Revolution of 1917 the Jews themselves requested it, in order to have the benefit of cultural autonomy.

I have always made every effort to have good personal relations with the Russians—like Vladimir Petrovitch Potemkin, Konstantin Oumansky, Maxim Litvinov, Gromyko, Dobrynin and Rosenberg, who was the Russian deputy secretary-general at the League of Nations before the war—for the Russian attitude towards the Jews is important for two reasons. The first is that there are more than three million Jews there, and that it is a community with a splendid past. If we include Poland, a Russian possession for a long time, it was one of the most creative in the world during the eighteenth and nineteenth centuries. The second reason is that it has always seemed obvious to me that the creation of a Jewish state was very much dependent on Russia.

The presence of millions of Jews in the USSR as well as in the other Communist countries is a decisive factor for world Jewry. There is a grave danger of losing them not by deportation or extermination, but by complete assimilation. That would be a real catastrophe for the whole of Jewish life, and I have the impression that its importance is under-estimated. Nearly all the agitation raised around the Russian Jews is focused on the problem of emigration, clearly as acute for Russia as it is for Israel, yet which concerns only a minority of Russian Jewry. It is totally unrealistic to think that several hundred thousand Jews will go to Israel, in the near future at any rate.

That could only happen if true antisemitism manifested itself in Russia, a threat to Jews there as such. That is certainly imaginable, but judgement must be made only on the existing conditions. As long as Israel knows no peace and its economic situation is in danger, the country is incapable of absorbing hundreds of thousands of emigrants—even supposing they wanted to be absorbed.

A lot of Jewish extremists advance a theory according to which there is no chance of obtaining facilities for those Jews who remain in Russia, from which they draw the conclusion that all hope of preserving that community should be abandoned in favour of concentrating every effort on the emigrants. I strongly object to this analysis, which, after the Nazi tragedy, amounts to renouncing more than one-fifth of the Jewish people at a stroke. And I have always maintained that a Jewish way of life is possible even under a Communist regime.

In the USSR there are more than a hundred minorities, each with the right to its own language, literature, theatre, press and schools. So even within such a highly centralized system the USSR recognizes the principle of minorities. The difficulty derives from the Jewish people yet again posing a problem *sui generis*. We are a scattered people which wants its own country, and in the USSR we are a scattered people which wants the same rights as other nationalities, although these have a territorial base.

The principle of the right to take part in the life of the nation, an accepted right of the Russian minorities, is built on territoriality. A minority of three hundred thousand people (which is a tenth of the Russian Jewish population) can receive administrative autonomy as soon as it is concentrated on a given territory. If that minority is more developed it can accede to the status of an autonomous territory and eventually even of a state within the framework of the Soviet Union. But the Jews are spread all over Russia, and every move to bring them together has failed.

It is well known that the USSR—to counteract Zionism as much as to apply the principle of the right of nationalities on the basis of territoriality—has offered the Jews the autonomous territory of Birobidzhan, in Siberia. Soviet diplomats have often told me: 'If the Jews were to settle in Birobidzhan they could even choose Hebrew as their national language.' The Jews have refused, because this province next door to Mongolia and China would remove them from the great urban centres where they like to live. I pointed that out to Gromyko—'Give them Kiev, Odessa, Leningrad, and they'll all want to go!' The Russians have created a colossal industry in Siberia, but that is not reason enough for the Jews; in America too they prefer to live in Philadelphia or Chicago rather than in the little rural towns. But after all, the Russians can't be blamed for that, and the Birobidzhan affair proves that the Russian leadership is not opposed to a Jewish way of life in principle.

After the Revolution of 1917 there was a very intense Jewish cultural life in Russia, both in Yiddish and in Hebrew. It should not be forgotten that Israel's present national theatre, Habima, was created in Russia. All that intellectual activity, fed by news-papers and books in Yiddish, only disappeared when Stalin became a half-mad dictator haunted by the menace of an inter-national Jewish conspiracy.

And a Jewish life goes on in various other Communist countries. In Romania, for example, where there are eighty thousand Jews, there are synagogues, a Yiddish theatre and ritual foodstuffs. The ritual slaughterers in Romania have some trouble in emigrating to Israel because the rabbis need them where they are, and the authorities persuade them that it is their duty to provide kosher meat for the Romanian Jewish community.

I have an amusing memory on that subject. On the occasion of one of my visits to Bucharest (it was before I knew Ceausescu), Chief Rabbi Rosen, a member of the Romanian parliament and the only Jewish leader in any of the Eastern countries to have achieved international standing, decided to give a big kosher banquet at the Athenaeum, Bucharest's most famous hotel. So he went to the director and told him: 'Have your kitchens vacated for two days; at my reception the food must be kosher.' The man was all set to throw this lunatic out, but Rabbi Rosen brought in the head of the government's religious department, who ordered the director to clear the place.

The dinner was a great success, and was attended by many

artists, writers, museum and art gallery directors, and musicians, as well as by the Orthodox archbishop and the same head of the religious department, a professor of philosophy and a very interesting man. As always in that kind of gathering, the problem was language. To use French would have required translation, and though most of those present would speak German it would be painful to use it, because of the sufferings undergone by the Nazis' Romanian Jewish victims. Everybody was curious to know how I would get round it.

I started my speech of thanks with these words: 'Ladies and Gentlemen, I am going to speak in the language of Schiller and of Heine . . .' (a few literary people clapped.) 'which is also the language of Marx and Engels . . .' (here all the Communists clapped.) 'and the language of Theodor Herzl.' Here there was an ovation. Later in the evening the head of the religious department took me aside and said: 'Mr Goldmann, I have just learned a valuable lesson in diplomacy!'

It is true that Romania is quite apart in the Communist bloc. It often embarrasses the Russians at European conferences and in their policy towards China, with which Ceausescu maintains excellent relations. The Russians know that they cannot coerce the Romanians, or intervene on their territory as they did in Hungary and in Czechoslovakia. That is the proof that Nicolae Ceausescu is a true statesman, a very brave and unusual man. In fact no other Communist leader has occupied as he has the three key positions in the regime: he is Secretary General of the Party, President of the Republic, and Prime Minister. Even Stalin did not manage that: he was either Secretary General or Prime Minister; as for Tito, who is President of Yugoslavia, he was Secretary General of the Party for a long time, but never Prime Minister. Ceausescu holds the positions of Brezhnev, Kosygin and Podgorny combined.

He once asked me for my honest opinion of himself, and I answered: 'There are two kinds of Communists, those who have become Communists, and those who always were. You are one of the latter.' And it is true: Ceausescu is a born Communist, not an extremist certainly, but very strict in his domestic policy. He has a sense of discipline, and he maintains the unity of Romania, which contains other minorities such as Hungarians, Germans and others, with some rigour. On the other hand he is nonconformist and very courageous in foreign policy. I have not had the occasion to talk ideology with him, but he has great political understanding. I was present at a brief impromptu talk where he spoke for less than an hour but gave a fascinating analysis of the international situation, together with a stunning display of erudition on the part of a man who had never been to university. 'My son is a professor at Harvard,' I told him, 'and he sometimes invites great political leaders. I am going to suggest inviting you. You would be heard by the world's finest political economists, and if you were to repeat what I have just heard you would receive a standing ovation.'

During the same period I also established relations with Marshal Tito, President of Yugoslavia. His first invitation coincided with the May Events in Paris in 1968, and I had trouble reaching Belgrade because all the air links from Paris had been cut, but I managed to get hold of enough petrol to drive to Brussels, where thanks to friends in the EEC I was able to find a seat on a plane to Zurich and Belgrade. Since then I have seen Tito often, and could not help being struck by his extraordinary personality, bravery and strength, and by his bold perspectives on the international political scene. He is the most eminent nonconformist in the Communist world, and the recent conference of the Communist parties in East Berlin, when Brezhnev embraced him, confirmed his final victory over the dictatorial policy of the USSR.

His attitude to the Jews has always been above reproach, and Yugoslavia's small Jewish community (which has shrunk from about one hundred thousand pre-war to less than ten thousand today) enjoys all the facilities of a national minority. Each of my visits to Belgrade has made me admire the will to survive of a community which maintains quite a thriving cultural life, keeps two choirs, and has an ongoing relationship with world Jewry and with Israel. Yugoslavia is in any case the most ideal state from the point of view of minority rights, because every national group enjoys a broad measure of cultural and even economic autonomy.

Tito's relations with Israel have followed a sorry course. Until the Six Day War he was the best friend Israel had inside the Communist bloc. With President Nasser and Chou En-lai he had been a founder-member of the 'group of non-aligned countries', and that is why, after the Sinai campaign, he broke off diplomatic relations with Israel—which subsequently prevented him from playing any role as mediator between Israel and the Arabs. Since then his attitude has become more and more negative, although he recognizes Israel's right to existence inside secure frontiers, and at international conferences Yugoslavia has argued for the withdrawal of Israel from all the occupied territories and has observed a very critical policy.

My personal relations with Tito have remained close and almost amicable throughout this time. He appreciates my views on solving the Arab–Israeli problem and my nonconformist policy. For my own part I find him still brimming with dynamism and energy, despite his great age, and each time I have the pleasure of meeting him I come away very impressed by this heroic figure.

As for the USSR, I repeat that the establishment of a real Jewish way of life on Soviet soil is very much dependent on curtailing the state of war between Israel and the Arab powers. As long as Israel stays in the American camp the Russians will consider it as an enemy and make no distinction between Judaism and Zionism. But if Israel becomes neutral, as I dearly hope, I am sure that the Soviets will go some way towards meeting our demands, which have brought no response hitherto.

That still leaves the question of determining what demands can be made. For example it would be absurd to require a system of Yiddish schools—for the simple reason that the younger generation does not want to learn Yiddish. But there is another motive for refraining: at the outset of the Communist regime in Romania there used to be a Jewish section of the Party, a *yevsektsya*, run by a man called Feldmann, which supervised the Yiddish schools. Well, Chief Rabbi Rosen told me that no good Jew would send his children to these schools because the teachers were so virulently anti-religious and anti-Zionist. They spent the day teaching the children that they ought not to believe in God, the Bible was a joke, Zionists were all reactionaries, and so on. In the non-Jewish schools, nobody bothered with all that. So from the point of view of Jewish education it was far better to enrol the children in a government school, and in the end the Yiddish schools were abolished. Insufficient thought has been given to the fact that Jewish schools are not in themselves a guarantee of the continuation of Judaism; it all depends on the teachers' motivations.

On the other hand it would undoubtedly be possible to obtain the right to build synagogues—and without even asking the state for the money, because many Eastern Jews would foot the bill. Bear in mind, incidentally, that the economic situation of the Russian Jews is not bad, and furthermore that in the big towns it is often better than that of non-Jews: one only has to work out the proportion of Jews occupying places in the liberal professions such as medicine and law.

All the same, there are jobs which are closed to Jews, but that is partly the fault of Israel's pro-American policy. The Russians do not always trust the Jews in 'positions of responsibility'.

Before the war, most Russian diplomats were Jews. A list of these representatives of the USSR is published every year, and some years ago I asked Robinson, of the Institute of Jewish Affairs, to examine it. Recently it has only contained two or three Jewish names. I took the list to Gromyko and asked why his diplomatic machinery was *judenrein*.

'That has nothing to do with antisemitism,' he replied. 'With a few exceptions you won't find any Ukrainians there either. Frankly, we are a closed society, not very democratic in the Western sense of the word. Now if we send a Jewish second secretary to the Russian embassy in Rio de Janeiro, for example, in his first week he'll discover that he has a cousin in Sao Paulo, a week later that he has an uncle in Curitiba, and so on. We don't like that; we don't want our diplomats to have personal international relations. Well, the Jewish people is international through and through. I am not saying that Jews are disloyal, but they have too many friends, relations and acquaintances for our liking. We take the same line with the Ukrainians, who have several communities living abroad.'

To return to the rights we should request, in addition to building synagogues, the right to constitute a proper seminary for rabbis must be obtained: the present substitute is a farce, with barely three or four students, because the authorities discourage candidates. Likewise the Jews should be allowed to take courses in Hebrew, whether they want to go to Israel or remain in Russia. These courses do exist at present in a few universities, but they need extending.

Lastly, it would be necessary to establish a representative 'address' for Russian Jewry, which is now the only such community in the world not to have its own headquarters. There was one in existence during the last war, the Antifascist Committee, chaired by Ilya Ehrenburg, with which the WJC had permanent relations. But it was dissolved when Stalin 'liquidated' the Jewish writers. I had a plan to reconstitute an organization of that kind, because when the question came up of my being invited to the USSR I asked where I could meet some Russian Jews and was told: 'But ... in the synagogues!' As I was anxious not to confine my contacts to religious Jews, I suggested the creation of a welcoming committee which would have contained people like Ehrenburg and the great economist Libermann, and which might have been a sort of correspondent of the WJC. But that could not be done prior to a global agreement between the Russians and ourselves.

I would like to come back to one essential point: if the USSR is accused, and often with good reason, of preventing emigration and making life difficult for its Jews, yet it should also be remembered that the Soviet government saved hundreds of thousands of our brothers by enabling them to escape from Nazism, and that without Russia the State of Israel would not exist today. Not so much because the Russians voted for its creation as because in 1948–9, at the time of the Arab invasion, all Israel's arms were of Communist origin. Israel must not forget what Ben Gurion, with his usual courage, never ceased to point out. 'If I am now receiving you in a Jewish state,' he used to tell Israeli TV reporters, 'it is a lot more thanks to the USSR than to

the United States, because during our war of independence, when
we were hemmed in by the Arab armies, we didn't get a single
rifle from America.'

Besides, Jews make a big mistake by treating the USSR as if it
were some minor country. Jews have no sense of proportion, and
they readily launch forth into clumsy condemnations of the second
greatest power in the world. This does not improve anything,
and confirms the Russians in their attitude of distrust and even of
hostility. The methods of those little radical groups who break
windows or demonstrate outside Russian embassies are utterly
wrong-headed, and I do not accept being saddled with these
young demonstrators—for whom I have to admit to a certain
esteem—as the sole defenders of Russian Jewry. I know many
Jews in the Eastern countries who deplore this kind of agitation.

What makes caution all the more necessary is that we are dealing
with a state which is on the way to liberalizing itself. The government is less brutal than it was in Stalin's day, but if it feels
threatened it does not hesitate to assert its power, as in Hungary
and Czechoslovakia. So what would happen if the Russians got
riled enough to deport a million Jews to Siberia? Would America
go to war to protect them? No, world Jewry decidedly has no
right to endanger the future of three million Jews, especially
when these have not given their consent.

It is time to acquire a sense of responsibility and to put a stop
to the hysterical agitation practised by Israel and still more by
American Jewry. Russian Jewry is not a tool for mobilizing the
young Jews of the United States. That is immoral and dangerous.
I do not even think that a rallying cry of that kind remains
effective for very long, and you will be seeing America's young
Jews turning away from it more and more. You cannot hold a
demonstration for every Jewish student imprisoned by the USSR.
On this subject a Harvard professor once said to me: 'You are a
really impossible people, the most egocentric in the world! For
every Jewish citizen arrested, somebody demands my signature
on a petition. Can you imagine anything like that for the two
million victims in Biafra, or the sufferers in Bangladesh? Does
every single Jew have some God-given right to call upon all the

world's lovers of justice?' Now this.professor is a fervent democrat; if we go too far, it is men like him who will get tired and eventually refuse to sign.

A number of liberal Russians, who are not themselves Jewish, also include equal rights for Jews and their freedom to emigrate among their demands. I admire these dissidents and I am fully in favour of developing our relations with them. However, I do not over-estimate their importance. Men like Solzhenitsyn, Sakharov and Amalrik are heroes, but their influence is very limited. I believe that the Russian people are quite satisfied with their government and that they approve of the economic and scientific progress being made. Certainly they would like to see an improved standard of living and more individual liberty. But don't let us inflate the internal audience of the dissidents, who in any case are too few to make a revolution. Having said that, I am happy that these liberals exist and that they support the Jewish claims.

I have said that once there is peace in the Near East the Soviet authorities are more likely to permit the development of Jewish cultural and religious life in the USSR. But the question has been put whether the government might not dissociate these problems. I believe this to be impossible. No government would do that: the anti-Israeli policy of any state has repercussions on its Jewish policy in general. For the Russians, the more Jewish a Jew becomes the more he supports Israel, and in fact Israel does constitute a part of Jewish religion and culture. You cannot honestly claim to be a good Jew and yet detest Israel, and this explains the Soviet rationale, which goes: 'As long as Israel, which is a satellite of the United States, is a country whose policy we oppose, we cannot help the Jews towards self-determination, because if we do that we are indirectly reinforcing the pro-Israeli front.'

So there are three sides to the Russian problem: the life of the Jews in Russia, which we have been discussing, the USSR's attitude towards Israel, and lastly emigration.

I have already referred to my conviction in 1948 that the Russians would vote in favour of the creation of the State of Israel. They did it partly to weaken the British, but after all there was no compulsion on them. 'Why should we help to create a Jewish state in Palestine,' they used to ask me, 'when we know for a fact that the state will be dependent on the United States? Your dependence will be obligatory, because all the money you will need will come from American Jewry.' Remember that this kind of discussion was taking place at the start of the cold war. But I used to reply: 'The Jewish state will depend on two factors: on the one hand the Russian Jews, who will make up a large part of the population and without whom the plan does not stand up; and on the other hand money, which will indeed come from the Western powers. That kind of balance will force the Jewish state to remain neutral.'

The Russians had accepted that reasoning, and nowadays they tend to blame us for not keeping that promise, even if it was not categorical. That is obviously a consequence of the war with the Arabs, and our sages of old were right when they said that 'one sin leads to another'. At the outset, Israel practised a policy of non-alignment backed by Moshe Sharett, Ben Gurion and many of its other leaders; even Rabbi Silver, who was an extremist, was in favour of neutrality so as to gain the backing of the Communist world.

But conflict broke out, and no one, neither the Russians nor the Americans, foresaw how long it would last. After a period when it benefited from Russian aid, Israel grew more and more dependent on Western arms, mainly French and American. The Russians then seized the opportunity to get into the Middle East by the Arab door. And if today they still have an interest in the existence of the Jewish state, it is paradoxically because it was Israel which brought them a political victory they had awaited for centuries, by enabling them to gain a foothold in the Mediterranean.

From the start, though, it was clear to me that Communist opposition to Zionism must be overcome, and I tried to win over a certain number of Soviet diplomats, but it was basically a matter of rather theoretical conversations. Potemkin, then Russian ambassador in Paris, certainly tried to get Stephen Wise and me invited to Moscow in 1936, but nothing came of it; later on he was recalled, and I completely lost touch with him.

Another initiative took place in Khrushchev's day. I had interested Dag Hammarskjöld, the secretary general of the United Nations, in the Jewish problem, and he advised me to meet Anatoly Dobrynin, the UN assistant secretary general. 'It is very important for you to see him immediately,' Hammarskjöld told me, 'because he's leaving for Moscow tomorrow. He could mention the matter to Khrushchev.' Dobrynin agreed to see me despite the lateness of the hour, and that first conversation marks the beginning of my friendship with that very talented, very brilliant man who will one day be Russia's foreign minister, I believe.

'I won't have much time,' he told me then, 'but I am prepared to talk to Khrushchev if the occasion arises. So tell me in one sentence what my answer should be if he asks me what the Jews want'.

'We want the USSR to treat its Jews at least as well as Yugoslavia and Romania do, because the anti-Jewish attitude of the Soviet government is not a Communist but a Russian affair.'

'Perfect,' said Dobrynin, 'that is an excellent formulation.'

But unfortunately he did not get to see Mr K.

Years later, Hammarskjöld was invited by Khrushchev to vacation in Sochi. He promised me to raise the Jewish case with him and to suggest inviting me to the USSR. I was then holding down the twin presidencies of the World Zionist Organization and the WJC. On his return Hammarskjöld relayed the conversation: 'Khrushchev would be delighted to ask you, but he warned me that there was one major difficulty: "Tell Goldmann that things would be easier if he came in the form of twin brothers, one president of the World Zionist Organization, the other president of the World Jewish Congress. Then they could be separated, and I would willingly invite the latter. But since he is as inseparable as Siamese twins and is president of the WZO I can't meet him. We are anti-Zionist, and it would annoy the Arabs." '

With the USSR's penetration into the Mediterranean, thanks to the Arab–Israeli conflict, the question has arisen whether the Russians do not run the risk of peace lessening their influence in the Near East. I do not believe this to be the case. The

Soviets are aware that that explosive situation cannot last for ever and that there is a risk of it precipitating a war liable to threaten the whole policy of détente. If they abandon the Arabs they lose their influence, but if they give them too much help they trigger hostilities with the Americans. But the Russians see détente as being much more important for them than the entire Near East. If they could make the period of the troubles endure for fifty years they might perhaps do it, but they know that it is impossible and that another war would nullify all their efforts for détente. That is what Brezhnev is afraid of, and what Kissinger and Carter have understood.

On the other hand if peace in the Near East was to be a 'pax Americana' the Russians would sabotage it, as in fact they openly admit. However, if the Americans and the Russians are the guarantors of such a peace, the Russian positions in this region will be accepted by the United States. That is why I have always been in favour of a neutralization of Israel, underwritten jointly by the USSR and the United States. Unfortunately neither side wanted anything to do with it, the Americans no more than the Russians: it is often forgotten, but the United States has never recognized the frontiers of Israel, not even those of 1967, or Jerusalem as its capital.

It is some time since I convinced Ben Gurion to try to obtain an American guarantee while I would do my best to get one from the Russians. Ben Gurion was never received officially by the government of the United States: when he went there he was either the guest of the Jewish community or of a university. Levi Eshkol was the first Israeli leader to be invited as such by the Americans.

So one day Brandeis University wanted to award a doctoral degree to Ben Gurion and he was given to understand that on the occasion of this visit Eisenhower would see him officially. The meeting did take place, and Ben Gurion explained: 'For the Arabs to accept Israel any hope that the Russians may help them to liquidate the Jewish state must be driven out of their minds. If the Americans and the Soviets give us their guarantee, the Arabs will give up their illusions.' Eisenhower promised to think it over, but some time later he sent his refusal, on the grounds that by becoming the co-signatory of such a guarantee the United States would, by the same token, be recognizing the equal status of the Russians and the legitimacy of their presence in the Near East.

Today, things have moved on. After the Six Day War I mentioned that conversation to one of the men responsible for American foreign policy, and he answered: 'If a guarantee could be obtained from the Russians, we would be happy to give you our own.' And Gromyko has stated that the USSR is prepared to give its most formal and concrete guarantee of the integrity of the State of Israel, but only after the signature of a peace treaty. That is a thoroughly realistic position, and the Americans will not refuse to be equal partners with the Russians, because they know that by themselves they cannot re-establish peace.

Gromyko does not actually decide Soviet policy in the Near East, but he does put it into practice. He is a first-class diplomatic technician, and the proof is that he has been foreign minister for close on twenty years: he has served under Stalin, Khrushchev, then Brezhnev, and today he is even a member of the Presidium. It is the first time that a Soviet foreign minister has been part of the supreme authority.

His broad culture extends far beyond the political arena, and all sorts of problems can be discussed with him. His manner is slightly curt, and he is equipped with a certain sense of humour and a sure sense of irony. He never loses his composure, reacts to everything with great deliberation and expresses himself with elegance. In addition he has shown some understanding of Jewish problems and of Israel. He supported the idea of partition for Palestine and I was convinced that he would. Certainly the decision did not come directly from him, but he used his influence with the Soviet government to procure the vote of the USSR. Unfortunately the fate of the Soviet Jews is not a matter of foreign policy, but I believe that as long as Gromyko has anything to say about it we can rely on his understanding of the problem, both because of his stint as ambassador to the United States and because of his experience of international politics.

On the subject of Soviet Jews, there are only a few tens of thousands who actually declare themselves as Jewish and want to leave for Israel. Even at the point when emigration reached its peak, that is when forty to fifty thousand Jews were leaving the Soviet Union every year, the birth-rate stayed high enough for there to be little diminution in the total number of Russian Jews. Anyway it is absurd to believe that the problem of the Jews of Russia can be settled only through emigration to Israel. Even supposing that they came in their tens or hundreds of thousands, perhaps even half a million, that would still leave all the others.

In order to improve their lives I have always thought it necessary to use two methods at once: public political pressure on the one hand, diplomatic contacts on the other. And we should bring into play the influence of those non-Jewish figures who have great moral authority and are respected by the Russians. About fifteen years ago I called the first international gathering on this subject in Paris, and for months the Russians tried in vain to prevent it. The philosopher Martin Buber and I were the main speakers, but we got telegrams of solidarity from Mrs Roosevelt, Bertrand Russell, Albert Schweitzer and many more. Also I have often tried to influence the Russians by way of the European Communist parties. The French and Italian parties in particular have helped us a lot, and Waldeck Rochet and Longo have made personal interventions with the Soviets.

But these political pressures must never be misused; it is impossible to force the Russians to do something, and the most that can be done is to persuade them. The accusations of antisemitism made against the USSR have been very much exaggerated, but it is true that there has not been a complete break with the sinister old antisemitic tradition of Russia. A hostile anti-Jewish potential has been building up there, and some Russians believe that their country's enemy is not so much capitalism as world Jewry. Fortunately that is not the ruling opinion in government circles, but one might tremble for the fate of the Russian Jews if another cold war were to set in.

Finally, emigration is complicated by the fact that Israel sometimes has trouble absorbing its arrivals from the USSR. I am afraid that many of them may quit Israel; the world crisis, which does not make it easy to obtain visas for other countries, prevents them from leaving at present. On top of that, if a Russian Jew wants to leave Israel he has to repay all the money advanced by the Jewish Agency for his departure from the USSR, which comes to twelve to fifteen thousand dollars. Most of them do not have that kind of money. A delegation of Russian Jews once came to me to protest against this arrangement. I attempted to reason with them by explaining that it was a logical one: if the Jewish state is to invest a lot of money to organize their departure, travel and assistance on arrival, and the beneficiaries then want to part company with that state, then they should either pay back the money themselves or find a friend or relation who will guarantee the repayment.

One of the factors that create difficulties for the absorption of the Russian Jews is their level of professional qualification. The Soviet Union is a country where some engineers are trained for very sophisticated machines which are practically unknown in Israel, which means that there is no work for them. It is the same with the doctors, who include many super-specialists.

At the same time, it is getting harder and harder for Russian Jews to leave the USSR. They lose their jobs as soon as they show signs of wanting to leave, their families are subject to harassment, and above all the Soviet authorities want to have the sole decision on their fate.

The Jackson affair was proof enough that they intend to remain the masters. Senator Jackson had got the American Congress to pass an amendment linking an important trade agreement which was very advantageous for the Soviet Union with freedom to emigrate for the Jews of the USSR. The result was that the Russians denounced the treaty and granted less than twelve thousand exit visas in 1975, compared with forty thousand in 1974. That's what you get for trying to put the screws on the second greatest power in the world.

8 *The Labyrinth of the Vatican*

IN THEIR RELATIONS with different nations the Jews have often encountered the Vatican, and beyond it the Catholic Church. My personal attitude towards Christianity is very reserved, not on the level of religious theory but of historical reality. Having said that, I generally view Catholicism with greater sympathy than Protestantism.

During one of my travels as a young man I was on a train in Italy and met an eminent Catholic dignitary (who also flirted with the girl I was with). What followed was my first really serious conversation on the subject, in which he told me: 'You have a false notion of the Catholic Church. The Church is not an individual matter, but a collective one. Its historic task is to guarantee order and harmony in the world through obedience. Without it, the masses would destroy civilization. The Church is the world's organizing force. Its design is so vast that what one of its members may do individually cannot concern the Church itself. And there have been two sorts of popes: some, who were saints, were ruinous for the Church; others, who led scandalous lives, were great statesmen, and the Church was a magnificent power under their rule.'

He might have added that one of the essential functions of the Church is to satisfy the metaphysical needs of the masses. From that angle, Catholicism is far more attractive than Protestantism, which does not possess its imaginative gifts: the best proof of that is the architectural poverty of the Protestant churches, which cannot be compared with the beauty of the Gothic or the Romanesque. But the monsignor was right: no other religion has succeeded more than Catholicism in building a political power which in return served the interests of the Church and which exerted a long-lasting dominance over the history of Europe.

Before tackling the relations between Judaism and Catholicism, allow me first to recall two personal anecdotes. The first took place a year or two after the First World War, when I had just gained a doctorate at Heidelberg University. In those days I was very friendly with the philosopher and psychoanalyst Erich Fromm, who was fairly pro-Zionist, although subsequently he totally changed his tune. I was returning to Frankfurt with him, on the way to see my parents, and a very elegant gentleman was sitting opposite us. Fromm and I got into a lively discussion on philosophical problems, and the traveller was listening attentively. At one point we ran out of cigarettes and he offered his own. Every time he spoke to me he addressed me as 'Herr Doktor'.

'How could you know that I am a doctor,' I asked him, 'seeing that my degree is only a few days old? Is it written on my face?'

'No, but I know that you are Nahum Goldmann.'

Feeling quite surprised, I asked who he was, and he simply handed me his card, on which I read: 'M. Rosen—Palazzo Pitti—Florence'. He was an art dealer, and had taken a few years' lease on the palace . . . When we reached Frankfurt he said to me: 'If you should ever need anything at all in Italy, write to me, and promise to come and see me if you're in Florence.'

Some years later a friend from Palestine wrote to me that she was in Rome and wanted to pay me a visit in Germany, but was having trouble obtaining a visa in time. Then I remembered Rosen and dropped him a line: 'This is the address of a friend of mine. Can you help her to get a visa?' Communications were unreliable, and I did not receive any reply, but a few days later my friend arrived in Berlin.

'How did you manage it?' I asked her.

'A man turned up on your behalf, took my passport, and brought it back two days later with all the visas in it.'

I thanked Mr Rosen, and went to see him on one of my trips to Italy. A Polish Jew from Lodz, he had built up a thriving business dealing mainly in medieval arms and furniture. He also ran a business specializing in the manufacture of ecclesiastical robes. Every bishop and cardinal bought from him, and paid dearly too, so he had his own channels to the Vatican, and took a malicious pleasure in describing and explaining many of its intrigues to me.

All the same, the attraction of Catholicism with all its ceremony can be immense, and a boyhood friend called Fischer, whom I had 'converted' to Zionism, became a very devout and active Catholic; before his early death he became one of the leaders of Germany's young Catholics and very influential. In my conversations with him I realized what an extraordinary impression the Roman Catholic religion can make, not only on the ignorant masses but likewise on brilliant intellectuals such as Fischer was.

As for the relations between Judaism and the Roman Catholic Church, I became involved with them fairly late in the day, just before, during and after the Second World War. Until then there was hardly any contact between Jewish organizations and the Vatican, although from time to time we developed links with certain bishops, particularly in Latin America, where the Church had great influence—and where it also displayed its antisemitism.

The World Jewish Congress had no global policy concerning the various churches, but the Zionist movement made several attempts to enlist the help of the Vatican, because many of the votes in the Council of the League of Nations belonged to Catholic countries. When the time came for the Council to ratify the Balfour Declaration on the British mandate in Palestine, we were afraid that several states would go against us because of official Catholic opposition. Nahum Sokolow, who was later to replace Weizmann as president of the Zionist Organization, was then a member of the Zionist Executive with responsibility for contacts with the Roman Catholics, but he did not manage to see the Pope.

As regards the conduct of Pius XII, who was accused of having Nazi sympathies, my own information on that subject comes from the mouth of Cardinal Tisserant, who was dean of the Sacred College. He told me that the Pope had not been pro-Nazi but pro-German, and that he had not dared to act in favour of the Jews. But after Tisserant's death somebody published a letter he had sent to Pius XII accusing him of having as good as sided with the Nazis by a policy which would remain a blot on the history of Catholicism. It is true that Cardinal Tisserant, who spoke Hebrew among his fifteen languages, was openly pro-Jewish and pro-Zionist.

I made my first approaches to the Roman Catholic hierarchy on the occasion of the Saar plebiscite. I have already described how helpful Mussolini was, but at the time I still did not know whether he would back us to the hilt, and I had decided to try to get the support of the Church. A lot of Saarlanders were Catholics, and the Catholics too tended to be discriminated against in Nazi Germany, so it seemed to me that it should be possible to compare the two cases and thereby persuade the hierarchy to collaborate with us.

I must say that it was harder to make these contacts than it would have been with any national government. The Roman Catholic Church has a diplomatic system which is two thousand years old, and fantastically elaborate. For example, if you are asking for an interview with the Pope, or the Vatican secretary of state, or even a simple cardinal, you generally have to indicate the topics you intend to discuss at least two weeks in advance. In that way, when you do meet the prelate, he is admirably well briefed. In the other chancelleries a minister seldom knows what you are going to say to him in advance, and the first conversation is not very productive.

In 1936 I had accreditation from the Jewish Agency with the French government, and had an office at 83 Avenue de la Grande Armée. One day a visiting card was brought to me with the message that an Austrian archduke wanted to see me. A man of typical Viennese charm, which is to say simultaneously superficial and engaging, he began: 'Sir, I am here on behalf of the family of Habsburg. I have spent months looking for the right man to approach. When I asked around for the name of the representative of the Jewish people I was given all sorts of names, Weizmann's among them, but then I learned that Chaim Weizmann was only concerned with the Palestine problem. That left two men—Stephen Wise, who is in America, and yourself.' I asked him what was the object of his visit, and he replied: 'Hitler is a threat to the seven hundred thousand Jews living in Germany. So I have a very simple solution to propose: you, the Jews, help us to restore the Habsburg dynasty, and in return we will authorize the settlement of those seven hundred thousand Jews in Austria.' The Habsburgs were in fact considered pro-Jewish, and they were very popular, in Galicia, for example. 'The Jews will bring their wealth, their industries and their ability,' he went on, 'and the Habsburgs will show their gratitude. You are too honest to accept money, I'm sure, but perhaps a title would please you . . .'

I saw him several times more, and on one occasion I said to him:

'Suppose that Austria, which is a small country, could actually absorb seven hundred thousand German Jews; it will not be easy to get the American Jews, who have a lot of democrats among them, not to mention liberals and socialists, to contribute towards restoring the Austrian monarchy.'

'Look,' he replied, 'a monarchy has a great advantage over a republic. Look at the French: they change governments every six months and everything has to be renegotiated each time. Whereas monarchy is stable: you pay once and it's settled.'

It was a whole philosophy of state! As I was objecting that the Jews could not bring off such an operation on their own, even supposing they wanted to, he answered: 'You will bring it off with the help of the Catholic Church. Together you make a powerful force.'

It sounded like an interesting notion, and I asked him whether he knew any Church VIPs. It turned out that he was close to Cardinal Innitzer of Vienna, so I asked him to write to Innitzer and inform him that I would like to meet him to find out to what extent the Catholic Church would cooperate with us. He wrote the letter and I went to Vienna to meet Innitzer, who was still fairly neutral at the time, but later became quite pro-Nazi and a supporter of the Anschluss.

He lived in a big palace near St Stephen's Cathedral. When I got there his secretary was waiting at the foot of the stairway and showed me in ahead of about fifty people who were hoping for an audience. So the Cardinal saw me at once, and when I asked him if the Church was really in favour of restoring the Habsburgs he replied:

'That's right. The Habsburgs are a great Catholic family and it is in our interests to encourage their ambitions. Still, don't take their attitude too seriously: these archdukes are young people very impatient to regain their castles and recover their fortunes, because they are in poor financial straits. They are pressing us to intervene, but we are moving with patience: you and I, Mr President, represent eternal powers, and we count in centuries, not in years.'

'Certainly, Your Eminence, and without knowing what you think of Judaism I believe that you will recognize what remarkable endurance we have shown in the course of history: we have been living under persecution for two thousand years!'

'Your patience is indeed admirable, but the Catholic Church has the same quality.'

'No doubt it has assimilated a few of our own characteristics,' I replied.

He nodded his head, then asked:

'May I take that as a compliment?'

'But of course.'

'In that case I thank you in the name of the Church.'

And he gave me an introduction to the Vatican, not to the secretary of state, who at that time was Pacelli, the future Pius XII, but to Father Leibel, a Biblical scholar, professor at the Gregorian University, and very influential in the Vatican.

We should bear in mind that Cardinal Pacelli was more German than Italian: he spoke German in private conversation, read a German Bible, and his housekeeper, Sister Angelina, whom he had met in Munich during his time as Papal Nuncio there, was German. Later he was Nuncio in Berlin. Father Leibel was to arrange a meeting for me with Pacelli, and before it the priest and I had a very instructive conversation. First we talked about Zionism in general, and his own doubts and reservations about it; I remember how often he referred to 'the great power of the Jews'. Finally I raised the main subject.

'I am here about a concrete problem,' I said, 'the problem of the

Saar. The League of Nations Council is to make its decision in a few weeks' time, and we want to obtain the right for anyone who wishes to do so to take their money in French francs and to leave. This concerns a minority of Jews and might concern a majority of Catholics. We therefore have interests in common.'

'Allow me to express my doubts,' he said after reflection. 'What effect will a League resolution have? Hitler scoffs at them.'

'You are forgetting the affair of the Silesian Jews,' I replied.

In fact, by the terms of a treaty between Poland and Germany guaranteeing equal rights for all minorities living in Silesia, Germany had been bound to grant these rights to the Silesian Jews. When Hitler took power and published the racist Nuremberg Laws he wanted to annul the treaty. We then addressed the famous Bernheim Petition to the League of Nations, and we won: until 1935, when it expired, Hitler had to respect the treaty.

Later on, when I met Pacelli, I reminded him too of that episode. 'If you, the representative of a big Jewish organization, submit a request to the League I can understand that it may be accepted,' he replied. 'As for us Catholics, I doubt whether our intervention would carry any weight.' This was so plainly in bad faith that I took offence. 'Instead of putting up a theoretical and time-consuming argument,' I told him, 'I'll make you a concrete suggestion: let us change places, not in terms of religion but of political power.'

He replied that what I said was certainly very witty, but that his own remark perhaps deserved to be taken more seriously. In a higher key, I went on: 'I have been trying to make contact with you for years. When I finally managed it, it still took six weeks between your receiving the recommendation and my getting to see you. I took the train, and I made a sixteen-hour journey to meet you. I have never seen a single one of your cardinals travel for sixteen hours to see me in Paris and ask me to protect some Catholic minority.' Pacelli's answer was categorical: 'If it had not been for protocol, there would have been and still will be occasions on which I might have to send one of my colleagues to ask for your support and protection for Catholic minorities in some countries.'

In the same period we were trying to establish ties with the three Catholic orders which had some political influence: the Franciscans, the Dominicans and the Jesuits. It quickly turned out the first two were sternly anti-Zionist. That left the Jesuits, who seemed fairly favourable to us.

The Society of Jesus is organized in the same way today as it was in the time of Ignatius of Loyola: there is the general, and immediately under him seven assistants—one for France, one for Spain, one for Asia, etc. The assistant for France was a very cultured man, because it takes twenty-one years of studies to become a high Jesuit dignitary: seven years of theology, seven of jurisprudence, seven of political science. This assistant, Father Gostagarzu, arranged a meeting between Father Jansen, the General of the Jesuits, and myself.

Father Jansen was a lean, austere-looking Belgian with a near-encyclopaedic mind. His residence near the Vatican was a building reserved for the Society of Jesus and which did not contain a single comfortable chair. The whole place was redolent of power and solemnity. I had a long interview with Jansen which started with having to resolve a question of protocol. The proper form of address for the general of the Jesuits was 'Very Reverend Father', while some assistants were entitled to 'Reverend Father' and others to the more modest 'Father'. Jansen had obviously been wondering about my own designation, and he chose 'Very Esteemed President'!

I wanted to break this rhetorical yoke, and when the General told me: 'You are the first Jew I have met officially,' I answered: 'You are the first father general I have met, and that puts me in a dilemma, because the Talmud recommends saying a blessing when one meets an important person. Only the Talmud does not specify what blessing is appropriate when a Jewish leader meets the General of the Jesuits!' The remark made him smile, and the atmosphere thawed. Now he began:

'Our attitude to the State of Israel and to Zionism is one of the Church's most complex problems. Theologically speaking you are the people accursed, the people which crucified Christ. Your dispersion is your punishment. Consequently how could we approve of the concept of a Jewish state? Our debate about you has been going on for seven years: how to reconcile the existence of Israel with the theological abomination which the Jews committed? Nevertheless, we have reached one conclusion: since God has allowed the Jews to establish a state, it is because He is providing the proof that their crime has been expiated. So that obstacle no longer exists, and it remains to investigate what is good or bad for the Church from a pragmatic point of view, since it has religious establishments in the Arab countries. Two reasons impel us to be favourable to your state, and I hope, very esteemed President, that their expression will not shock you. The first is negative.. Throughout its history, in fact, it has been evident to the Church that the dispersion of the Jews was not in its favour. Distributed as they are among most of the world's nations, the Jews are often liberals, atheists, socialists, even communists. It is not good for us that there should be so many focuses of irreligion throughout the world, and it is all the more dangerous because yours is a very influential people. Therefore it suits us better if it is reunited into a single country. The second reason is this: the Church can conceive the hope that if the Jews are brought together once again in the land of the Lord, a day will come when His spirit will master them and they will become converts to Christianity.'

'You are very optimistic,' I replied, 'and that is a long-term policy . . .'

'Indeed,' he said, 'we count in centuries. But let uss um up: we are unable to help you publicly, because the Jesuits remain tied to the other orders. However, we are His Holiness's political advisers. I shall explain what we can do. You are to request an audience by way of the secretary of state. There are two secretaries of state, Cardinals Montini [the present Pope Paul VI] and Tardini. Montini is the more likable, but he is a weakling. As for Tardini, he is totally anti-Zionist, if not antisemitic. So the interview will be refused. But since its creation the order of Jesuits has had one privilege: four times a year it can directly solicit an audience with the Pope. So we shall ask for one on your behalf.'

Some time later, in fact, I received a telegram in London informing me that I was to be received on a Monday by the Pope in 'private audience', meaning that the news of the meeting would not be published. Father Jansen asked me to be in Rome by the previous Saturday so that he could advise me how to speak to Pius XII. I caught the next flight, and arriving in Rome about five in the afternoon I had time to stop at my hotel for a shower. There I was informed that Father Gostagarzu wanted to see me straight away. As soon as I set eyes on him I knew that there was a problem. He appeared very concerned as he explained: 'We had not informed the secretary of state of our request for an audience for you, and we were hoping that he would not get to hear about it. But Tardini heard the news yesterday afternoon, and he has asked His Holiness to cancel the interview on the grounds that the Arabs would be angry enough to take retaliatory measures against the Catholic communities in their own countries.' The Pope had objected that I was already on my way, but Tardini had suggested the following scenario: once a month, the Pope celebrated Mass in St Peter's then received a number of people at a rate of one every five or ten minutes. These interviews are completely formal, they are announced in *L'Osservatore Romano*, and there is no question of raising any serious problem in them. Tardini therefore proposed substituting some such meeting for my private audience on Monday. I at once decided not to attend.

Gostagarzu blanched when I told him.

'But you can't refuse an invitation from the Holy Father!' he exclaimed.

'First of all he is your Holy Father, not mine,' I replied. 'Secondly, it is an insult to alter the nature of an interview. If the Pope is too weak to resist Tardini's injunctions that is his own business, but I don't want *L'Osservatore Romano* writing that I went to see Pius XII for an audience of five minutes.'

'Mr President, think,' the Jesuit insisted. 'It is probably the first time in the history of the Catholic Church that an audience has been refused!'

'Well, that's fine. So I have created an historic precedent and I will become famous.'

'At least let me ask Father Jansen's advice.'

'Do that, but be sure to tell him that whatever he advises I shall not go.'

He returned an hour later, distinctly relieved: 'Father Jansen wants me to say that you are not only brave but very wise to have refused. As for the order of Jesuits, it does not accept this decision and means to lodge a complaint against Cardinal Tardini: it is a violation of our privileges, and we cannot accept his dictatorial attitude.' The affair became famous, and a long time afterwards when I met a Catholic diplomat I heard him exclaim: 'So you are Doctor Goldmann, the man who refused to see the Pope! You had the whole Vatican buzzing!'

As they had said they would, the Jesuits lodged a complaint, and the Pope appointed a three-man commission to investigate it. I told them in advance that they would lose: 'Literally speaking you are right, but what is the basic notion behind your privilege? It is that the Jesuits should have direct access to the Pope, not that Zionists or Jews should use you as a lever to see Pius XII.' I was right: the complaint was rejected.

Much later, in the time of Pope John XXIII, the Pope's confessor, Cardinal Bea, who was a Jesuit, asked to meet me in order, he said, to pass on a message from His Holiness. So I stopped off in Rome on the way back from Israel and saw the Cardinal. He was a very interesting, exceptionally kind and tolerant man, and a great Biblical scholar, who spoke Hebrew fluently and knew a lot about Judaism. A German by birth, and a professor of Biblical studies, he was a liberal, something of a progressive and pro-Israeli.

'It's hard to negotiate with the Jews,' he told me, 'because one does not know who best represents them. For us, there is the Vatican; for the Protestants, there is the World Council of Churches; but when I investigated the present-day structures of Jewry I discovered that there were Orthodox, Conservative and Reformed Jews, and Zionists too. It was so complicated that I asked other Jesuits for advice. They told me that you were the ideal man to see, practically the Pope of the Jews!'

'Your Eminence,' I replied, 'since I hope to see you again often,

I would rather put my cards on the table: the Pope of the Jews does not believe in celibacy!'

The quip made Bea roar with laughter, then he came to the point: 'His Holiness John XXIII has decided to list the Jewish problem on the agenda of the Ecumenical Council, and this in the teeth of all opposition. He wants the Council to vote in favour of a text absolving the Jews from the accusation of having crucified Christ and thereby committed an unatonable crime. [This was, quite simply, a revolutionary decision.] The Holy Father has instructed me to deal with the matter,' Bea went on, 'because he knows of my sympathies for the Jews. But from the protocol point of view we cannot take the initiative: we need a memorandum signed by a majority of the Jewish organizations asking us to discuss the question. Can you arrange that?' I accepted, of course, and Cardinal Bea promised that I would always be dealing directly with himself, so that the matter should be handled at the highest level.

When I got back to New York I realized that the main thing was to gain the consent of the Orthodox Jews, for whom negotiating with the Catholics bordered upon blasphemy. This led to my meeting with Rabbi Joseph Soloveitchik, of New York.

Soloveitchik is the greatest Talmudist in the world. He is never called Rabbi Soloveitchik, just 'the Rabbi'. Coming from a family that numbers four generations of Talmudic geniuses, from his great-grandfather downwards, he is nevertheless the complete opposite of a clerical and never confuses religious interests with political requirements. He studied in Germany for years, can sustain his end of any conversation on, say, Sartre or Heidegger, and writes a fine classical English style. In my view this man is the world's noblest representative of religious Jewry. He has educated an entire generation of Orthodox Jews by teaching three days a week at the New York Yeshiva University, and for the rest of the week he lives in Boston, where he is the rabbi of a small community.

When I go to America I never fail to look him up for a few hours' conversation, although he is well aware that I am not

Orthodox. But at the time of the Ecumenical Council I did not yet know him personally, so I asked a mutual friend to ask Soloveitchik to call me on the phone. I was actually very busy, and rather embarrassed about inviting the greatest rabbi in the world! I knew that his home was a long way from my office, and therefore suggested meeting him half-way, but he replied:

'Doctor Goldmann, do you know the Talmud?'

'Only slightly,' I confessed.

'Very slightly indeed, because you should know that Talmudic law says that the king has priority over the prophet. I am no prophet, but you are a sort of king, so I will come all the way to your place; there's no problem.'

When I explained the Vatican request he told me that he was favourable to it, on condition that no religious problem should be raised during the discussions. 'Talk about antisemitism, or the struggle against poverty, but whatever you do, don't enter into any theological question. You can negotiate, Mr Goldmann, because you are not a rabbi. A rabbi would not be able to restrain himself from talking religion, and that would probably mean trouble.'

We did our best to follow his advice, but the text passed by the Council, which had been the subject of Byzantine disputations, was seriously watered down. Since then there has been a composite commission of Catholics and Jews which meets three times a year to delete or modify controversial passages in the various Catholic books—from the elementary catechism to the textbooks used in Catholic universities and seminaries, by way of the liturgy and, most of all, the service for Good Friday. The work is very slow, because the independence of every bishop has to be respected and because the texts with antisemitic blemishes can be counted in hundreds. They therefore have to be expurgated country by country, language by language, and that will take years.

When I eventually met the Pope, it was Pope Paul VI. My position as president of the World Jewish Congress was a hindrance, because the Vatican said: 'We can negotiate with Jewry as a religion, but the Congress is a political organization.' In the end our meeting came about by accident.

You remember the day when the Israelis raided Beirut airport, destroying twelve aircraft on the ground. The Lebanon is a half Christian country and the Pope made a statement severely condemning the Israeli action but not breathing a word about Arab terrorism. Jerusalem was furious, and felt that Paul vi ought at least to have condemned both sides alike. It does seem that the Pope intervened on his own initiative.

The World Jewish Congress was holding a meeting in Rome when the Pope made his speech. The Israeli press reacted furiously in the next few days. Now the Vatican had recently set up a department with special responsibility for Jewish questions, under the direction of a Dutch theologian, Father Rijk. I had just closed one of our sittings when an excited Father Rijk arrived and told me:

'I'm here on behalf of the acting secretary for foreign affairs, Bonelli. I am to inform you that the Pope would like to see you tomorrow.'

'Tomorrow is impossible,' I replied.

'But why?'

'Listen, I am sure that he has sent me this invitation because of the Israeli reaction. If it was only a matter for the Congress, there would be no problem, but in this case I must telephone Prime Minister Eshkol to get his consent. I am not the official representative of Israel, so invite the ambassador.'

'Impossible.'

'Then you'll have to wait: there's a meeting of the Israeli cabinet tomorrow morning, and I can't get through to Eshkol.'

'That's a nuisance,' Rijk replied, 'because the Pope is engaged all day on Monday: he is to consecrate twelve bishops.'

'Then Monday is out!'

'Tuesday, then?'

'No,' I told him, 'on Tuesday I have to go to Israel for an important meeting. But there's no urgency. I'll come back during the week and see him when it suits him.'

Father Rijk shuttled back and forth between Cardinal Bonelli and me, giving me time to get hold of Eshkol on the phone. He told me to agree to see the Pope, provided I had the right to check the final communiqué and that it contained a condemnation of all terrorism. On the Sunday night, Rijk told me: 'The Pope has cancelled one of tomorrow's ceremonies in order to see you.' I answered that I wanted to be accompanied by Dr Riegner, the secretary general of the WJC, and by my friend Rabbi Prinz, who was then chairman of the Governing Council of the WJC. He returned to tell me that this could be arranged, but that since the audience was reserved for me, the other two must not open their mouths.

Protocol is decidedly a juicy subject for the novelists. Although I had no official standing I was received in the courtyard by the Swiss Guard, every soldier wearing a uniform of the era of Raphael. Then we were shown through nine immense rooms, each of them presided over by a high official. As I walked, I remarked to myself that the rabbinate of Jerusalem was a cottage by comparison. The Pope was waiting for us in the tenth salon. He gave me the impression of being weak, almost ill. He rose courteously to his feet, asked us to be seated, and said: 'You will permit me to read you a speech of welcome.'

He read out a document, in French, which contained a great many personal compliments but not a word about Israel. At one point he referred to the 'Hebraic people', which is a misnomer, then stopped, looked at me, and said: 'May one not say "Hebraic people"?' I answered that it might be said at a pinch, but that 'Jewish people' was more appropriate. 'Permit me to make one remark on this occasion,' he said. 'The Catholic Church has a long history and has maintained centuries-long relationships with many peoples in the world. But its relations with the Jewish people are very recent, because our past contacts can hardly be called "relations". We therefore lack experience in this field; that is why we make mistakes such as the one which led me to use the word "Hebraic". Be patient, sir, and allow us time to learn to negotiate with the Jews.'

That was a likable response. He finished his speech, then gave us gifts in accordance with protocol: something in gold for me, one in silver for each of my companions. When we took our leave of him he told us: 'I want to ask you for a favour. We belong to different religions, but we believe in the same God. Permit me then to give you a blessing in the name of that common God.' He raised his hands and intoned:

'I wish you happiness and success in all you undertake.'

'Your Holiness,' I replied, 'it would be arrogant on my part to want to bless you in my turn, since I am not even a rabbi. But allow me to wish you happiness.'

'When you want to see me,' he concluded, 'these doors will always be open to you.'

Since then, the representative of the World Jewish Congress in Rome has no longer had any problem with the Vatican . . .

9 *Geneva and Hope*

THE MOST EAGERLY AWAITED CHAPTER of this book—the one dealing with the Arab–Jewish conflict—I have kept till last. My views are unorthodox and are less well known than the official Israeli line.

To begin with, when discussing Israeli territorial claims, one has to look back at least as far as the creation of the State of Israel. Without the Jews, the Arabs who lived in Palestine would never have left their native land. That is an historical fact. But in 1945 there were nearly six hundred thousand Jewish survivors of the German concentration camps that no other country would take in. That too is an historical fact. Without Israel, it might have been all over for the Jewish people. And the whole of mankind has a certain interest in the non-disappearance of the Jewish people.

Naturally the world can live without the Jews; I am no fanatic, and I dislike talking about the chosen people. There are about fourteen million of us today. Before Hitler, there were eighteen million. But at certain periods in history—in the seventeenth century, for instance—there were scarcely more than a million Jews, perhaps a million and a half. We are a small people, therefore, and in proportion to their modest numbers the Jews have made a vast contribution to world culture and civilization. What humanity would have lost without the prophets, without monotheism, without Spinoza, Marx, Freud, Einstein, is beyond measure—I say it again.

In everything the Jews have created there is always a specifically Jewish element. It is almost impossible to explain what makes Goethe German, Voltaire French and Shakespeare English, but it can be felt. Similarly, without their Jewishness Spinoza would not have been Spinoza, nor Marx Marx, nor Einstein Einstein. That is why it is in the interest of all for the Jewish people to possess a homeland of its own, not only to harbour and protect individuals who are physically threatened, but to safeguard values which concern all humanity. That is one reason that can justify us even before the Arabs.

If it was not a question of the material and spiritual survival of the Jewish people, the Arabs would have a perfect right to resent its being achieved at their expense. A socialist MP once raised the question of Zionism with Chou En-lai, at my suggestion, and the Chinese prime minister told him: 'Zionism is absurd. If God has promised the Jews a homeland, then let Him give them one, since God is all-powerful. But what has that to do with the Arabs? If the Jews needed a homeland because of Hitler, then let the Germans grant them one of their own provinces, instead of paying them off in millions of marks!' From a strictly logical angle, Chou En-lai was right, but from the point of view of culture, philosophy and history, Israel constitutes the sole means of enabling the Jewish people to continue its contribution to human civilization. Humanity does in fact have the right to say to the Arabs: 'We ask you to sacrifice one per cent of your territories in the service of us all.'

If we now go into details, I am not personally opposed to Israel keeping Hebron. I am a Jew, I have learned the Bible and Jewish history, so I know that it is the town of the patriarchs of our religion, the founders of our people. In the middle of the last war, at the time of the debate for or against partition, I am sure that deep in its heart the majority of the Zionist movement was against. At that time my argument in favour of partition was that time was not on our side: I used to make the point that the numerical superiority of the Arabs could only increase, and that since the British would not allow any massive Jewish immigration our minority position would become more and more glaring until it finally deprived us of the right to ask for a state of our own. I remember quoting our great humorist Sholom Aleichem, who said: 'A Jew has to sell his last shirt to become a millionaire.' In the same way we had to sacrifice half of Palestine to become a state.

Later on, at the Zionist Congress, I had a discussion with the Herut leader, Menahem Begin, and I said to him:

'If you can keep Bethlehem, Hebron and even Samaria at no risk to the existence of Israel, I'll have a whole forest planted in your honour!'

'We certainly have more right to Hebron than to Jaffa,' he retorted.

And he was quite right: in Jewish ancient history, Jaffa does not play any part, whereas Bethlehem and Hebron are crucially important. But there it is—it is not enough to be right either historically or logically, and since it is impossible for us to have and hold the entire territory of Palestine it is pointless to get over-excited about the subject.

In any case, Israeli territorial expansion would still involve a growing Arab population, and that is the decisive argument which all the annexationists come up against. In 1967, one or two weeks after the Israeli victory in the Six Day War, I saw Eshkol. Although he himself had announced that he wanted no territorial expansion, plenty of Israelis were in favour of keeping the whole West Bank. Eshkol showed me a memorandum signed by Israel's most eminent statistician, Bachi; what emerged from this study was that if Israel kept the West Bank and the Gaza Strip, then in six to eight years the territory would contain about fifty per cent Jews and fifty per cent Arabs—there would be a sort of binational state. But after ten or twelve years the majority of the population would be Arabs and Israel would become a *de facto* Arab state with a Jewish minority: in other words, the total negation of Zionism.

When you say this to Begin, who has inherited the Jabotinsky theory calling for absolute equality of rights for the Arabs, his answer is: 'Once we have the whole of Palestine there will be an additional annual immigration of two or three hundred thousand Jews and we will remain in the majority.' Not that this is impossible, but you can't build anything on sheer hypotheses.

As for Dayan, he has come up with a method, an immoral and unacceptable method, by which Arabs living in Israeli occupied territories would not be Israeli citizens. They might be working in

Israel, but they would remain Jordanian citizens. So the Jewish people, which is in a minority all over the world, is to descend to taking South Africa as a model? That would mean undermining all the ideological foundations of Zionism.

I am absolutely against the Israeli attempt to colonize a territory stretching between the Gaza Strip and Sinai, and the plans to construct the town of Yamit. The idea will have to be discarded once peace has been made. The Arabs will not accept it, and many Israelis themselves are hostile to it. This kind of enterprise is the result of a miscalculation on the part of the Israeli government, which is under the impression that if Israel presents the world with a *fait accompli*, the world will swallow it. This may hold true for many countries which ten years after the end of the troubles in the Near East will be facing other problems—coexistence, race riots, nuclear armament, pollution, etc. The Arabs, though, have the same historical memory as the Jews. The Semitic race is a stubborn one; it forgets nothing.

At a big meeting in Sydney, Australia, I once said that Israel's bad luck was to have the Arabs for enemies instead of the British. In fact the British have a genius for forgetting; in the space of a generation they have lost the world's greatest empire, and despite that they are very happy: for some time their main popular concern was over who was to marry the princess ... Can you imagine the Jews in the same situation? The Temple in Jerusalem was destroyed two thousand years ago, and we observe an annual day's fasting in remembrance. If we had lost an empire equivalent to the British we would have had to fast twice a week for those twenty centuries!

And the Arabs are like ourselves. It is utterly simple-minded to believe that in the end they will forget our presence in Palestine and come to terms with our occupation of the Golan or Sinai. They have proved that they will prolong the war until they regain their lands. So this whole policy of the *fait accompli* represents an enormous waste. How many hundred million dollars did Israel spend on the Bar Lev Line along the Suez Canal, which was smashed in a matter of hours? How many villages are being built right now which some day will have to be wiped off the map?

On the other hand, if a genuine peace is concluded it is possible to look forward to some improvement in relations in a year or two, and to some sort of arrangement for free movement. Jews would move into the Gaza Strip, Arabs into Israel, there would be open frontiers and perhaps an economic confederation. On the West Bank, the Jews would be foreigners authorized by a treaty to exercise their rights to make homes there and circulate freely, as happens inside the Common Market. There would be no question of building towns, which the Arabs would not permit, but the possibility of agricultural villages would be considered. At the same time tens of thousands of Arabs would have the opportunity to come and work in Israel, where they would earn more money than they do in their own countries. But that kind of approach would only bear fruit in a climate of peace, not in the context of a *fait accompli* policy imposed by military occupation.

As for the Gaza Strip itself, it must be given up, either to Jordan or to a Palestinian state in the West Bank, in the event of its creation, but in either case with a corridor to Gaza, which would become a free port under the terms of the peace treaty. The Gaza Arabs could work in Israel if they so wished, and their daily comings and goings would reduce the hostility between the parties.

To those who dismiss me as a daydreamer when I air this plan, I can only reply that if they do not believe that Arab hostility can some day be alleviated then we might just as well liquidate Israel at once, so as to save the millions of Jews who live there. On this point I am categorical: there is no hope for a Jewish state which has to face another fifty years of struggle against Arab enemies. How many will there be, fifty years from now?

But I feel sure that we can live as friends within the framework of a genuine alliance. Certainly it has become a lot harder after thirty years of hidebound, ingrown Israeli policy which is largely the fault of Ben Gurion. Yet there is still time to convince the Arabs that the Jews would bring them an immense contribution with their knowledge and technology, their two thousand years' experience throughout Europe. There are no great policies without great designs.

A major section of Israeli public opinion and some influential leaders adhere to a theory according to which the Arab character will never allow them to suffer the presence of the State of Israel willingly. They back up this hypothesis by stressing the intolerance of the Arabs and their negative attitude to all minorities. I reject this theory utterly.

I do so, first, because if it were true there would be no hope of a future for the State of Israel: an Arab world of over a hundred million inhabitants would necessarily end up by annihilating the little Jewish state if the Arabs were not prepared to accept it.

Secondly, I repudiate this idea, which is based on a racist concept. The character of a race or people undoubtedly plays an important, but never a decisive role in its history. In the conflict between racism and the environment (see Taine and Gobineau), nature and nurture, I make no final judgement, but I do think that the two elements carry different weights in different eras. During the 'golden age' of their Spanish domination, for example, the Arabs were more tolerant towards the Jews than the Christian world ever was, and the same spirit characterized them too at other times—even as regards the Christians. And if proof is needed to show how absurd it is to ascribe an immutable character to any people, one has only to cite the example of Israel: in the course of two or three generations the Israelis have become the opposite of what the Jews were supposed to be during the two thousand years of Diaspora. The stereotype Jew was a brilliant businessman but a poor and rather cowardly soldier. In Israel today it is precisely the contrary: the Israelis are excellent fighters but fairly average businessmen.

It is the different living conditions in the Diaspora and in an independent state which have produced so striking a change in so short a lapse of time. The same could happen with the Arabs, once liberated from the complexes of colonial domination and restored to a sense of security and human respect.

The first condition of success is, of course, that the Jews should adapt to the Arab world. Take the oil question for example. In my opinion the oil producers were quite right; they behaved brutally, but we must not forget that the capitalist world was exploiting them cynically. Western governments were making far more out of the re-sale of oil than the Arabs were making from the price of crude. It is thanks to the exploitation of the Third World that the Western countries went through an era of unprecedented prosperity. Well, on this point in particular Israel should have taken the side of the Arabs and not lined up with America and the exploiters. Its position on this problem has had a disastrous consequence, because the Arabs said to themselves: 'Israel is decidedly a foreign element. It is an agent of imperialism and we've got to eliminate it.'

The clinching proof for the Arabs that the State of Israel was interfering with their international policy and so was not to be tolerated was provided by the Sinai war. They could not accept either the Israeli attack which sparked off the conflict or, still less, the collusion with the French and British, who in retaliation against Nasser for nationalizing the Suez Canal used Israel as a spearhead. I consider that war as one of Ben Gurion's major mistakes.

I have often defended the notion of a confederation uniting all the states in the Near East, Israel included. Each state would be sovereign in its domestic policy, but when it comes to foreign policy the Jews would have to adapt to the main lines laid down by the Arab majority. I have had hours of discussions on this subject, and have drawn the following conclusions: what disturbs the really responsible Arab leaders is not that Israel possesses half of Palestine; actually this is of little interest to them, especially if the Palestinians are granted a state of their own. No, what troubles them is the Jews setting themselves up as an independent minority inside the Arab world.

I had a close friendship with the late Dag Hammarskjöld, the secretary general of the United Nations: I was one of ten people, I discovered, who were on first-name terms with him. 'Go and see Nasser for me,' I once suggested to him, 'and propose this solution to him: let him recognize Israel and make peace, and Israel will become a member of a confederation of Near Eastern states including not only the Arab countries but Turkey as well. In that way the Jews will form a minority, which means that they will not be able to conduct an individual policy determined by the Americans, the British or the French, but will have to bow to the collective decision. Israel will have to adapt, just as the members of the EEC do, like it or not.'

Hammarskjöld passed on the message and Nasser replied: 'This actually may be a solution. The Arabs will steel themselves to accept the partition of Palestine, because we have vast amounts of land available which will take centuries to develop. But we will never accept Israel as a wedge inside the Arab world. Our plan is to form a bloc stretching from Morocco to Iraq. Unfortunately at the centre of that bloc there is an Israeli state which does not care a rap for our plans. We want to create a policy of non-alignment and Israel practises a pro-capitalist policy. We cannot tolerate that.' It was a very good answer, and a year later, when I submitted my suggestion to Nehru, he was so impressed by it that he altered his schedule of visits and stopped in Cairo to talk it over with Nasser. 'I have already discussed it with Hammarskjöld,' Nasser told him, 'and I instructed him to let Nahum Goldmann know that it really was a valid idea. Only, this Mr Goldmann cannot deliver the goods. It is Ben Gurion who makes the decisions, not Goldmann, and we will never sign an accord with Ben Gurion, who is a brutal man, an aggressor and an imperialist!'

A good friend of mine is Roger Garaudy, whose courage and free-ranging opinions I very much admire. Asked to deliver a series of lectures at the university of El Azhar in Cairo on the relations between modern socialism and religion, which is his favourite subject, he was invited to dinner by Nasser and spent four hours in conversation with him. Garaudy noticed that the Egyptian head of state was more familiar with Jewish and Zionist questions than some of Israel's own leaders.

'I desire peace,' Nasser told him, 'because I know that in my own lifetime at least we will be unable to destroy Israel. My great aim is to build a modern, socialist Egypt and to unite the Arab world. To achieve that, the Israeli problem must be resolved, not by eradicating but by accepting Israel.'

'If you do sign a peace,' asked Garaudy, 'will it be a true peace, allowing for freedom of movement and communication, trade treaties and some degree of cooperation?'

And Nasser, who lacked neither charm nor humour, told him: 'Of course; only I shall have one big worry: every Sunday the Israelis will flock into Port Said in their thousands and empty our shops, and we shall have to replenish our stocks every Monday!'

But the reality of the present moment is taking us daily farther from this solution. I have often been publicly critical of the Zionist economic policy. The Jerusalem government should have brought the Israeli Arabs into the economy right from the start. Banks were created: why not grant thirty per cent of the shares to the Arabs? Big industries were created: why not get them involved? Like everybody else, Jews do not like to give something for nothing, and that is a very human reflex. The slogan 'Jewish labour to create a Jewish state' brought about a revaluation of manual and agricultural labour in Israel, and that was a fine thing, but it also excluded the Arabs from the development of Palestine.

The big mistake of the Zionists was their insistence on monopolizing all the positions of power. Yet just imagine the combination of the Jewish financial and commercial acumen with the Arab billions! The Near East could become one of the wealthiest regions in the world. We unquestionably took the wrong direction from the start, and did not pay enough attention to the warnings of a far-sighted Zionist minority (people like Buber, Kalvariski, Arlosorof and others) who sensed what a false step it was. I often point out that had we put twenty per cent of the energy we expended on influencing the British, American, German and French governments into influencing the Arabs instead, there would never have been a war. But we said to ourselves: 'What do these Bedouins matter? Better to convince Balfour, Wilson and Roosevelt.' An expensive mistake.

Most Palestinians are now reduced to living in refugee camps, which raises the question that keeping them there now provides the Arab governments with a good excuse for evading their domestic problems—underdevelopment, food shortages and excessively high birthrates. In my opinion there are two answers to that question. First, the Arabs are definitely exploiting the refugees for the purpose of anti-Israeli propaganda—this much is certain. And until peace is signed they will pursue this policy, which constitutes an internationally very convincing argument. Then again, most of the Arab countries have no intention of absorbing these refugees. Although some countries actually need them—for example Kuwait and Saudi Arabia—Egypt is already overpopulated and Syria would be hampered by such an influx. Iraq would be the ideal destination, and with that much more manpower the country irrigated by the Tigris and Euphrates could become very rich.

So what is to be done? From the moment when peace is proclaimed, the camps will have to be run down and closed. The Arabs can certainly afford to do so by themselves, but I don't think they want to foot the entire bill, so some sort of international loan will have to be considered. The Jews will pay millions of dollars to be rid of the camps, and that would also make a very impressive gesture. America will subscribe some hundreds of millions, and the Germans have told me that they were ready to make a major contribution.

If there is a Palestinian state in existence by then, it can take in most of the refugees. I admit that not all the Arabs who left Israel can be allowed to return, but if they are promised bases for the installation of agricultural and industrial infrastructures on the West Bank, their future looks favourable to me. The West Bank is a lot more fertile than Israel and thanks particularly to the water supply, new farms stand more chance of succeeding there?

At present, then, the Arab countries are using the refugees to demonstrate the brutality of Israel, and as long as the war goes on they will go on preventing any relocation of the Palestinians—who in any case are not supported by them, but by UN subsidies, in particular from the United States, Germany and France. But as soon as peace comes into force, what interest will they have in keeping three hundred thousand Arabs in hardship in Gaza? Furthermore, the new Palestinian state cannot fail to invite the refugees to join it, because the Palestinian leaders are often very intelligent and know that the state could not exist without them.

It is not a certainty that the peaceful solution envisaged pre-supposes the existence of an independent Palestinian state. However, it does become a possibility from the moment when Israel evacuates the West Bank. As Carter has said on several occasions, the Americans are in favour of a homeland for the Palestinians; they would rather see it linked with Jordan, but cannot deny the Palestinians the right to express their own wishes on the subject. A top official in the American State Department mentioned to me a possible plan for the West Bank once the Israelis had moved out. Rather than bring back the Jordanian administration the United Nations would set up a temporary administration and organize a plebiscite in which all Palestinians —West Bankers and others—would take part. The alternatives would be as follows:

1. Do you want a sovereign Palestinian state?
2. Or do you want a confederation with Jordan, guaranteeing full economic and domestic autonomy, but with one central authority deciding foreign policy and questions relative to the army and territorial security?

It is reasonable to hope that the majority would vote in favour of confederation, because the Palestinians will realize that an independent state would be economically and militarily weak as compared with Israel. But in the event of a confederation I believe that it would be right for Israel to suggest taking part in it so as to form the nucleus of a Near Eastern Common Market— Jordan/Palestine/Israel.

In my view, negotiation is urgent now. I don't much like phrases such as 'last chance' or 'only chance', but honestly we are living through a decisive moment in Jewish history. I have some friends who insist that in five years' time no state in the Arab world will be prepared to deal with Israel, because their power will be so much greater by then. Today there is a good opportunity to open negotiations. For two reasons: first, because the Arabs have realized that Israel has come through four successive wars intact; they may come out on top in half a century, but no policy can be based on such a long term. The second reason is that the Arabs are becoming much more interested in developing their own countries—their present unexpected wealth may prove either a negative or a positive factor. Negative because it endows the Arabs with great influence in a world whose policies are so bound up with oil. Positive because Israel is like a bone stuck in their throats, which they would like to cough up as fast as possible so as to be able to start exploiting their own lands. Here I am merely repeating what any number of Arabs have told me.

But the decisive reason in my view lies elsewhere: it has to do with the whole policy of détente, which concerns the entire world. We are living in a century in which nothing can be achieved without the two superpowers. We may regret this, but we have to be realistic. When the Israelis say: 'No meddling in our affairs!' they are daydreaming. My friend Eban is an expert in philology, and very good at hitting on some resounding formula and believing that he has thereby solved the problem—but the problem remains, no matter how good the formula. That is the case with his slogan 'No imposed peace': it is an illusion. No peace will hold without the agreement and respect of the two superpowers. The Arabs would very much like to follow Sadat's example and rid themselves of the powerful Soviet influence, but as long as the war continues, they are dependent on the Russians—just as Israel depends upon the Americans, even though Vietnam proved that the US guarantee is not always enough.

As far as Europe is concerned, I do not believe that Israel can count very much on the Europeans. On the guarantees of Israel's existence, everybody is in agreement—not only would the Americans go to war to prevent its annihilation, but the Russians would not allow the Arabs to attempt it. Giscard d'Estaing has categorically stated: 'We are prepared formally to guarantee the existence of Israel.' There are only a few extremists left with their minds set on another holocaust, but they do not count in the concert of nations.

On the other hand, when it comes to the stand taken by the Israeli government, everybody except the Americans is against it, some totally, others more or less reservedly. But the difference between the British and the French, for example, is minimal: both in London and in Paris, everything depends on oil and on the Arabs' financial strength. All the Western capitals are on their knees to the Arabs: Wall Street, the Chase Manhattan, the City Bank and big industry are at their mercy. Take just one example out of hundreds: I have heard that Abu Dhabi, which is not the richest emirate, has placed some billions of pounds sterling in London. If Great Britain does anything to displease the emirate, it will transfer those funds to Zurich and the pound will go into free fall. McCloy, the former American high commissioner in Germany, is the big oil companies' number one lawyer, and it is some years since he informed me of the staggering growth of the power of the oil-rich states. I reported the conversation to Golda Meir, but she only shrugged her shoulders: 'You're letting the jurists get at you! Everybody has oil. It's propaganda . . .'

So Israel will remain isolated as long as there is no peace. But if it agrees to restore the occupied territories, international opinion will swing round: if the Arabs still refused to negotiate then, the world's governments would be on Israel's side in spite of oil.

As for Jerusalem, it is unthinkable for the old town to be handed back to the Arabs and the city divided once again. I am convinced that none of the big powers, Russia included, has any such possibility in mind, and I believe that most of the Arabs themselves have realized that another partition of Jerusalem would be quite absurd. On the other hand it is hard to imagine the Arabs putting up with the legal annexation of the old town by Israel. So a solution will have to be considered whereby Jerusalem will remain a single administrative unit while the old town which is sacred to three great religions becomes some sort of special legal entity. The holy places might constitute a kind of neutral enclave, with administration and public services (gas, electricity, etc.) an Israeli responsibility, and local autonomy for the Armenian, Arab and other quarters.

Some European powers are still behind Israel, for example Holland, but I believe too much has been made of this. The Dutch are an upright, honest, hard-working people, and I have a high opinion of them, but if the Israelis have spotlighted their attitude it is mainly because of their own acute sense of isolation. They overlook the other side of the coin: the Dutch may have indicated that they will not add their signatures to documents mentioning a boycott of Israel, but their foreign ministry has stated that it agreed with the other European countries that Israel should restore the occupied territories.

The *Realpolitik* of the European powers is taking a smoother tone than in the days of de Gaulle, but it remains in force. I do not believe that there is any real danger of the Arabs attempting to expel Israel from the United Nations, and they certainly would not stand a chance of getting any such proposal through the Assembly or the Security Council, because in any case the United States, and perhaps even France, would use their right of veto. The fact remains that the very possibility is morally repugnant.

Although the present conflict necessarily involves the Palestinians, I have not met any of their leaders. However, the opportunity did present itself in 1969. I was holidaying in Italy when I received a phone call from Jean Daniel, editorial director of the *Nouvel Observateur*, an old and valued friend, informing me of a message from the secretariat of King Hassan II of Morocco, who wanted to see me. I consulted a few leading Israelis, in particular Moshe Dayan, and they all spoke in favour of talking to him, so I went with Jean Daniel to Rabat, where the King received me as his personal guest.

Having asked me for my own analysis of the situation, Hassan II came to the main point: he told me that the Palestinian movement was gaining in importance, that he knew Yasser Arafat personally and considered him as a moderate, and that it was very important for me to see Arafat, and he, the King, was prepared to arrange such a meeting in Algiers. He neglected to inform me that in fact he had already arranged it, with the consent of Nasser, Arafat and some other Arab leaders—I found this out later.

I told the King in reply that there were two major obstacles to my agreement. The first was that Arafat was operating a policy of blind terrorism, directed more often against Israeli civilians than against soldiers. The second was that there was little basis for discussion with a man who by his demands for a unified Palestinian state was consequently calling for the liquidation of the Jewish state. The King smiled before answering: 'Come now, Mr Goldmann, do you think that I am so naive as to suppose that after fifty years of Zionist activities you would be prepared to negotiate about the removal of the State of Israel? If I suggest a meeting with Arafat it is because I have grounds for believing that he is ready to concede the principle of the continuance of Israel.' I then asked him why the interview should take place in Algiers and not in Rabat, where I would be under his royal protection. 'I could even arrange it for Rabat,' he told me.

Moshe Dayan was then the Israeli minister of defence, and I immediately called him on the phone. He said that he was not opposed to the meeting in principle, but this was not the opportune moment: the clash between the PLO and King Hussein of Jordan was only a few months in the future, and Dayan had got wind of it. 'I don't know whether Arafat will still be Arafat in a few months' time,' he said. 'So wait a bit, and we'll discuss it again.' So I informed Hassan II of my refusal, much to his disappointment.

When this sort of proposal fails, it only leaves the Geneva Conference, which is more a symbol than the basis of any concrete solution. But this symbol has an exemplary character: the Conference would survey the problem in its entirety, and bring together all the interested parties, including the Palestinians, at least once certain conditions had been fulfilled. It would also allow for the presence of the superpowers, and I hope that the European nations will eventually be invited, because no long-term solution is possible without them.

But let's get one thing straight: no conference has ever created a line of action; all they do is to solemnly formalize results achieved in the course of prior talks in small committees and during unofficial get-togethers. In fact this statement reflects my general attitude towards any so-called collective wisdom: the more collective, the less wise. So the Conference could not take the place of bilateral discussions between America and Israel, America and Egypt, and hopefully between Israel and the other Arab states, whether military or not. As for the technique of bringing about such a Conference, generally speaking I have great confidence in the step-by-step policy. In the course of my career I have often been blamed for being a temporizer, but I attach the utmost importance to preparing the psychological ground. From this point of view the gradualist policy enables the right atmosphere to be created; you start with the easiest details, build small bridges across the gulfs between the adversaries, and slowly put them into a more conciliatory state of mind.

This is all very sensible, no doubt, but first it requires having enough time available. For twenty-five years the Near Eastern situation was neglected by superpowers which either remained inactive or else practised a policy of stops and starts. Their mistakes and the stubbornness of the Jews and Arabs have created a real powder-keg which urgently needs defusing.

Then again, gradualism is an appropriate policy for more or less rational peoples for which passion and emotion are not decisive factors. That is hardly the case with the Arabs and the Jews, who resemble one another in their impatience and sensitivity. Take this example from life: when it came to evacuating the two Sinai passes, Israeli public opinion broke into such an outburst of demonstrations and agitation that it might have been the whole of Sinai that was being abandoned.

In any case Kissinger's step-by-step policy is no longer operative, as the Carter administration is now advocating a total solution. I am in favour of this policy, which aims at getting the Arabs to recognize Israel and sign a formal peace agreement in exchange for Israel's withdrawal from the greater part of the occupied territories, except for the town of Jerusalem, for which a solution acceptable to all the different peoples and religions will have to be found, because a further division of the town would be intolerable. Kissinger was afraid of a radical solution because he feared the pro-Israeli lobby and Jewish opinion in the United States. I once told him: 'Let yourself be abused once and for all, and then the Jewish people will make you one of its heroes because you will have brought peace. But if you go step by step you will accumulate so much hatred against yourself that you'll be seen as a second Haman.' And I quoted a very wise German proverb: 'Better an end with great fear than a great fear without end.' If the whole thing is not settled in one sweep, then nothing will be settled, so many and convoluted are the interests involved. To the religious Jews who cling to God's promises and want Hebron and Bethlehem because they are sacred towns, how is the strategic importance of a given pass to be explained? And when it comes to the problem of the West Bank, everything overlaps: historical tradition, important security considerations, fear of committing a mortal sin, and so on.

As regards the step-by-step policy I once made Kissinger roar with laughter by telling him a Jewish story which illustrates the situation. One night a Jew is kneeling down in the street looking for something under a street-lamp. Another Jew comes along, and because the Bible recommends helping one's neighbour he kneels down and starts looking too. In a little while, not having found anything, he asks the first man:

'What exactly have you lost?'

'My wallet.'

'And you're sure you dropped it here?'

'Not at all: I lost it over there, at the corner of the street.'

'Then why look here?'

'Because there's more light!'

'That is your technique,' I told Kissinger. 'You look where there is a little light, but what matters are those broad areas of shadow.'

The question has arisen whether this gradualist policy might be adopted at the Geneva Conference with each point being examined and debated individually When I was a student of philosophy, we were taught then that there were two methods in logic: the inductive and the deductive. Induction is the gradualist policy—you start with the tiniest fact and work your way up to the solution. Deduction starts with the big problem requiring to be solved. This will be the case with the Geneva Conference, which will last the comparatively short time of a year or two.

What matters is to compel the Israelis and Arabs to take two decisions right from the beginning: the Israelis must commit themselves to evacuating the occupied territories, except for Jerusalem, generally agreed to be a problem apart; and the Arabs must formally recognize the Jewish state. Once these goals are achieved, the rest will follow.

From the point when the Israelis know that they have to restore the conquered lands, there will be an end to the months of wrangling about each individual hill. That will be the time to work out how to prevent the Arabs from using Sharm el Sheikh to stop Israeli shipping reaching Eilat. An Arab leader close to Nasser once told me: 'I know that the Israelis are afraid that we will cheat and secretly arm Sharm el Sheikh so as to violate the peace and interdict their shipping. Well, there's one very simple answer: let the Israelis build hotels there and give us a half-share. Instead of sending real head waiters they can put in disguised officers who can observe whether or not we are trying to trick them on the spot.' That was very typical of Arab thinking, but when I passed on the proposal to Dayan he did not just laugh it off.

Another example is the Golan heights: once Israel evacuates them a way will have to be found to permanently demilitarize that part of the Golan where Syrian artillery could fire on the kibbutzim. But as soon as the principle is agreed, there will be a spate of solutions. On the other hand, if the step-by-step inductive method is used, the Messiah will come long before the conflict is over.

I am relying very much on the superpowers to speed things up. Without them, neither Israel nor the Arab countries can exist in the long term. So the superpowers have got to be very firm and say: 'We can't risk the peace of the world and face the danger of nuclear war just because of your quarrels.' After all, the future of Israel does not depend on Sharm el Sheikh, nor the future of the Arabs on the existence of a Jewish state. The world has far more difficult and important problems than these!

The argument has been put forward that the Geneva Conference is too much in the public eye, whereas the gradualist policy allows contacts to be made with greater discretion. I believe this to be just poor journalism. Only the formal conference is public— and that does not prevent more intimate discussions. As for the discretion of the gradualist policy, it is a joke: we know everything that goes on, and secret agreements are common knowledge even before they are written down. No, the supporters of the closed door make that criticism of the Geneva Conference because they are afraid of being asked the real questions there: 'Do you or do you not want peace? Do you or do you not agree to evacuation?' The Arabs and Israelis are afraid of being pinned down.

Other adversaries of the Conference go along with the pro-position that the presence of the Palestinians might harden the Arab position, but that really is the reasoning of lesser diplomats. What does the participation of the Palestinians depend on? First, on relinquishing the idea of a unified binational state superseding Israel; nowadays the majority of them understand that this con-cept is unrealistic, even though they may hesitate to say so in order to avoid splitting their movements. After that, if Israel does not accept a Palestinian state it's hard to see why the Palestinians should accept an Israeli state.

When these two points are settled, and they have put a stop to their terrorist activities, the Palestinians can sit at the Geneva table. Bear in mind that they have been reducing their terrorism outside Israel: they want to become responsible people, recog-nized by the whole world. On the other hand they will concentrate their terrorism on Israeli territory as long as Israel remains unwill-ing to negotiate. But if the Palestinians themselves were to recog-nize Israel, how could the other Arabs take a more extremist line?

There is one last argument which must not be given too much weight: the fact that Libya, Iraq and undoubtedly Algeria will not take part in the Conference. This is unimportant because they are not Israel's neighbours. Neither Kadhafi, nor Assad, nor Boumedienne is in a position to make a direct attack, so it is enough for the Lebanon, Jordan, Egypt, Syria and the Palestinians to appear at Geneva with Israel. Never has the danger been so grave, but never have I had so much confidence in a possibility of peace. It is true that I am an incorrigible optimist . . .

What of the future of the Jewish people? I tend to believe in an optimistic one, as much out of rational conviction as some unshakable faith, but it is impossible to ignore the hypothesis of a pessimistic scenario.

In fact the likelihood of a severe setback is greater in the present century than in any other period of Jewish history. It is one of the paradoxes of Jewish destiny that in the twentieth century, when the Jews of the Diaspora have gained equal rights almost everywhere and enjoy almost unprecedented economic, political and cultural prosperity, and when the sovereign State of Israel has come into being, their future should be more endangered than in any other epoch. The reason for that is that it is always the interior front that finally determines the fate of a people, and although the Jewish exterior front now seems stronger than ever (or perhaps because of that very fact), the interior front is weaker. Equality, with the consequence of increasing assimilation, and the concentration of millions of Jews into a state of their own, under the threat of destruction by the Arabs, therefore render the pessimistic scenario more credible than it was in the past.

This pessimistic forecast is based on the idea that there will be no final peace with the Arab world. My own opinion is different, but a great many Israelis, and plenty of Jews and non-Jews all over the world, despair of ever concluding a peace settlement. If they are right, this is how things will happen.

First, Israel will have to concentrate the bulk of its efforts—military, financial, economic, social and even spiritual—on its own defence in order to remain stronger than the Arabs—which in my view is just about impossible in the long run. The consequences of this absolute necessity, a matter of life or death for Israel, will be growing political isolation in the world and ever more total dependence on the United States: of course it is hard to foresee how much longer the Americans will be prepared to run the risk of a world-wide conflagration for the sake of Israel.

Second, it will be impossible for Zionism to fulfil its essential task, which is to make the sovereign state a spiritual centre for Jews the whole world over, for maintaining the Jewish identity of the greater part of the younger generation, and for guaranteeing the solidarity of the Diaspora with Israel.

With Israel concentrating on its own defence, the state will be unable to constitute a source of new inspiration, and that will eventually bring about a weakening of the specifically Jewish spiritual nature of the Diaspora. On the other hand, a small minority (and the symptoms are already starting to make themselves felt today) will display more fanatical and rigid religious feelings directed against the Jewish *status quo* and even in part against the State of Israel.

Even if this scenario is not seen as culminating in the disappearance of the Jewish people, its future would then be of a minor sect with no influence on world culture, huddled into a corner of international life and praying for the salvation which is to be brought by the Messiah.

Perhaps I am influenced by wishful thinking, but the main basis of my optimistic scenario is an early peace with the Arab world, not only in a formal, legalistic sense, but as the beginning of a genuine acceptance of the State of Israel by its neighbours and the start of an era of cooperation between Israelis and Arabs, inaugurating a renaissance in the Near East. It should never be forgotten that modern civilization traces its origins to Egypt and Babylonia; the earthly paradise from which Adam and Eve were expelled is believed to have been located in Mesopotamia; and not only in ancient times but even at the start of the Middle Ages, the Near East was one of the cultural, economic and political centres of the world. The awakening of Arab nationalism and the wealth and ever-increasing importance of these nations are that many more reasons for a belief in a period of renaissance for this vital region. If peace is established, Israel can take part in that renaissance together with the Arabs.

I only want to make the very briefest mention of the three great syntheses which Israel will have to achieve in order to fulfil its fundamental tasks. The first must be the synthesis of present-day Israeli culture with the culture created during the two thousand years of dispersion: so like and yet so unlike as they are, it is in Israel that they must find a final symbiosis. The second will be a synthesis of the cultural creativity of the Israelis and the cultural contribution of the Jews of the Diaspora: by virtue of that synthesis Israel will become the source of inspiration for contemporary Jewry and avoid the danger of a kind of Israeli provincialism; by way of the Jewish communities of the Diaspora, all the great currents of the world culture of today and tomorrow may be integrated into a specifically Israeli culture. Lastly, Israel will be the great link between world culture, on the one hand, and the new culture of the Near East on the other; historically, this could constitute the most important cultural contribution of the State of Israel.